CLASSIC TEXTS SERIES

Science for Everyone

APTITUDE TEST PROBLEMS IN PHYSICS

SS KROTOV

arihant
SUCCESS AND NOTHING LESS

ARIHANT PRAKASHAN (Series), MEERUT

Administrative & Production Offices

Regd. Office

'Ramchhaya' 4577/15, Agarwal Road, Darya Ganj, New Delhi -110002
Tele: 011- 47630600, 43518550

Head Office

Kalindi, TP Nagar, Meerut (UP) - 250002
Tel: 0121-7156203, 7156204

Sales & Support Offices

Agra, Ahmedabad, Bengaluru, Bareilly, Chennai, Delhi, Guwahati, Hyderabad, Jaipur, Jhansi, Kolkata, Lucknow, Nagpur & Pune.

PRICE ₹140.00

PO No. : TXT-59-T070011-3-26

Published by Arihant Publications (India) Ltd.

For further information about the books published by Arihant, log on to www.arihantbooks.com or e-mail at info@arihantbooks.com

Follow us on

PREFACE

The present state of science and technology is such that a large number of scientists and engineers must be educated at an advanced level. This cannot be done without significantly raising the level of teaching physics, with an emphasis on the individual and special efforts to detect and nurture budding talents. In this respect, physics olympiads for students at secondary school and vocational training colleges are important in bringing to light the brightest students and in correctly guiding them in their choice of profession.

This book, which is a collection of physics aptitude test problems, draws on the experience of the physics olympiads conducted during the last fifteen years among the schoolchildren of Moscow. A Moscow physics olympiad includes three preliminary theoretical rounds at the regional, city and qualifying levels, followed by a final practical round. After the final round, a team of Moscow schoolchildren is selected for participation in the all-Union olympiad. The complexity of the problems set for each round increases gradually, starting from the simplest problems at regional level, problems which can be solved simply by having a thorough knowledge of the basic laws and concepts of physics. The problems at the qualifying stage are much more complicated. Some of the problems at this level involve a certain amount of research (as a rule, the problems make participation in the olympiads even more challenging).

This collection contains problems from the theoretical rounds only. The structure of the book reflects the emphasis given to it in different sections of the physics course at such competitions. The number of problems set at an olympiad and the fraction allotted to a particular topic in the book are determined by the number of years the topic is taught at school. A detailed classification of different topics is not given since some are represented by only one or two problems, while other topics have dozens of problems.

Most of the problems are original, and a considerable proportion of them was composed by the authors. The most difficult problems are marked by asterisks. Being the product of a close group of authors, the book reflects certain traditions and experience drawn from Moscow olympiads only. A feature of the book is that it presents the scientific views and working style of a group of like-minded scientists.

In view of all this, the book should attract a large circle of readers. The best way to use it is as a supplementary material to the existing collections of problems in elementary physics. It will be especially useful to those who have gone through the general physics course, and want to improve their knowledge, or try their strength at nonstandard problems, or to develop an intuitive approach to physics. Although it is recommended primarily for high-school students, we believe that college students in junior classes will also find something interesting in it.

The book will also be useful for organizers of physics study circles, lecturers taking evening and correspondence courses, and for teachers conducting extracurricular activities.

This book would have never been put together without the inspiration of Academician I.K. Kikoin, who encouraged the compilation of such a collection of problems. For many years, Academician Kikoin headed the central organizing committee for the all-Union olympiads for schoolchildren and chaired the editorial board of the journal *Kvant (Quant)* and the series "Little Quant Library". The book is a mark of our respect and a tribute to the memory of this renowned Soviet scientist.

The authors would like to place on record their gratitude to their senior colleagues in the olympiad movement. Thanks are due to V.K. Peterson, G.E. Pustovalov, G.Ya. Myakishev, A.V. Tkachuk, V.I. Grigor'ev, and B.B. Bukhovtsev, who helped us in the formation of our concepts about the physical problem. We are also indebted to the members of the jury of recent Moscow olympiads, who suggested a number of the problems included in this book. Finally, it gives us great pleasure to express our gratitude to G.V. Meledin, who read through the manuscript and made a number of helpful remarks and suggestions for improving both the content and style of the book.

CONTENTS

Problems

1. Mechanics

For the problems of this chapter, the free-fall acceleration g (wherever required) should be taken equal to 10 m/s^2.

1.1. A body with zero initial velocity moves down an inclined plane from a height h and then ascends along the same plane with an initial velocity such that it stops at the same height h. In which case is the time of motion longer?

1.2. At a distance $L = 400$ m from the traffic light, brakes are applied to a locomotive moving at a velocity $v = 54$ km/h.

Determine the position of the locomotive relative to the traffic light 1 min after the application of brakes if its acceleration $a = -0.3$ m/s^2.

1.3. A helicopter takes off along the vertical with an acceleration $a = 3$ m/s^2 and zero initial velocity. In a certain time t_1, the pilot switches off the engine. At the point of take-off, the sound dies away in a time $t_2 = 30$ s.

Determine the velocity v of the helicopter at the moment when its engine is switched off, assuming that the velocity c of sound is 320 m/s.

1.4. A point mass starts moving in a straight line with a constant acceleration a. At a time t_1 after the beginning of motion, the acceleration changes sign, remaining the same in magnitude.

Determine the time t from the beginning of motion in which the point mass returns to the initial position.

1.5. Two bodies move in a straight line towards each other at initial velocities v_1 and v_2 and with constant accelerations a_1 and a_2 directed against the corresponding velocities at the initial instant.

What must be the maximum initial separation l_{max} between the bodies for which they meet during the motion?

1.6. Two steel balls fall freely on an elastic slab. The first ball is dropped from a height $h_1 = 44$ cm and the second from a height $h_2 = 11$ cm τ s after the first ball. After the passage of time τ, the velocities of the balls coincide in magnitude and direction.

Determine the time τ and the time interval during which the velocities of the two balls will be equal, assuming that the balls do not collide.

1.7*. Small balls with zero initial velocity fall from a height $H = R/8$ near the vertical axis of symmetry on a concave spherical surface of radius R. Assuming that the impacts of the balls against the surface are perfectly elastic, prove that after the first impact each ball gets into the lowest point of the spherical surface (the balls do not collide).

1.8. A small ball thrown at an initial velocity v_0 at an angle α to the horizontal strikes a vertical wall moving towards it at a horizontal velocity v and is bounced to the point from which it was thrown.

Determine the time t from the beginning of motion to the moment of impact, neglecting friction losses.

1.9*. A small ball moves at a constant velocity v along a horizontal surface and at point A falls into a vertical well of depth H and radius r. The velocity v of the ball forms an angle α with the diameter of the well drawn through point A (Fig. 1, top view).

Determine the relation between v, H, r, and α for which the ball can "get out" of the well after elastic impacts with the walls. Friction losses should be neglected.

1.10. A cannon fires from under a shelter inclined at an angle α to the horizontal (Fig. 2). The cannon is at point A at a distance l from the base of the shelter (point B). The initial velocity of the shell is v_0 and its trajectory lies in the plane of the figure.

Determine the maximum range L_{max} of the shell.

1.11. The slopes of the windscreen of two motorcars are $\beta_1 = 30°$ and $\beta_2 = 15°$ respectively.

At what ratio v_1 / v_2 of the velocities of the cars will their drivers see the hailstones bounced by the windscreen of their cars in

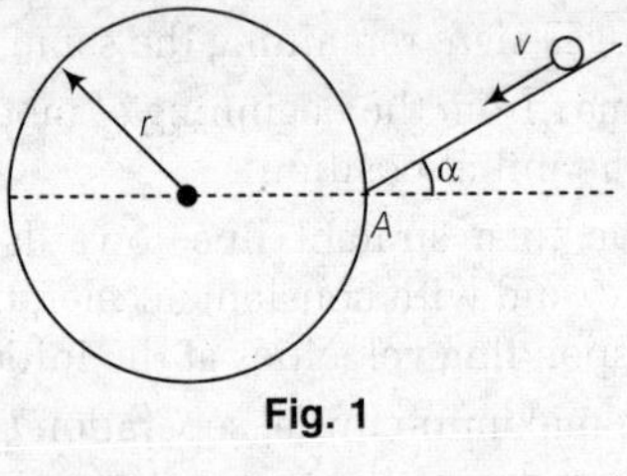

Fig. 1

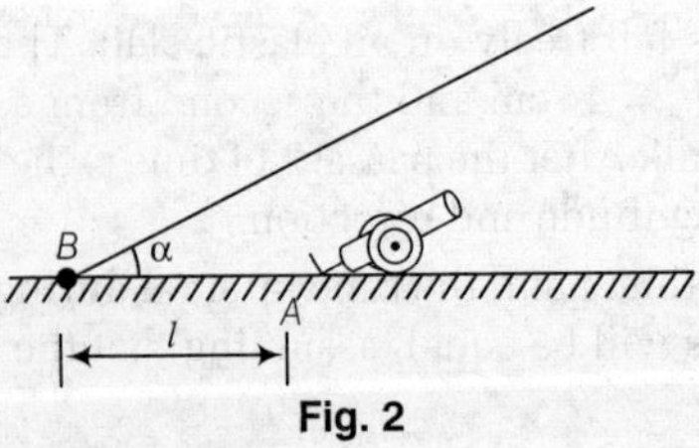

Fig. 2

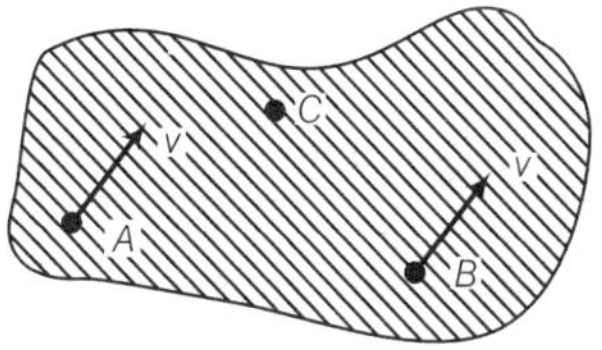

Fig. 3

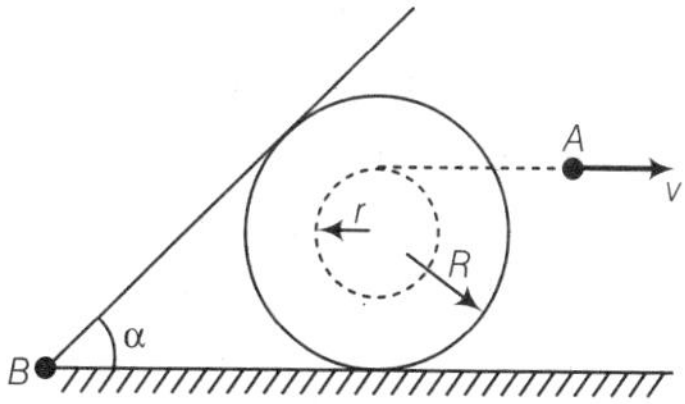

Fig. 4

the vertical direction? Assume that hailstones fall vertically.

1.12. A sheet of plywood moves over a smooth horizontal surface. The velocities of points A and B are equal to v and lie in the plane of the sheet (Fig. 3).

Determine the velocity of point C.

1.13. A car must be parked in a small gap between the cars parked in a row along the pavement.

Should the car be driven out forwards or backwards for the manoeuvre if only its front wheels can be turned?

1.14*. An aeroplane flying along the horizontal at a velocity v_0 starts to ascend, describing a circle in the vertical plane. The velocity of the plane changes with height h above the initial level of motion according to the law $v^2 = v_0^2 - 2a_0h$. The velocity of the plane at the upper point of the trajectory is $v_1 = v_0 / 2$.

Determine the acceleration a of the plane at the moment when its velocity is directed vertically upwards.

1.15. An open merry-go-round rotates at an angular velocity ω. A person stands in it at a distance r from the rotational axis. It is raining, and the raindrops fall vertically at a velocity v_0.

How should the person hold an umbrella to protect himself from the rain in the best way?

1.16*. A bobbin rolls without slipping over a horizontal surface so that the velocity v of the end of the thread (point A) is directed along the horizontal. A board hinged at point B leans against the bobbin (Fig. 4). The inner and outer radii of the bobbin are r and R respectively.

Determine the angular velocity ω of the board as a function of an angle α.

1.17. A magnetic tape is wound on an empty spool rotating at a constant angular velocity. The final radius r_f of the winding was found to be three times as large as the initial radius r_i (Fig. 5). The winding time of the tape is t_1.

What is the time t_2 required for winding a tape whose thickness is half that of the initial tape?

1.18. It was found that the winding radius of a tape on a cassette was reduced by half in a time $t_1 = 20$ min of operation.

In what time t_2 will the winding radius be reduced by half again?

1.19. Two rings O and O' are put on two vertical stationary rods AB and $A'B'$ respectively. An inextensible thread is fixed at point A' and on ring O and is passed through ring O' (Fig. 6).

Assuming that ring O' moves downwards at a constant velocity v_1, determine the velocity v_2 of ring O, if $\angle AOO' = \alpha$.

1.20. A weightless inextensible rope rests on a stationary wedge forming an angle α with the horizontal (Fig. 7). One end of the rope is fixed to the wall at point A. A small load is attached to the rope at point B. The wedge starts moving to the right with a constant acceleration a.

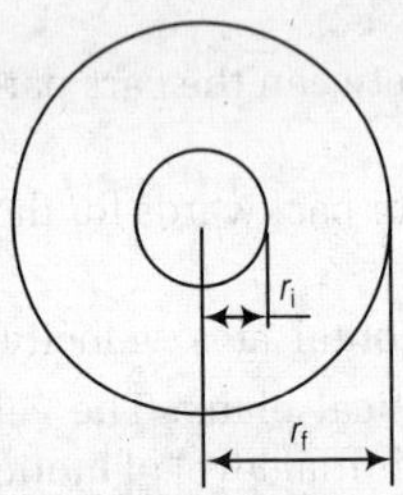

Fig. 5

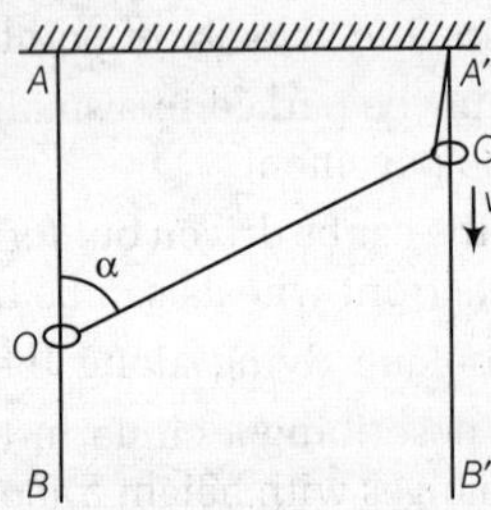

Fig. 6

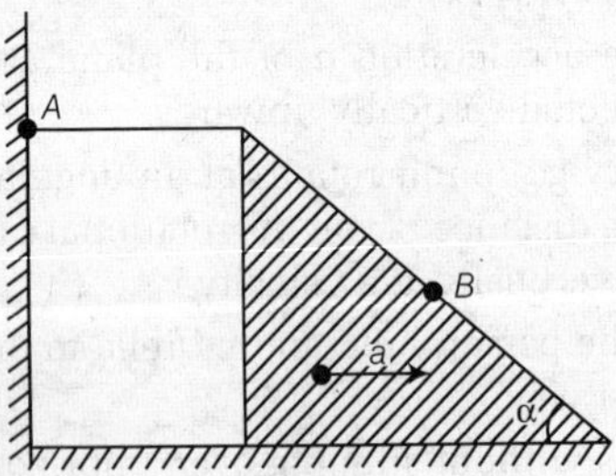

Fig. 7

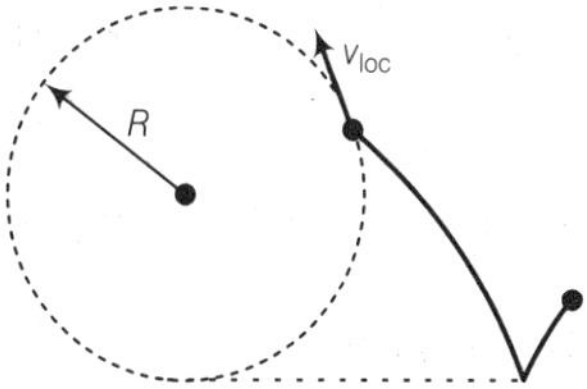

Fig. 8

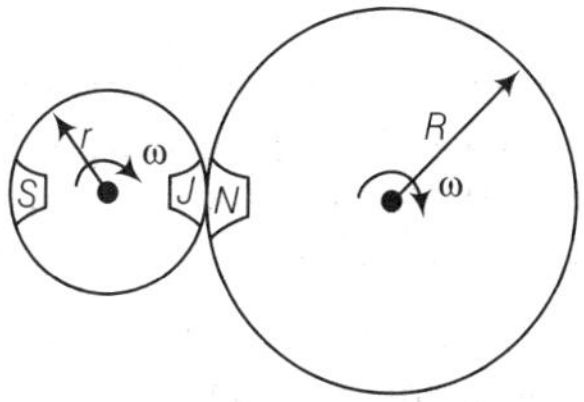

Fig. 9

Determine the acceleration a_1 of the load when it is still on the wedge.

1.21. An ant runs from an ant-hill in a straight line so that its velocity is inversely proportional to the distance from the centre of the ant-hill. When the ant is at point A at a distance $l_1 = 1$ m from the centre of the ant-hill, its velocity $v_1 = 2$ cm/s.

What time will it take the ant to run from point A to point B which is at a distance $l_2 = 2$ m from the centre of the ant-hill?

1.22. During the motion of a locomotive in a circular path of radius R, wind is blowing in the horizontal direction. The trace left by the smoke is shown in Fig. 8 (top view).

Using the figure, determine the velocity v_{wind} of the wind if it is known to be constant, and if the velocity v_{loc} of the locomotive is 36 km/h.

1.23*. Three schoolboys, Sam, John, and Nick are on merry-go-round. Sam and John occupy diametrically opposite points on a merry-go-round of radius r. Nick is on another merry-go-round of radius R. The positions of the boys at the initial instant are shown in Fig. 9.

Considering that the merry-go-round touch each other and rotate in the same direction at the same angular velocity ω, determine the nature of motion of Nick from John's point of view and of Sam from Nick's point of view.

1.24. A hoop of radius R rests on a horizontal surface. A similar hoop moves past it at a velocity v.

Determine the velocity v_A of the upper point of "intersection" of the hoops as a function of the distance d between their centres, assuming that the hoops are thin, and the second hoop is in contact with the first hoop as it moves past the latter.

1.25. A hinged construction consists of three rhombus with the ratio of sides 3:2:1 (Fig. 10). Vertex A_3 moves in the horizontal direction at a velocity v.

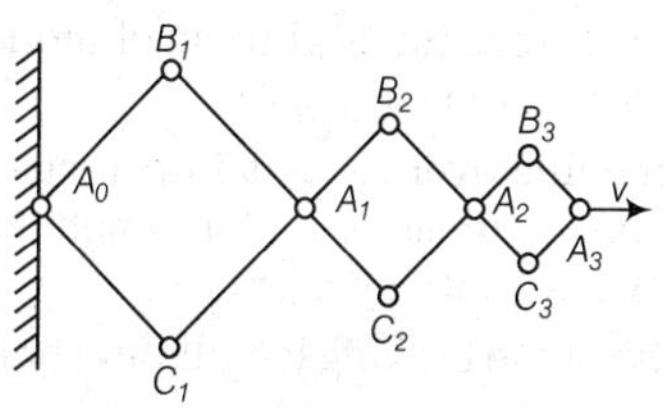

Fig. 10

Determine the velocities of vertices A_1, A_2, and B_2 at the instant when the angles of the construction are 90°.

1.26. The free end of a thread wound on a bobbin of inner radius r and outer radius R is passed round a nail A hammered into the wall (Fig. 11). The thread is pulled at a constant velocity v.

Find the velocity v_0 of the centre of the bobbin at the instant when the thread forms an angle α with the vertical, assuming that the bobbin rolls over the horizontal surface without slipping.

1.27. A rigid ingot is pressed between two parallel guides moving in horizontal directions at opposite velocities v_1 and v_2. At a certain instant of time, the points of contact between the ingot and the guides lie on a straight line perpendicular to the directions of velocities v_1 and v_2 (Fig. 12).

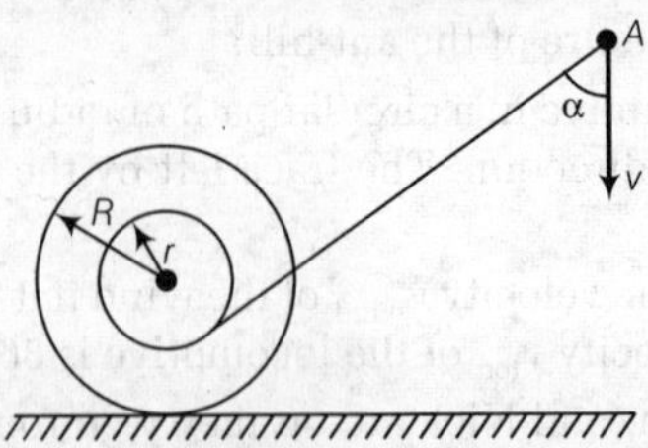

Fig. 11

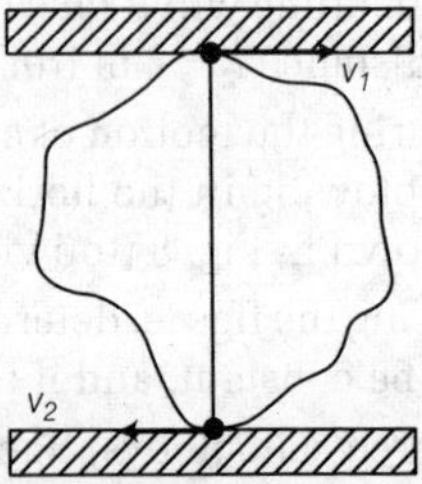

Fig. 12

What points of the ingot have velocities equal in magnitude to v_1 and v_2 at this instant?

1.28. A block lying on a long horizontal conveyer belt moving at a constant velocity receives a velocity $v_0 = 5$ m/s relative to the ground in the direction opposite to the direction of motion of the conveyer. After $t = 4$ s, the velocity of the block becomes equal to the velocity of the belt. The coefficient of friction between the block and the belt is $\mu = 0.2$.

Determine the velocity v of the conveyer belt.

1.29. A body with zero initial velocity slips from the top of an inclined plane forming an angle α with the horizontal. The coefficient of friction μ between the body and the plane increases with the distance l from the top according to the law $\mu = bl$. The body stops before it reaches the end of the plane.

Determine the time t from the beginning of motion of the body to the moment when it comes to rest.

1.30. A loaded sledge moving over ice gets into a region covered with sand and comes to rest before it passes half its length without turning. Then it acquires an initial velocity by a jerk.

Determine the ratio of the braking lengths and braking times before the first stop and after the jerk.

1.31. A rope is passed round a stationary horizontal log fixed at a certain height above the ground. In order to keep a load of mass $m = 6$ kg suspended on one end of the rope, the maximum force $T_1 = 40$ N should be applied to the other end of the rope.

Determine the minimum force T_2 which must be applied to the rope to lift the load.

1.32. Why is it more difficult to turn the steering wheel of a stationary motorcar than of a moving car?

1.33. A certain constant force starts acting on a body moving at a constant velocity v. After a time interval Δt, the velocity of the body is reduced by half, and after the same time interval, the velocity is again reduced by half.

Determine the velocity v_f of the body after a time interval $3\Delta t$ from the moment when the constant force starts acting.

1.34. A person carrying a spring balance and a stopwatch is in a closed carriage standing on a horizontal segment of the railway. When the carriage starts moving, the person sitting with his face in the direction of motion (along the rails) and fixing a load of mass m to the spring balance watches the direction of the deflection of the load and the readings of the balance, marking the instants of time when the readings change with the help of the stopwatch.

When the carriage starts moving and the load is deflected during the first time interval $t_1 = 4$ s towards the observer, the balance indicates a weight $1.25mg$.

During the next time interval $t_2 = 3$ s, the load hangs in the vertical position, and the balance indicates a weight mg. Then the load is deflected to the left (across the carriage), and during an interval $t_3 = 25.12$ s, the balance again indicates a weight $1.25mg$. Finally, during the last time interval $t_4 = 4$ s, the load is deflected from the observer, the reading of the balance remaining the same.

Determine the position of the carriage relative to its initial position and its velocity by this instant of time, assuming that the observer suppresses by his hand the oscillations resulting from a change in the direction of deflection and in the readings of the balance.

1.35. Two identical weightless rods are hinged to each other and to a horizontal beam (Fig. 13). The rigidity of each rod is k_0 and the angle between them is 2α.

Determine the rigidity k of the system of rods relative to the vertical displacement of a hinge A under the action of a certain force F, assuming that displacements are small in comparison with the length of the rods.

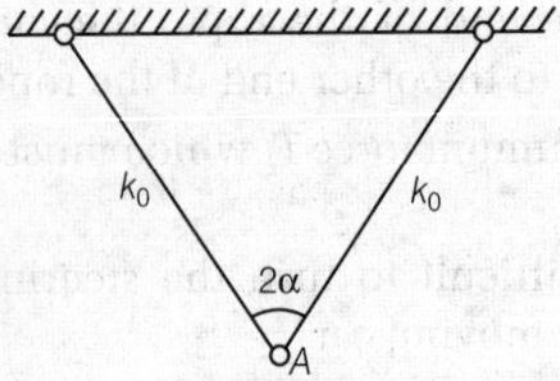

Fig. 13

1.36. Two heavy balls are simultaneously shot from two spring toy-guns arranged on a horizontal plane at a distance $s = 10$ m from each other. The first ball has the initial vertical velocity $v_1 = 10$ m/s, while the second is shot at an angle α to the horizontal at a velocity $v_2 = 20$ m/s. Each ball experiences the action of the force of gravity and the air drag $F = \mu v$, $\mu = 0.1$ g/s.

Determine the angle α at which the balls collide in air.

1.37. A light spring of length l and rigidity k is placed vertically on a table. A small ball of mass m falls on it.

Determine the height h from the surface of the table at which the ball will have the maximum velocity.

1.38*. A heavy ball of mass m is tied to a weightless thread of length l. The friction of the ball against air is proportional to its velocity relative to the air: $F_{fr} = \mu v$. A strong horizontal wind is blowing at a constant velocity v.

Determine the period T of small oscillations, assuming that the oscillations of the ball attenuate in a time much longer than the period of oscillations.

1.39. A rubber string of mass m and rigidity k is suspended at one end.

Determine the elongation Δl of the string.

1.40. For the system at rest shown in Fig. 14, determine the accelerations of all the loads immediately after the lower thread keeping the system in equilibrium has been cut. Assume that the threads are weightless and inextensible, the springs are weightless, the mass of the pulley is negligibly small, and there is no friction at the point of suspension.

1.41. A person hoists one of two loads of equal mass at a constant velocity v (Fig. 15). At the moment when the two loads are at the same height h, the upper pulley is released (is able to rotate without friction like the lower pulley).

Indicate the load which touches the floor first after a certain time t, assuming that the person continues to slack the rope at the same constant velocity v. The masses of the pulleys and the ropes and the elongation of the ropes should be neglected.

1.42. A block can slide along an inclined plane in various directions (Fig.16).

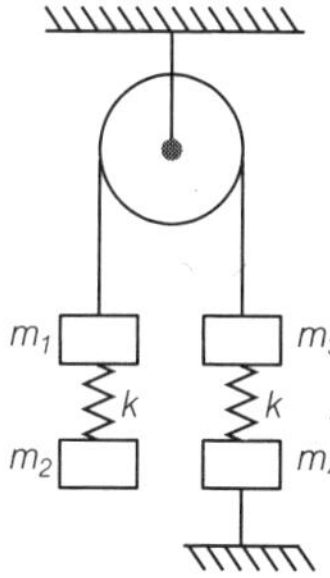

Fig. 14

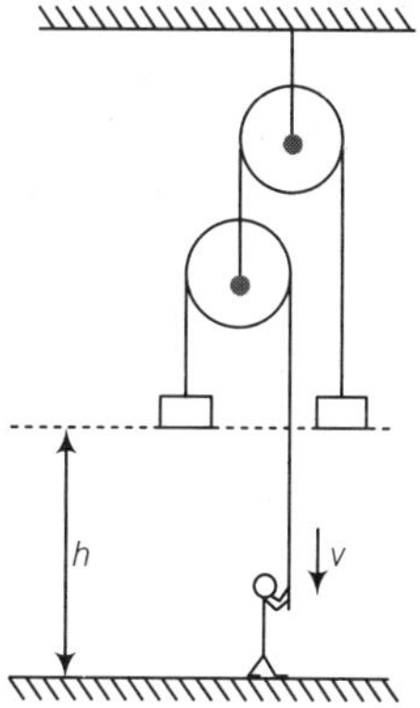

Fig. 15

If it receives a certain initial velocity v directed downwards along the inclined plane, its motion will be uniformly decelerated, and it comes to rest after traversing a distance l_1.

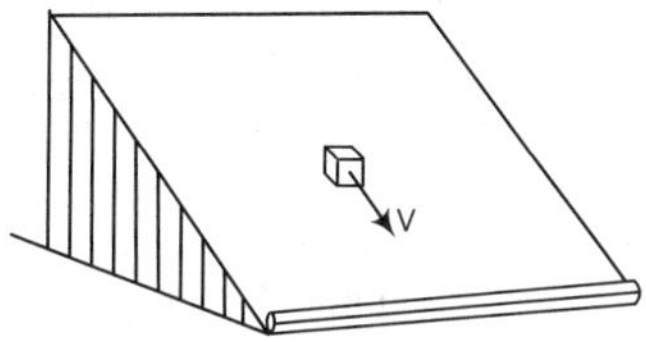

Fig. 16

If the velocity of the same magnitude is imparted to it in the upward direction, it comes to rest after traversing a distance l_2. At the bottom of the inclined plane, a perfectly smooth horizontal guide is fixed.

Determine the distance l traversed by the block over the inclined plane along the guide if the initial velocity of the same magnitude is imparted to it in the horizontal direction.

1.43. A block is pushed upwards along the roof forming an angle α with the horizontal. The time of the ascent of the block to the upper point was found to be half the time of its descent to the initial point.

Determine the coefficient of friction μ between the block and the roof.

1.44. Two balls are placed as shown in Fig. 17 on a "weightless" support formed by two smooth inclined planes each of which forms an angle α with the horizontal. The support can slide without friction along a horizontal plane. The upper ball of mass m_1 is released.

Determine the condition under which the lower ball of mass m_2 starts "climbing" up the support.

1.45. A cylinder of mass m and radius r rests on two supports of the same height (Fig. 18). One support is stationary, while the other slides from under the cylinder at a velocity v.

Determine the force of normal pressure N exerted by the cylinder on the stationary support at the moment when the distance between points A and B of the supports is $AB = r\sqrt{2}$, assuming that the supports

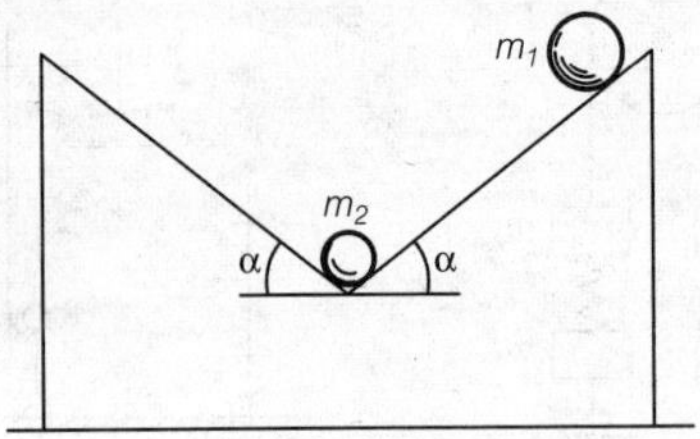

Fig. 17

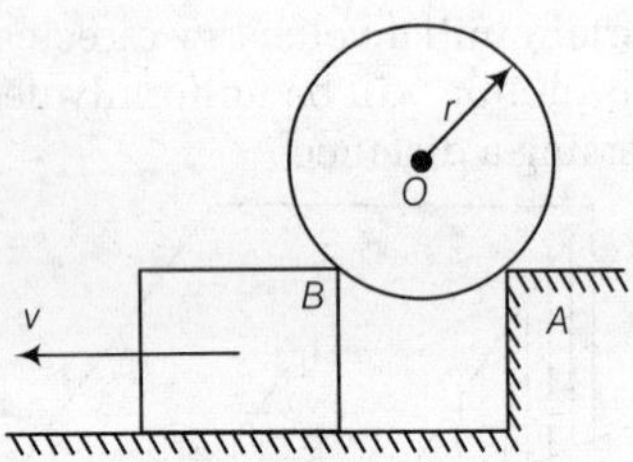

Fig. 18

Fig. 19

were very close to each other at the initial instant. The friction between the cylinder and the supports should be neglected.

1.46. A cylinder and a wedge with a vertical face, touching each other, move along two smooth inclined planes forming the same angle α with the horizontal (Fig. 19). The masses of the cylinder and the wedge are m_1 and m_2 respectively.

Determine the force of normal pressure N exerted by the wedge on the cylinder, neglecting the friction between them.

1.47. A weightless rod of length l with a small load of mass m at the end is hinged at point A (Fig. 20) and occupies a strictly vertical position, touching a body of mass M. A light jerk sets the system in motion.

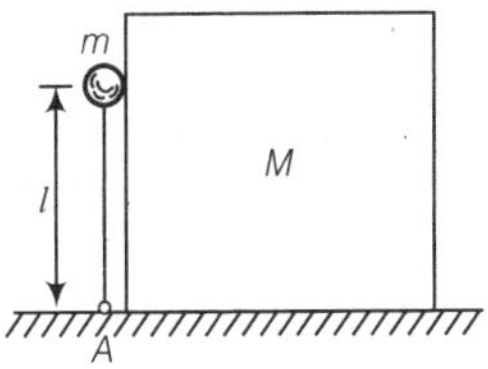

Fig. 20

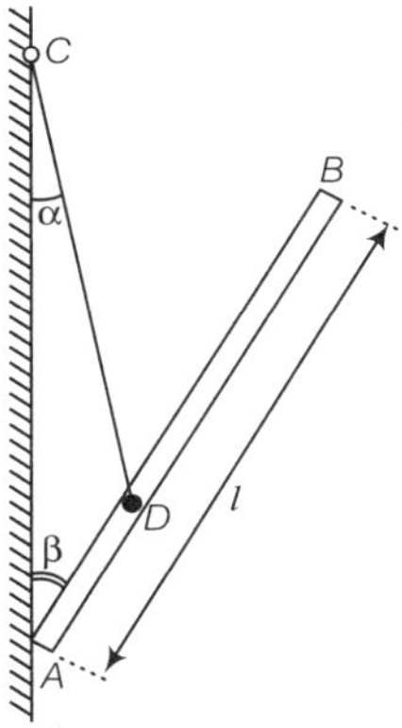

Fig. 21

For what mass ratio M/m will the rod form an angle $\alpha = \pi/6$ with the horizontal at the moment of the separation from the body? What will be the velocity u of the body at this moment? Friction should be neglected.

1.48. A homogeneous rod AB of mass m and length l leans with its lower end against the wall and is kept in the inclined position by a string DC (Fig. 21). The string is tied at point C to the wall and at point D to the rod so that $AD = AB/3$. The angles formed by the string and the rod with the wall are α and β respectively. Find all possible values of the coefficient of friction μ between the rod and the wall.

1.49*. A massive disc rotates about a vertical axis at an angular velocity Ω. A smaller disc of mass m and radius r, whose axis is strictly vertical, is lowered on the first disc (Fig. 22). The distance between the axes of the discs is d ($d > r$), and the coefficient of friction between them is μ.

Determine the steady-state angular velocity ω of the smaller disc. What moment of force M must be applied to the axis of the larger disc to maintain its velocity of rotation constant? The radius of the larger disc is $R > d + r$. The friction at the axes of the discs should be neglected.

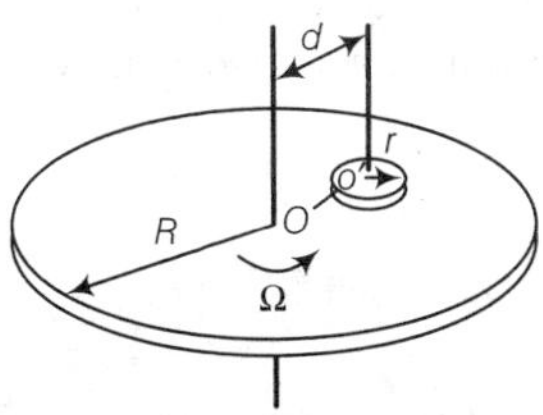

Fig. 22

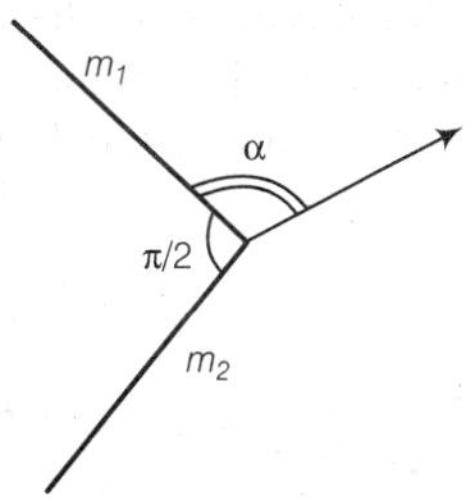

Fig. 23

1.50. Two rigidly connected homogeneous rods of the same length and mass m_1 and m_2 respectively form an angle $\pi/2$ and rest on a rough horizontal surface (Fig. 23). The system is uniformly pulled with the help of a string fixed to the vertex of the angle and parallel to the surface.

Determine the angle α formed by the string and the rod of mass m_1.

1.51. A ball moving at a velocity $v = 10$ m/s hits the foot of a football player.

Determine the velocity u with which the foot should move for the ball impinging on it to come to a halt, assuming that the mass of the ball is much smaller than the mass of the foot and that the impact is perfectly elastic.

1.52. A body of mass m freely falls to the ground. A heavy bullet of mass M shot along the horizontal hits the falling body and sticks in it.

How will the time of fall of the body to the ground change? Determine the time t of fall if the bullet is known to hit the body at the moment it traverses half the distance, and the time of free fall from this height is t_0. Assume that the mass of the bullet is much larger than the mass of the body ($M >> m$). The air drag should be neglected.

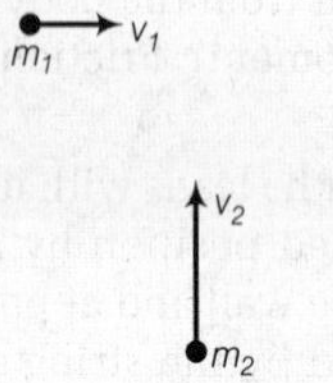

Fig. 24

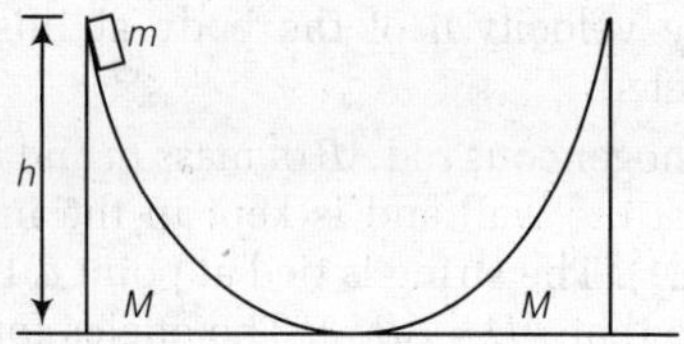

Fig. 25

1.53. Two bodies of mass $m_1 = 1$ kg and $m_2 = 2$ kg move towards each other in mutually perpendicular directions at velocities $v_1 = 3$ m/s and $v_2 = 2$ m/s (Fig. 24). As a result of collision, the bodies stick together. Determine the amount of heat Q liberated as a result of collision.

1.54. The inclined surfaces of two movable wedges of the same mass M are smoothly conjugated with the horizontal plane (Fig. 25). A washer of mass m slides down the left wedge from a height h.

To what maximum height will the washer rise along the right wedge? Friction should be neglected.

1.55. A symmetric block of mass m_1 with a notch of hemispherical shape of radius r rests on a smooth horizontal surface near the wall (Fig. 26).

A small washer of mass m_2 slides without friction from the initial position.

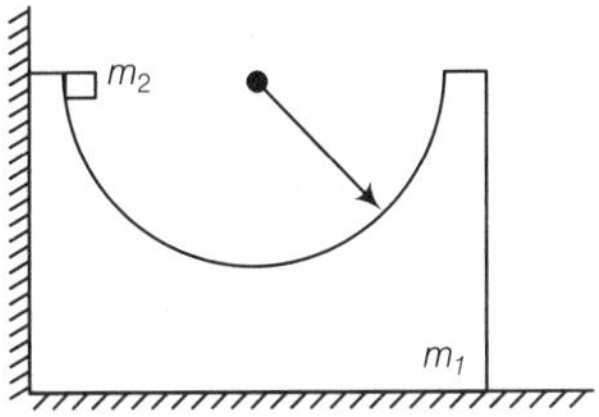

Fig. 26

Find the maximum velocity of the block.

1.56. A round box of inner diameter D containing a washer of radius r lies on a table (Fig. 27). The box is moved as a whole at a constant velocity v directed along the lines of centres of the box and the washer. At an instant t_0, the washer hits the box.

Determine the time dependences of the displacement x_{wash} of the washer and of its velocity v_{wash} relative to the table, starting from the

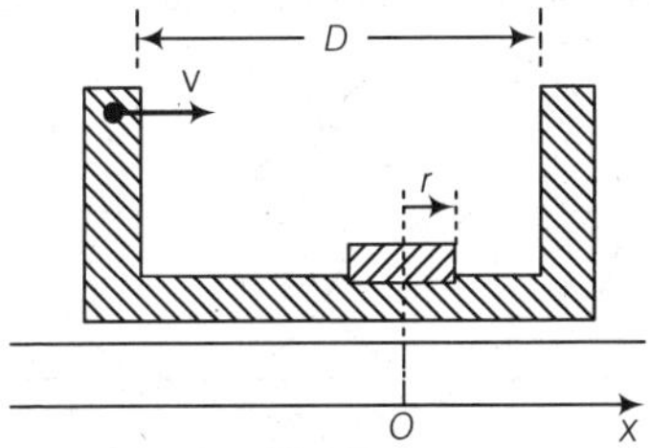

Fig. 27

instant t_0 and assuming that all the impacts of the washer against the box are perfectly elastic. Plot the graphs $x_{wash}(t)$ and $v_{wash}(t)$. The friction between the box and the washer should be neglected.

1.57. A thin hoop of mass M and radius r is placed on a horizontal plane. At the initial instant, the hoop is at rest.

A small washer of mass m with zero initial velocity slides from the upper point of the hoop along a smooth groove in the inner surface of the hoop.

Determine the velocity u of the centre of the hoop at the moment when the washer is at a certain point A of the hoop, whose radius vector forms an angle ϕ with the vertical (Fig. 28). The friction between the hoop and the plane should be neglected.

1.58. A horizontal weightless rod of length $3l$ is suspended on two vertical strings. Two loads of mass m_1 and m_2 are in equilibrium at equal distances from each other and from the ends of the strings (Fig. 29).

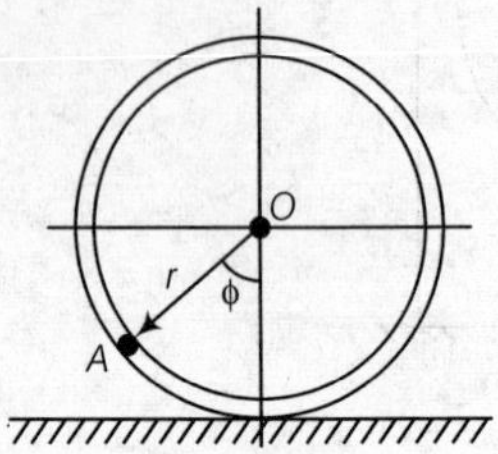

Fig. 28

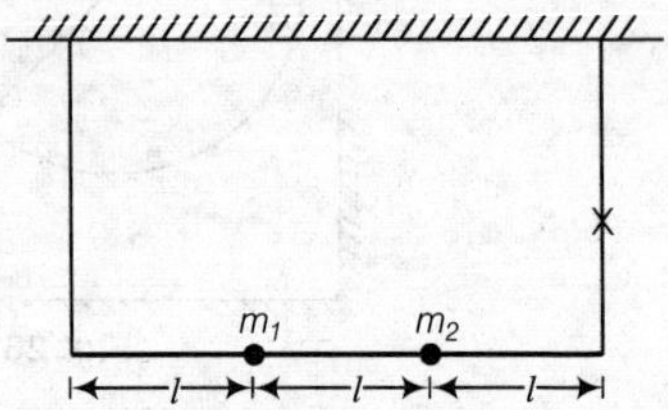

Fig. 29

Determine the tension T of the left string at the instant when the right string snaps.

1.59. A ring of mass m connecting freely two identical thin hoops of mass M each starts sliding down. The hoops move apart over a rough horizontal surface.

Determine the acceleration a of the ring at the initial instant if

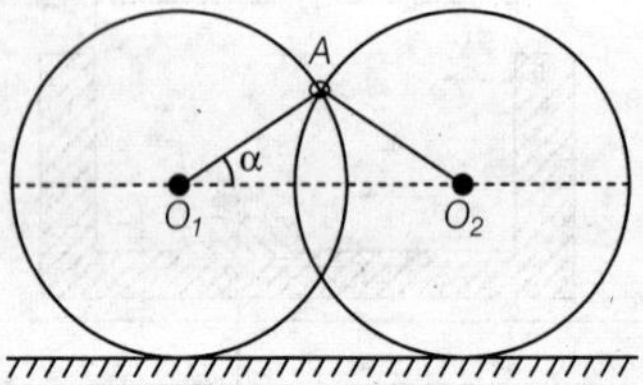

Fig. 30

$\angle AO_1O_2 = \alpha$ (Fig. 30), neglecting the friction between the ring and the hoops.

1.60. A flexible pipe of length l connects two points A and B in space with an altitude difference h (Fig. 31). A rope passed through the pipe is fixed at point A.

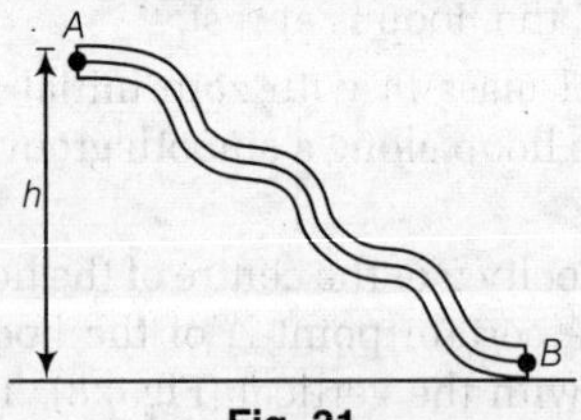

Fig. 31

Determine the initial acceleration a of the rope at the instant when it is released, neglecting the friction between the rope and the pipe walls.

1.61. A smooth washer impinges at a velocity v on a group of three smooth identical blocks resting on a smooth horizontal surface as shown in Fig. 32. The mass of each block is equal to the mass of the washer.

The diameter of the washer and its height are equal to the edge of the block.

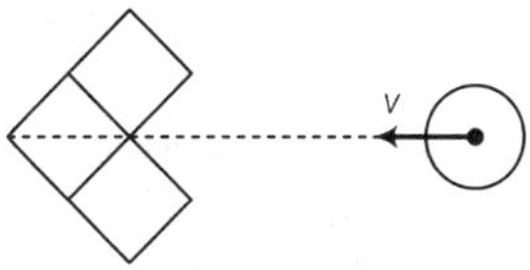

Fig. 32

Determine the velocities of all the bodies after the impact.

1.62. Several identical balls are at rest in a smooth stationary horizontal circular pipe. One of the balls explodes, disintegrating into two fragments of different masses.
Determine the final velocity of the body formed as a result of all collisions, assuming that the collisions are perfectly inelastic.

1.63. Three small bodies with the mass ratio 3:4:5 (the mass of the lightest body is m) are kept at three different points on the inner surface of a smooth hemispherical cup of radius r. The cup is fixed at its lowest point on a horizontal surface. At a certain instant, the bodies are released.
Determine the maximum amount of heat Q that can be liberated in such a system. At what initial arrangement of the bodies will the amount of liberated heat be maximum? Assume that collisions are perfectly inelastic.

1.64. Prove that the maximum velocity imparted by an α-particle to a proton during their collision is 1.6 of the initial velocity of the α-particle.

1.65. Why is it recommended that the air pressure in motorcar tyres be reduced for a motion of the motorcar over sand?

1.66. A long smooth cylindrical pipe of radius r is tilted at an angle α to the horizontal (Fig. 33). A small body at point A is pushed upwards along the inner surface of the pipe so that the direction of its initial velocity forms an angle ϕ with generatrix AB.
Determine the minimum initial velocity v_0 at which the body starts moving upwards without being separated from the surface of the pipe.

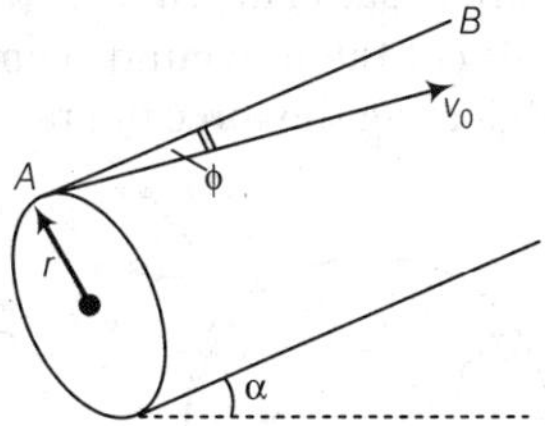

Fig. 33

1.67*. An inextensible rope tied to the axle of a wheel of mass m and radius r is pulled in the horizontal direction in the plane of the wheel. The wheel rolls without jumping over a grid consisting of parallel horizontal rods arranged at a distance l from one another ($l \ll r$).

Determine the average tension T of the rope at which the wheel moves at a constant velocity v, assuming the mass of the wheel to be concentrated at its axle.

1.68. Two coupled wheels (i.e. light wheels of radius r fixed to a thin heavy axle) roll without slipping at a velocity v perpendicular to the boundary over a rough horizontal plane changing into an inclined plane of slope α (Fig. 34).

Determine the value of v at which the coupled wheels roll from the horizontal to the inclined plane without being separated from the surface.

1.69. A thin rim of mass m and radius r rolls down an inclined plane of slope α, winding thereby a thin ribbon of linear density ρ (Fig. 35). At the initial moment, the rim is at a height h above the horizontal surface.

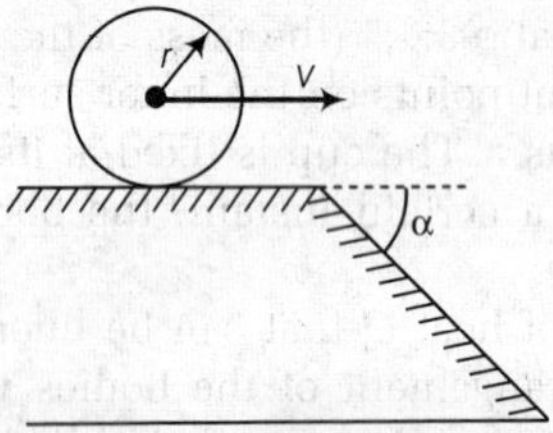

Fig. 34

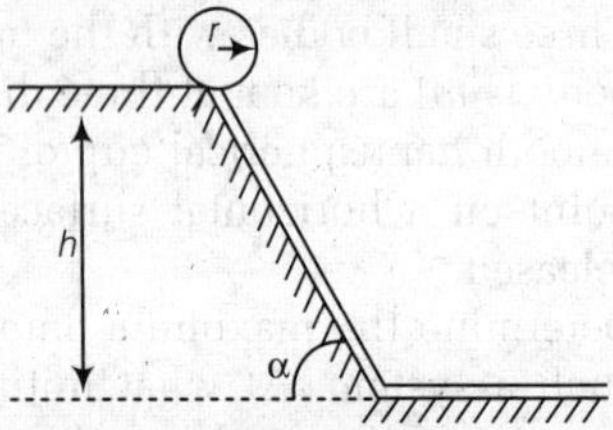

Fig. 35

Determine the distance s from the foot of the inclined plane at which the rim stops, assuming that the inclined plane smoothly changes into the horizontal plane.

1.70. Two small balls of the same size and of mass m_1 and $m_2 (m_1 > m_2)$ are tied by a thin weightless thread and dropped from a balloon.

Determine the tension T of the thread during the flight after the motion of the balls has become steady-state.

1.71*. A ball is tied by a weightless inextensible thread to a fixed cylinder of radius r. At the initial moment, the thread is wound so that the ball touches the cylinder. Then the ball acquires a velocity v in the radial direction, and the thread starts unwinding (Fig. 36).

Determine the length l of the unwound segment of the thread by the instant of time t, neglecting the force of gravity.

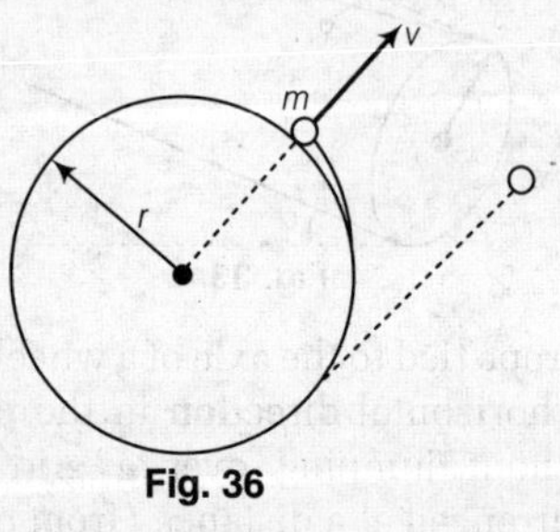

Fig. 36

1.72. Three small balls of the same mass, white (w), green (g), and blue (b), are fixed by weightless rods at the vertices of the equilateral triangle with side l. The system of balls is placed on a smooth horizontal surface and set in rotation about the centre of mass with period T. At a certain instant, the blue ball tears away from the frame.

Determine the distance L between the blue and the green ball after the time T.

1.73. A block is connected to an identical block through a weightless pulley by a weightless inextensible thread of length $2l$ (Fig. 37). The left block rests on a table at a distance l from its edge, while the right block is kept at the same level so that the thread is unstretched and does not sag, and then released.

What will happen first: will the left block reach the edge of the table (and touch the pulley) or the right block hit the table?

1.74. Two loads of the same mass are tied to the ends of a weightless inextensible thread passed through a weightless pulley (Fig. 38).

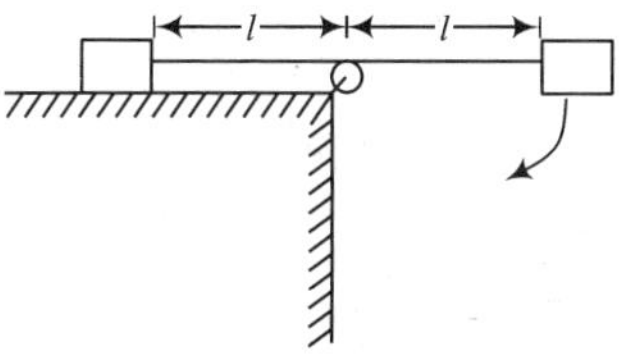

Fig. 37

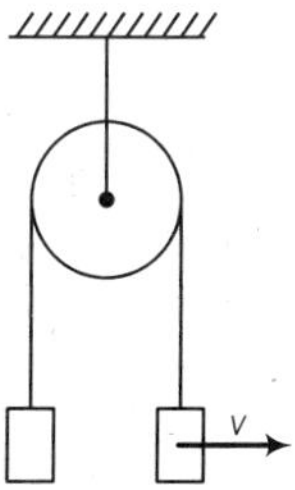

Fig. 38

Initially, the system is at rest, and the loads are at the same level. Then, the right load abruptly acquires a horizontal velocity v in the plane of the figure.

Which load will be lower in a time?

1.75. Two balls of mass $m_1 = 56$ g and $m_2 = 28$ g are suspended on two threads of length $l_1 = 7$ cm and $l_2 = 11$ cm at the end of a freely hanging rod (Fig. 39).

Determine the angular velocity ω at which the rod should be rotated about the vertical axle so that it remains in the vertical position.

1.76. A weightless horizontal rigid rod along which two balls of the same mass m can move without friction rotates at a constant angular velocity ω about a vertical axle. The balls are connected by a weightless spring of rigidity k, whose length in the undeformed state is l_0. The ball which is closer to the vertical axle is connected to it by the same spring.

Determine the lengths of the springs. Under what conditions will the balls move in circles?

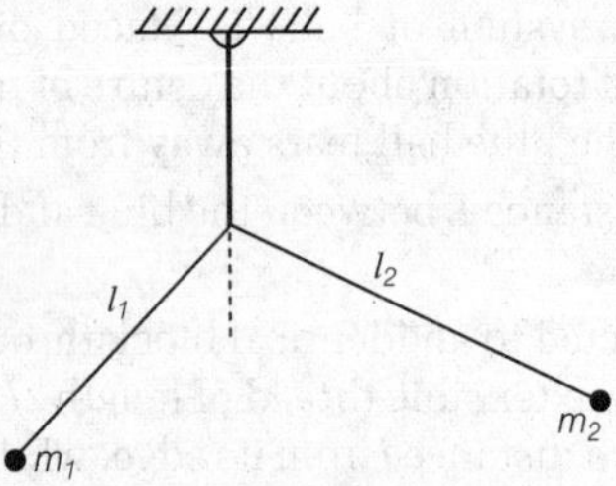

Fig. 39

1.77. Figure 40 shows the dependence of the kinetic energy W_k of a body on the displacement s during the motion of the body in a straight line. The force $F_A = 2$ N is known to act on the body at point A.

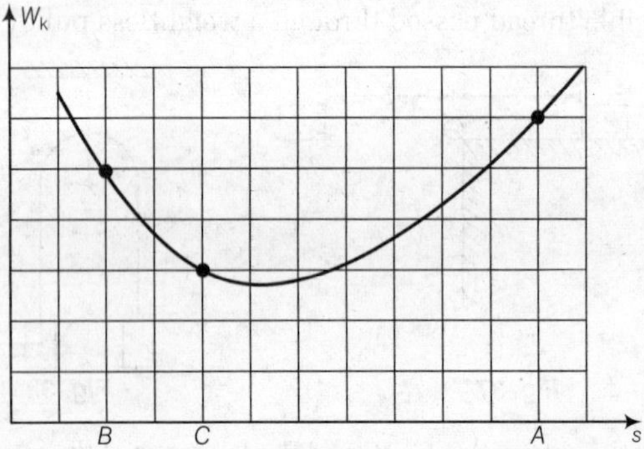

Fig. 40

Determine the forces acting on the body at points B and C.

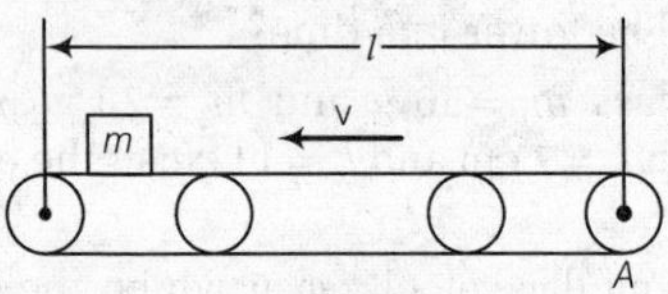

Fig. 41

1.78. A conveyer belt having a length l and carrying a block of mass m moves at a velocity v (Fig. 41).

Determine the velocity v_0 with which the block should be pushed against the direction of motion of the conveyer so that the amount of heat liberated as a result of deceleration of the block by the conveyer belt is maximum.

What is the maximum amount of heat Q if the coefficient of friction is μ and the condition $v < \sqrt{2\mu l g}$ is satisfied?

1.79. A heavy pipe rolls from the same height down two hills with different profiles (Figs. 42 and 43). In the former case, the pipe rolls down without slipping, while in the latter case, it slips on a certain region.

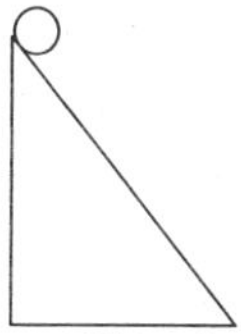

Fig. 42

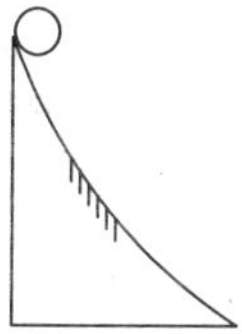

Fig. 43

In what case will the velocity of the pipe at the end of the path be lower?

1.80. A heavy load is suspended on a light spring. The spring is slowly pulled down at the midpoint (a certain work A is done thereby) and then released. Determine the maximum kinetic energy W_k of the load in the subsequent motion.

1.81. The masses of two stars are m_1 and m_2, and their separation is l. Determine the period T of their revolution in circular orbits about a common centre.

1.82. A meteorite approaching a planet of mass M (in the straight line passing through the centre of the planet) collides with an automatic space station orbiting the planet in the circular trajectory of radius R. The mass of the station is ten times as large as the mass of the meteorite. As a result of collision, the meteorite sticks in the station which goes over to a new orbit with the minimum distance $R/2$ from the planet.

Determine the velocity u of the meteorite before the collision.

1.83. The cosmonauts who landed at the pole of a planet found that the force of gravity there is 0.01 of that on the Earth, while the duration of the day on the planet is the same as that on the Earth. It turned out besides that the force of gravity on the equator is zero.

Determine the radius R of the planet.

1.84. The radius of Neptune's orbit is 30 times the radius of the Earth's orbit. Determine the period T_N of revolution of Neptune around the Sun.

1.85. Three loads of mass m_1, m_2 and M are suspended on a string passed through two pulleys as shown in Fig. 44. The pulleys are at the same distance from the points of suspension.

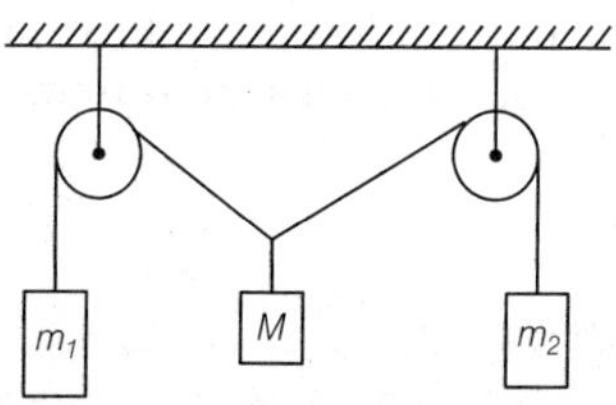

Fig. 44

Find the ratio of masses of the loads at which the system is in equilibrium. Can these conditions always be realized? The friction should be neglected.

1.86. Determine the minimum coefficient of friction μ_{min} between a thin homogeneous rod and a floor at which a person can slowly lift the rod from the floor without slippage to the vertical position, applying to its end a force perpendicular to it.

1.87. Three weightless rods of length l each are hinged at points A and B lying on the same horizontal and joint through hinges at points C and D (Fig. 45). The length $AB = 2l$. A load of mass m is suspended at the hinge C.

Determine the minimum force F_{min} applied to the hinge D for which the middle rod remains horizontal.

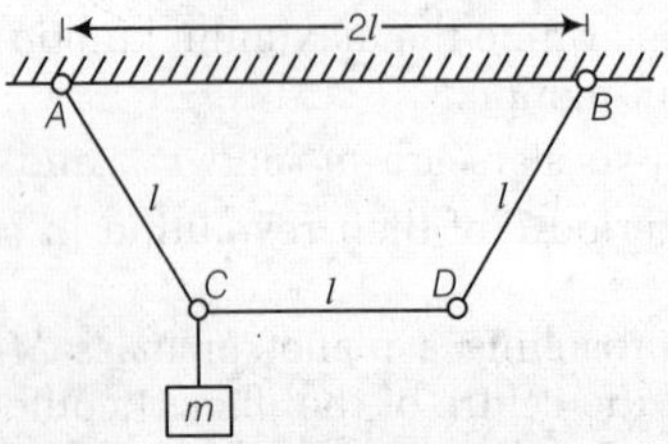

Fig. 45

1.88. A hexagonal pencil placed on an inclined plane with a slope α at right angles to the generatrix (i.e. the line of intersection of the plane and the horizontal surface) remains at rest. The same pencil placed parallel to the generatrix rolls down the plane.

Determine the angle ϕ between the axis of the pencil and the generatrix of the inclined plane (Fig. 46) at which the pencil is still in equilibrium.

1.89. A homogeneous rod of length $2l$ leans against a vertical wall at one end and against a smooth stationary surface at another end.

What function $y(x)$ must be used to describe the cross section of this surface for the rod to remain in equilibrium in any position even in the absence of friction? Assume that the rod remains all the time in the same vertical plane perpendicular to the plane of the wall.

1.90. A thin perfectly rigid weightless rod with a point-like ball fixed at one end is deflected through a small angle α from its equilibrium position and then released.

At the moment when the rod forms an angle $\beta < \alpha$ with the vertical, the ball undergoes a perfectly elastic collision with an inclined wall (Fig. 47).

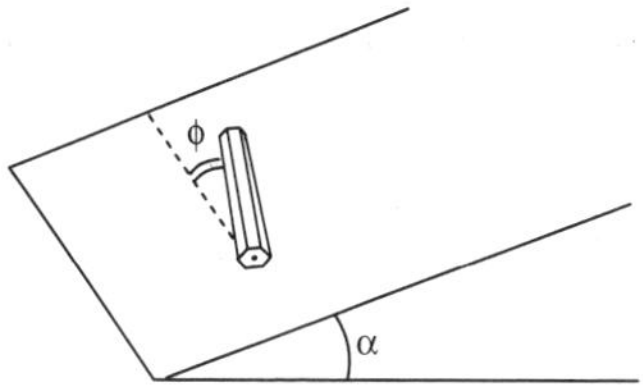

Fig. 46

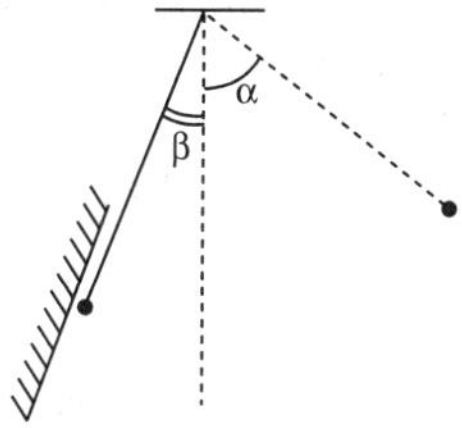

Fig. 47

Determine the ratio T_1 / T of the period of oscillations of this pendulum to the period of oscillations of a simple pendulum having the same length.

1.91*. A ball of mass m falls from a certain height on the pan of mass M ($M >> m$) of a spring balance. The rigidity of the spring is k.

Determine the displacement Δx of the point about which the pointer of the balance will oscillate, assuming that the collisions of the ball with the pan are perfectly elastic.

1.92. A bead of mass m can move without friction along a long wire bent in a vertical plane in the shape of a graph of a certain function. Let l_A be the length of the segment of the wire from the origin to a certain point A. It is known that if the bead is released at point A such that $l_A < l_{A_0}$, its motion will be strictly harmonic: $l(t) = l_A \cos \omega t$.

Prove that there exists a point B ($l_{A_0} \le l_B$) at which the condition of harmonicity of oscillations will be violated.

1.93. Two blocks having mass m and $2m$ and connected by a spring of rigidity k lie on a horizontal plane.

Determine the period T of small longitudinal oscillations of the system, neglecting friction.

1.94. A heavy round log is suspended at the ends on two ropes so that the distance between the points of suspension of the ropes is equal to the diameter of the log. The length of each vertical segment of the ropes is l.

Determine the period T of small oscillations of the system in a vertical plane perpendicular to the log.

1.95. A load of mass M is on horizontal rails. A pendulum made of a ball of mass m tied to a weightless inextensible thread is suspended to the load. The load can move only along the rails.

Determine the ratio of the periods T_2 / T_1 of small oscillations of the pendulum in vertical planes parallel and perpendicular to the rails.

1.96. Four weightless rods of length l each are connected by hinged joints and form a rhombus (Fig. 48). A hinge A is fixed, and a load is suspended to a hinge C. Hinges D and B are connected by a weightless spring of length $1.5l$ in the undeformed state. In equilibrium, the rods form angles $\alpha_0 = 30°$ with the vertical. Determine the period T of small oscillations of the load.

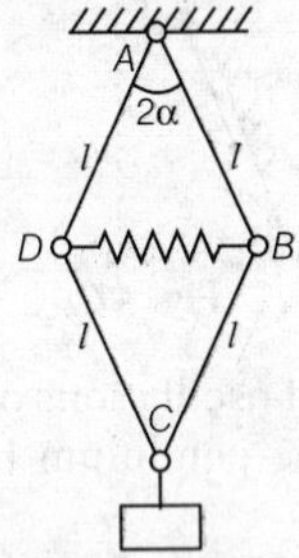

Fig. 48

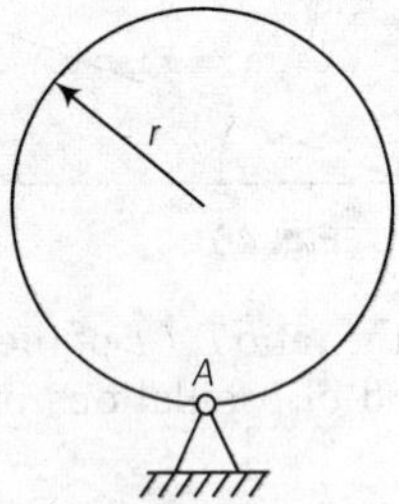

Fig. 49

1.97. A thin hoop is hinged at point A so that at the initial moment its centre of mass is almost above point A (Fig. 49). Then the hoop is smoothly released, and in a time $\tau = 0.5$ s, its centre of mass occupies the lowest position. Determine the time t in which a pendulum formed by a heavy ball B fixed on a weightless rigid rod whose length is equal to the radius of the hoop will return to the lowest equilibrium position if initially the ball was near the extreme upper position (Fig. 50) and was released without pushing.

1.98. A weightless rigid rod with a load at the end is hinged at point A to the wall so that it can rotate in all directions (Fig. 51).

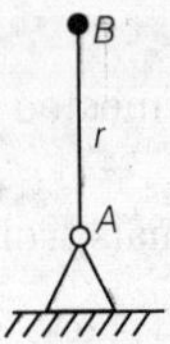

Fig. 50

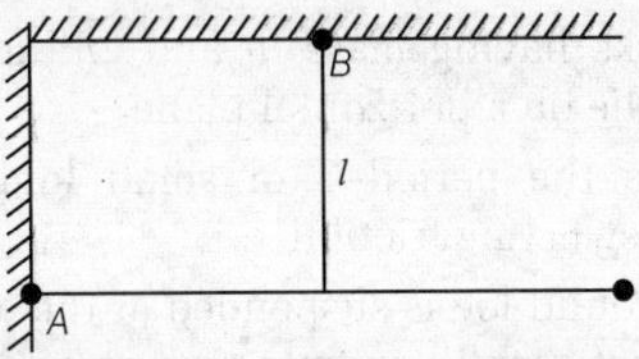

Fig. 51

The rod is kept in the horizontal position by a vertical inextensible thread of length l, fixed at its midpoint. The load receives a momentum in the direction perpendicular to the plane of the figure. Determine the period T of small oscillations of the system.

1.99. One rope of a swing is fixed above the other rope by b. The distance between the poles of the swing is a. The lengths l_1 and l_2 of the ropes are such that $l_1^2 + l_2^2 = a^2 + b^2$ (Fig. 52).

Determine the period T of small oscillations of the swing, neglecting the height of the swinging person in comparison with the above lengths.

1.100. Being a punctual man, the lift operator of a skyscraper hung an exact pendulum clock on the lift wall to know the end of the working day. The lift moves with an upward and downward accelerations during the same time (according to a stationary clock), the magnitudes of the accelerations remaining unchanged.

Will the operator finish his working day in time, or will he work more (less) than required?

1.101. The atmospheric pressure is known to decrease with altitude. Therefore, at the upper storeys of the Moscow State University building the atmospheric pressure must be lower than at the lower storeys. In order to verify this, a student connected one arm of a U-shaped manometer to the upper auditorium and the other arm to the lower auditorium.

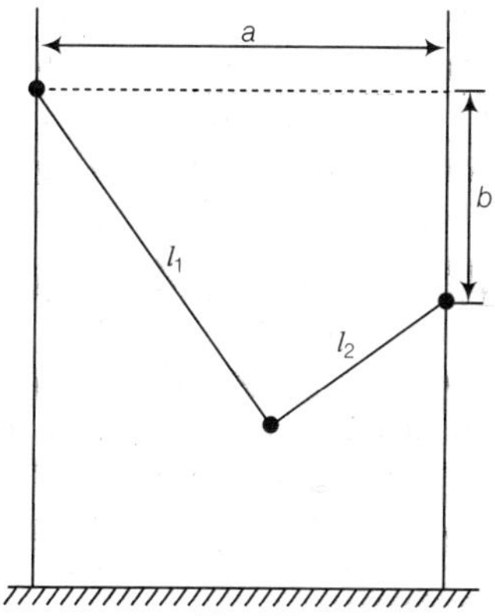

Fig. 52

What will the manometer indicate?

1.102. Two thin-walled tubes closed at one end are inserted one into the other and completely filled with mercury. The cross-sectional areas of the tubes are S and $2S$.

The atmospheric pressure is $p_0 = \rho_{mer} gh$, where ρ_{mer} is the density of mercury, g is the free-fall acceleration, and h is the height. The length of each tube is $l > h$.

What work A must be done by external forces to slowly pull out the inner tube? The pressure of mercury vapour and the forces of adhesion between the material of the tubes and mercury should be neglected.

1.103. Two cylinders with a horizontal and a vertical axis respectively rest on a horizontal surface. The cylinders are connected at the lower parts through a thin tube.

The "horizontal" cylinder of radius r is open at one end and has a piston in it

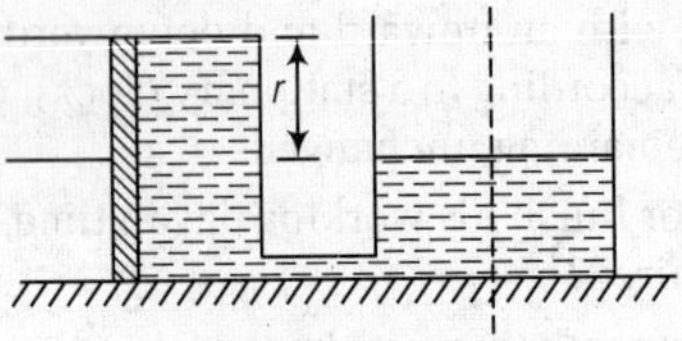

Fig. 53

(Fig. 53). The "vertical" cylinder is open at the top. The cylinders contain water which completely fills the part of the horizontal cylinder behind the piston and is at a certain level in the vertical cylinder.

Determine the level h of water in the vertical cylinder at which the piston is in equilibrium, neglecting friction.

1.104. An aluminium wire is wound on a piece of cork of mass m_{cork}. The densities ρ_{cork}, ρ_{al}, and ρ_w of cork, aluminium, and water are $0.5 \times 10^3 kg/m^3$, 2.7×10^3 kg/m^3, and 1×10^3 kg/m^3 respectively.

Determine the minimum mass m_{al} of the wire that should be wound on the cork so that the cork with the wire is completely submerged in water.

1.105. One end of an iron chain is fixed to a sphere of mass $M = 10$ kg and of diameter $D = 0.3$ m ,(the volume of such a sphere is $V = 0.0141$ m^3), while the other end is free. The length l of the chain is 3 m and its mass m is 9 kg. The sphere with the chain is in a reservoir whose depth $H = 3$ m.

Determine the depth at which the sphere will float, assuming that iron is 7.85 times heavier than water.

1.106. Two bodies of the same volume but of different masses are in equilibrium on a lever.

Will the equilibrium be violated if the lever is immersed in water so that the bodies are completely submerged?

1.107. A flat wide and a high narrow box float in two identical vessels filled with water. The boxes do not sink when two identical heavy bodies of mass m each are placed into them.

In which vessel will the level of water be higher?

1.108. A steel ball floats in a vessel with mercury.

How will the volume of the part of the ball submerged in mercury change if a layer of water completely covering the ball is poured above the mercury?

1.109. A piece of ice floats in a vessel with water above which a layer of a lighter oil is poured.

How will the level of the interface change after the whole of ice melts? What will be the change in the total level of liquid in the vessel?

1.110. A homogeneous aluminium ball of radius $r = 0.5$ cm is suspended on a weightless thread from an end of a homogeneous rod of mass $M = 4.4$ g. The rod is placed on the edge of a tumbler with water so that half of the ball is submerged in water when the system is in equilibrium (Fig. 54). The densities ρ_{al} and ρ_w of aluminium and water are 2.7×10^3 kg/m^3 and 1×10^3 kg/m^3 respectively.

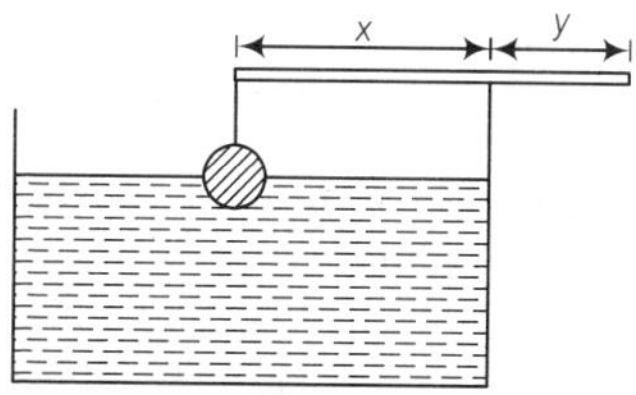

Fig. 54

Determine the ratio y/x of the parts of the rod to the brim, neglecting the surface tension on the boundaries between the ball and water.

1.111. To what division will mercury fill the tube of a freely falling barometer of length 105 cm at an atmospheric pressure of 760 mm Hg?

1.112. A simple accelerometer (an instrument for measuring acceleration) can be made in the form of a tube filled with a liquid and bent as shown in Fig. 55. During motion, the level of the liquid in the left arm will be at a height h_1, and in the right arm at a height h_2.

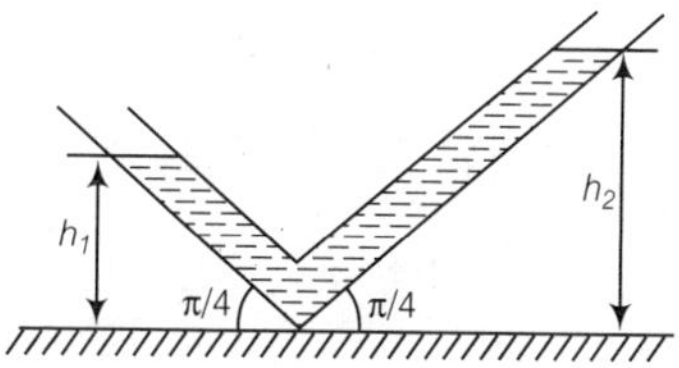

Fig. 55

Determine the acceleration a of a carriage in which the accelerometer is installed, assuming that the diameter of the tube is much smaller than h_1 and h_2.

1.113. A jet plane having a cabin of length $l = 50$ m flies along the horizontal with an acceleration $a = 1$ m/s^2. The air density in the cabin is $\rho = 1.2 \times 10^{-3}$ g/cm^3.

What is the difference between the atmospheric pressure and the air pressure exerted on the ears of the passengers sitting in the front, middle, aud rear parts of the cabin?

1.114. A tube filled with water and closed at both ends uniformly rotates in a horizontal plane about the OO'-axis. The manometers fixed in the tube wall at distances r_1 and r_2 from the rotational axis indicate pressures p_1 and p_2 respectively (Fig. 56).

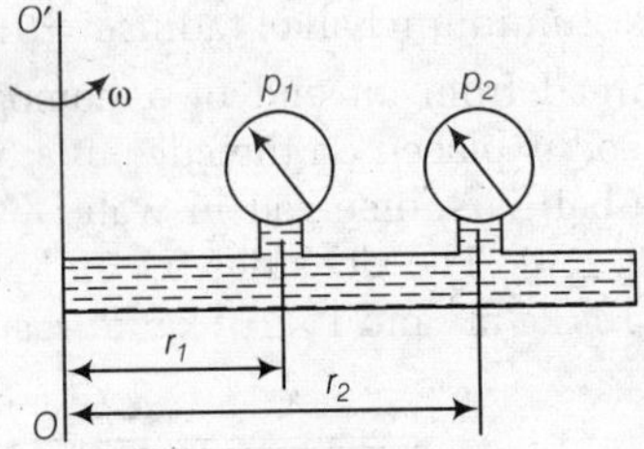

Fig. 56

Determine the angular velocity ω of rotation of the tube, assuming that the density ρ_w of water is known.

1.115. Let us suppose that the drag F to the motion of a body in some medium depends on the velocity v of the body as $F = \mu v^{\alpha}$, where $\alpha > 0$.

At what values of the exponent α will the body pass an infinitely large distance after an initial momentum has been imparted to it?

1.116. The atmospheric pressure on Mars is known to be equal to 1/200 of the atmospheric pressure on the Earth. The diameter of Mars is approximately equal to half the Earth's diameter, and the densities ρ_E and ρ_M of the planets are 5.5×10^3 kg/m^3 and 4×10^3 kg/m^3.

Determine the ratio of the masses of the Martian and the Earth's atmospheres.

2. Heat and Molecular Physics

For the problems of this chapter, the universal gas constant R (wherever required) should be taken equal to 8.3 J/(mol · K).

2.1. Two vertical communicating cylinders of different diameters contain a gas at a constant temperature under pistons of mass $m_1 = 1$ kg and $m_2 = 2$ kg. The cylinders are in vacuum, and the pistons are at the same height $h_0 = 0.2$ m.

What will be the difference h in their heights if the mass of the first piston is made as large as the mass of the second piston?

2.2. The temperature of the walls of a vessel containing a gas at a temperature T is T_{wall}.

In which case is the pressure exerted by the gas on the vessel walls higher: when the vessel walls are colder than the gas ($T_{wall} < T$) or when they are warmer than the gas ($T_{wall} > T$)?

2.3. A cyclic process (cycle) 1-2-3-4-1 consisting of two isobars 2-3 and 4-1, isochor 1-2, and a certain process *3-4* represented by a straight line on the *p-V* diagram (Fig. 57) involves n moles of an ideal gas. The gas temperatures in states 1, 2, and 3 are T_1, T_2, and T_3 respectively, and points 2 and 4 lie on the same isotherm.

Determine the work A done by the gas during the cycle.

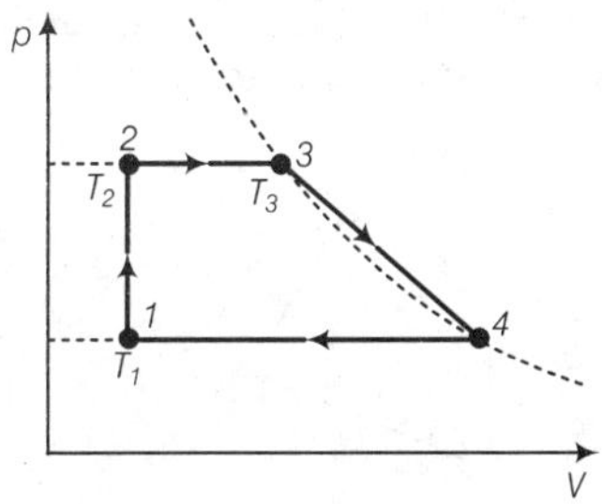

Fig. 57

2.4. Three moles of an ideal monatomic gas perform a cycle shown in Fig. 58. The gas temperatures in different states are

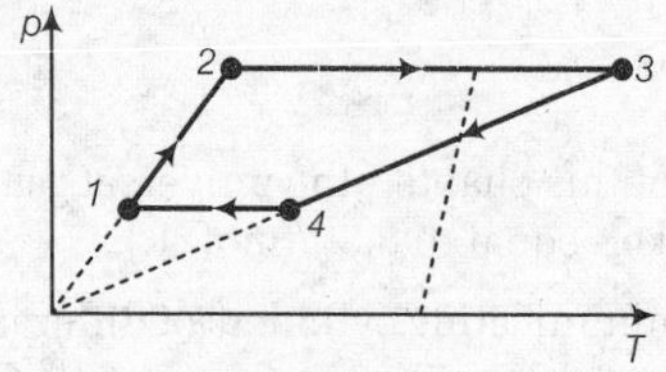

Fig. 58

$T_1 = 400\,\text{K}, T_2 = 800\,\text{K}, T_3 = 2400\,\text{K}$, and $T_4 = 1200\,\text{K}$.

Determine the work A done by the gas during the cycle.

2.5. Determine the work A done by an ideal gas during a closed cycle $1 \to 4 \to 3 \to 2 \to 1$ shown in Fig. 59 if $p_1 = 10^5$ Pa, $p_0 = 3 \times 10^5$ Pa, $p_2 = 4 \times 10^5$ Pa, $V_2 - V_1 = 10\,\text{l}$, and segments 4-3 and 2-1 of the cycle are parallel to the V-axis.

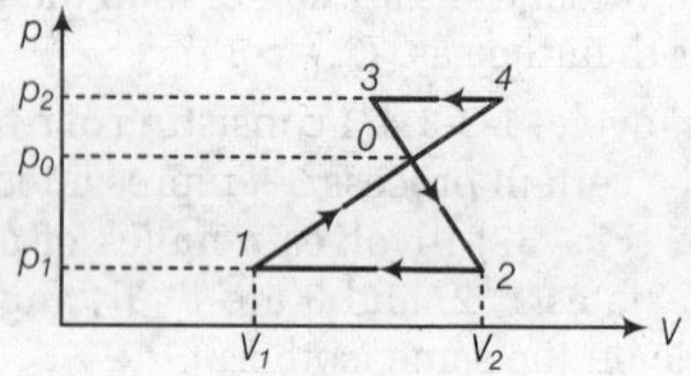

Fig. 59

2.6. A gas takes part in two thermal processes in which it is heated from the same initial state to the same final temperature.

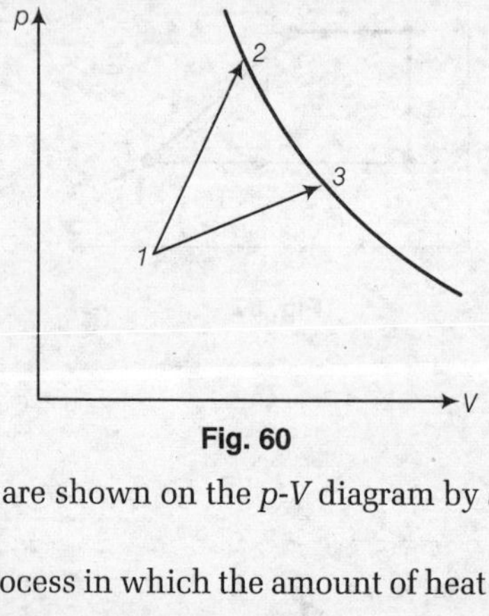

Fig. 60

The processes are shown on the p-V diagram by straight lines 1-3 and 1-2 (Fig. 60).

Indicate the process in which the amount of heat supplied to the gas is larger.

2.7. A vessel of volume $V = 30$ l is separated into three equal parts by stationary semipermeable thin particles (Fig. 61).

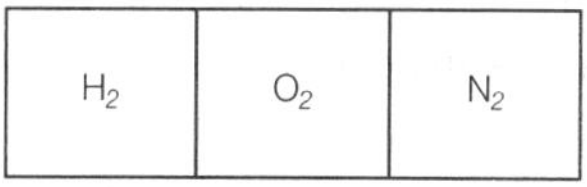

Fig. 61

The left, middle, and right parts are filled with $m_{H_2} = 30$ g of hydrogen, $m_{O_2} = 160$ g of oxygen, and $m_{N_2} = 70$ g of nitrogen respectively. The left partition lets through only hydrogen, while the right partition lets through hydrogen and nitrogen.
What will be the pressure in each part of the vessel after the equilibrium has been set in if the vessel is kept at a constant temperature $T = 300$ K?

2.8*. The descent module of a spacecraft approaches the surface of a planet along the vertical at a constant velocity, transmitting the data on outer pressure to the spacecraft. The time dependence of pressure (in arbitrary units) is shown in Fig. 62. The data transmitted by the module after landing are: the temperature $T = 700$ K and the free-fall acceleration $g = 10\ \text{m/s}^2$.

Determine (a) the velocity v of landing of the module if the atmosphere of the planet is known to consist of carbon dioxide CO_2, and (b) the temperature T_h at an altitude $h = 15$ km above the surface of the planet.

2.9. A vertical thermally insulated cylinder of volume V contains n moles of an ideal monatomic gas under a weightless piston.

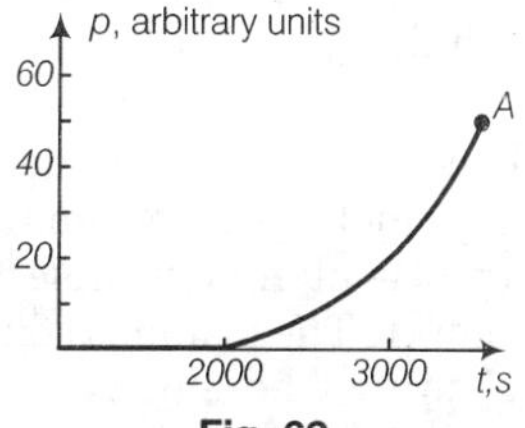

Fig. 62

A load of mass M is placed on the piston, as a result of which the piston is displaced by a distance h.
Determine the final temperature T_f of the gas established after the piston has been displaced if the area of the piston is S and the atmospheric pressure is p_0.

2.10. A vertical cylinder of cross-sectional area S contains one mole of an ideal monatomic gas under a piston of mass M. At a certain instant, a heater which transmits to a gas an amount of heat q per unit time is switched on under the piston.

Determine the established velocity v of the piston under the condition that the gas pressure under the piston is constant and equal to p_0, and the gas under the piston is thermally insulated.

2.11*. The product of pressure and volume (pV) of a gas does not change with volume at a constant temperature only provided that the gas is ideal.

Will the product pV be higher or lower under a very strong compression of a gas if no assumption is made concerning the ideal nature of the gas?

2.12*. A horizontal cylindrical vessel of length $2l$ is separated by a thin heat-insulating piston into two equal parts each of which contains n moles of an ideal monatomic gas at a temperature T. The piston is connected to the end faces of the vessel by undeformed

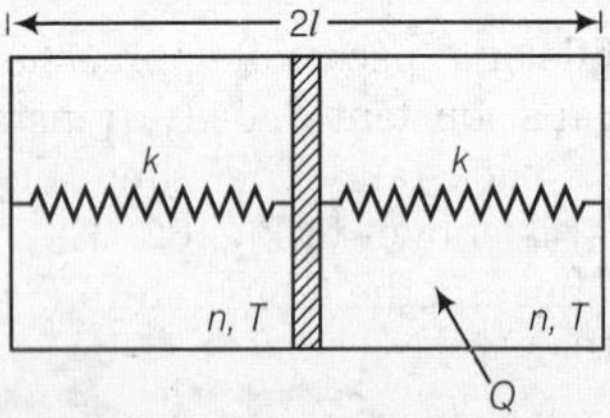

Fig. 63

springs of rigidity k each (Fig. 63). When an amount of heat Q is supplied to the gas in the right part, the piston is displaced to the left by a distance $x = l/2$.

Determine the amount of heat Q' given away at the temperature T to a thermostat with which the gas in the left part is in thermal contact all the time.

2.13. A thermally insulated vessel is divided into two parts by a heat-insulating piston which can move in the vessel without friction. The left part of the vessel contains one mole of an ideal monatomic gas, and the right part is empty. The piston is connected to the right wall of the vessel through a spring whose length in free state is equal to the length of the vessel (Fig. 64).

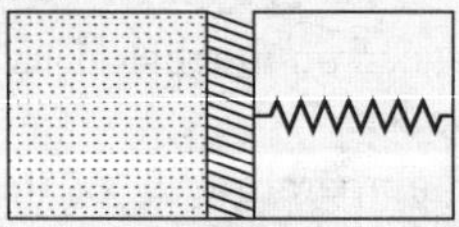

Fig. 64

Determine the heat capacity C of the system, neglecting the heat capacities of the vessel, piston, and spring.

2.14. Prove that the efficiency of a heat engine based on a cycle consisting of two isotherms and two isochors is lower than the efficiency of Carnot's heat engine operating with the same heater and cooler.

2.15*. Let us suppose that a planet of mass M and radius r is surrounded by an atmosphere of constant density, consisting of a gas of molar mass μ.

Determine the temperature T of the atmosphere on the surface of the planet if the height of the atmosphere is h ($h << r$).

2.16. It is known that the temperature in the room is + 20°C when the outdoor temperature is – 20 °C, and + 10 °C when the outdoor temperature is – 40 °C.

Determine the temperature T of the radiator heating the room.

2.17. A space object has the shape of a sphere of radius R. Heat sources ensuring the heat evolution at a constant rate are distributed uniformly over its volume. The amount of heat liberated by a unit surface area is proportional to the fourth power of thermodynamic temperature.

In what proportion would the temperature of the object change if its radius decreased by half?

2.18*. A heat exchanger of length l consists of a tube of cross-sectional area $2S$ with another tube of cross-sectional area S passing through it (Fig. 65).

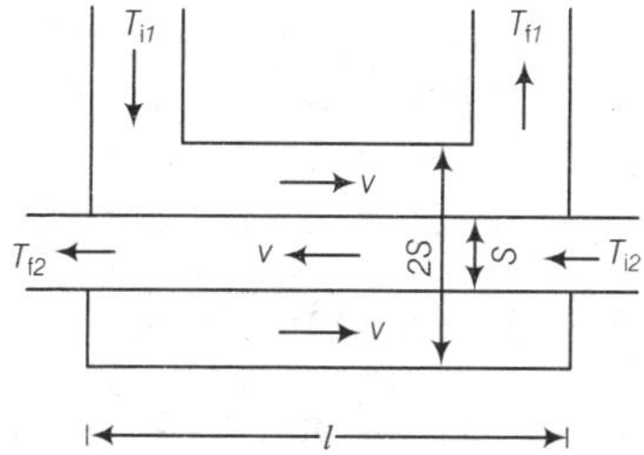

Fig. 65

The walls of the tubes are thin. The entire system is thermally insulated from the ambient. A liquid of density ρ and specific heat c is pumped at a velocity v through the tubes. The initial temperatures of the liquid in the heat exchanger are T_{i1} and T_{i2} respectively.

Determine the final temperatures T_{f1} and T_{f2} of the liquid in the heat exchanger if the liquid passes through the tubes in the counterflow, assuming that the heat transferred per unit time through a unit area element is proportional to the temperature difference, the proportionality factor being k. The thermal conductivity of the liquid in the direction of its flow should be neglected.

2.19*. A closed cylindrical vessel of base area S contains a substance in the gaseous state outside the gravitational field of the Earth, The mass of the gas is M and its pressure is p such that $p \ll p_{sat}$, where p_{sat} is the saturated vapour pressure at a given temperature. The vessel starts moving with an acceleration a directed along the axis of the cylinder. The temperature is maintained constant.

Determine the mass m_{11q} of the liquid condensed as a result of motion in the vessel.

2.20. The saturated water vapour pressure on a planet is $p_0 = 760$ mmHg. Determine the vapour density ρ.

2.21. In cold weather, water vapour can be seen in the exhaled air. If the door of a warm hut is opened on a chilly day, fog rushes into the hut. Explain these phenomena.

2.22*. A vessel of volume $V = 2$l contains $m_{H_2} = 2$ g of hydrogen and some amount of water. The pressure in the vessel is, $p_i = 17 \times 10^5$ Pa. The vessel is heated so that the pressure in it increases to $P_f = 26 \times 10^5$ Pa, and water partially evaporates. The molar mass of water vapour is $\mu = 18 \times 10^{-3}$ kg/mol.

Determine the initial T_i and final T_f temperature of water and its mass Δm.

Hint. Make use of the following temperature dependence of the saturated water vapour pressure:

T, °C	100	120	133	152	180
p_{sat}, $\times 10^5$ Pa	1	2	3	5	10

2.23. The lower end of a capillary of radius $r = 0.2$ mm and length $l = 8$ cm is immersed in water whose temperature is constant and equal to $T_{low} = 0°$ C. The temperature of the upper end of the capillary is $T_{up} = 100°$C.

Determine the height h to which the water in the capillary rises, assuming that the thermal conductivity of the capillary is much higher than the thermal conductivity of water in it. The heat exchange with the ambient should be neglected.

Hint. Use the following temperature dependence of the surface tension of water :

T, °C	0	20	50	90
σ, mN/m	76	73	67	60

2.24. A cylinder with a movable piston contains air under a pressure p_1 and a soap bubble of radius r. The surface tension is σ, and the temperature T is maintained constant.

Determine the pressure p_2 to which the air should be compressed by slowly pulling the piston into the cylinder for the soap bubble to reduce its size by half.

2.25. Why is clay used instead of cement (which has a higher strength) in laying bricks for a fireplace? (*Hint.* Red-clay bricks are used for building fireplaces.)

2.26. A thermally insulated vessel contains two liquids with initial temperatures T_1 and T_2 and specific heats c_1 and c_2, separated by a nonconducting partition. The partition is removed, and the difference between the initial temperature of one of the liquids and the temperature T established in the vessel turns out to be equal to half the difference between the initial temperatures of the liquids.

Determine the ratio m_1 / m_2 of the masses of the liquids.

2.27. Water at 20 °C is poured into a test tube whose bottom is immersed in a large amount of water at 80°C. As a result, the water in the test tube is heated to 80°C during a time t_1. Then water at 80 °C is poured into the test tube whose bottom is immersed in a large amount of water at 20 °C. The water in the test tube is cooled to 20 °C during a time t_2.

What time is longer: t_1 or t_2?

2.28. The same mass of water is poured into two identical light metal vessels. A heavy ball (whose mass is equal to the mass of water and whose density is much higher than that of water) is immersed on a thin non-conducting thread in one of the vessels so that it is at the centre of the volume of the water in the vessel. The vessels are heated to the boiling point of water and left to cool. The time of cooling for the vessel with the ball to the temperature of the ambient is known to be k times as long as the time of cooling for the vessel without a ball.

Determine the ratio c_b / c_w of the specific heats of the ball material and water.

2.29. Two identical thermally insulated cylindrical calorimeters of height $h = 75$ cm are filled to one-third. The first calorimeter is filled with ice formed as a result of freezing water poured into it, and the second is filled with water at $T_w = 10$ °C. Water from the second calorimeter is poured into the first one, and as a result it becomes to be filled to two-thirds. After the temperature has been stabilized in the first calorimeter, its level of water increases by $\Delta h = 0.5$ cm. The density of ice is $\rho_{ice} = 0.9\rho_w$, the latent heat of fusion of ice is $\lambda = 340$ kJ/kg, the specific heat of ice is $c_{ice} = 2.1$ (kJ/kg · K), and the specific heat of water is $c_w = 4.2$ kJ/(kg · K).

Determine the initial temperature T_{ice} of ice in the first calorimeter.

2.30*. A mixture of equal masses of water and ice ($m = m_w = m_{ice} = 1$ kg) is contained in a thermally insulated cylindrical vessel under a light piston. The pressure on the piston is slowly increased from the initial value $p_0 = 10^5$ Pa to $p_1 = 2.5 \times 10^6$ Pa. The specific heats of water and ice are $c_w = 4.2$ kJ/(kg · K) and $c_{ice} = 2.1$ kJ /(kg · K), the latent heat of fusion of ice is $\lambda = 340$ kJ/kg, and the density of ice is $\rho_{ice} = 0.9\rho_w$ (where ρ_w is the density of water).

Determine the mass Δm of ice which melts in the process and the work A done by an external force if it is known that the pressure required to decrease the fusion temperature of ice by 1°C is $p = 14 \times 10^6$ Pa, while the pressure required to reduce the volume of a certain mass of water by 1% is $p' = 20 \times 10^6$ Pa.

(1) Solve the problem, assuming that water and ice are incompressible.

(2) Estimate the correction for the compressibility, assuming that the compressibility of ice is equal to half that value for water.

2.31. It is well known that if an ordinary water is salted, its boiling point rises.

Determine the change in the density of saturated water vapour at the boiling point.

2.32. For many substances, there exists a temperature T_{tr} and a pressure p_{tr} at which all the three phases of a substance (gaseous, liquid, and solid) are in equilibrium. These temperature and pressure are known as the triple point. For example, $T_{tr} = 0.0075$ °C and $p_{tr} = 4.58$ mmHg for water.

The latent heat of vaporization of water at the triple point is $q = 2.48 \times 10^3$ kJ/kg, and the latent heat of fusion of ice is $\lambda = 0.34 \times 10^3$ kJ/kg.

Find the latent heat v of sublimation. (i.e. a direct transition from the solid to the gaseous state) of water at the triple point.

2.33. The saturated vapour pressure above an aqueous solution of sugar is known to be lower than that above pure water, where it is equal to p_{sat}, by $\Delta p = 0.05\, p_{sat} c$,

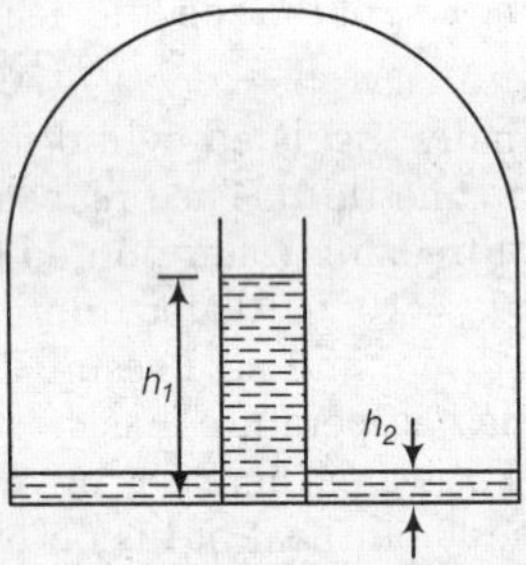

Fig. 66

where c is the molar concentration of the solution. A cylindrical vessel filled to height $h_1 = 10$ cm with a sugar solution of concentration $c_1 = 2 \times 10^{-3}$ is placed under a wide bell. The same solution of concentration $c_2 = 10^{-3}$ is poured under the bell to a level $h_2 << h_1$ (Fig. 66).

Determine the level h of the solution in the cylinder after the equilibrium has been set in. The temperature is maintained constant and equal to 20°C. The vapour above the surface of the solution contains only water molecules, and the molar mass of water vapour is $\mu = 18 \times 10^{-3}$ kg/mol.

2.34. A long vertical brick duct is filled with cast iron. The lower end of the duct is maintained at a temperature $T_1 > T_{melt}$ (T_{melt} is the melting point of cast iron), and the upper end at a temperature $T_2 < T_{melt}$.) The thermal conductivity of molten (liquid) cast iron is k times higher than that of solid cast iron.

Determine the fraction of the duct filled with molten metal.

2.35*. The shell of a space station is a blackened sphere in which a temperature $T = 500$ K is maintained due to the operation of appliances of the station. The amount of heat given away from a unit surface area is proportional to the fourth power of thermodynamic temperature.

Determine the temperature T_x of the shell if the station is enveloped by a thin spherical black screen of nearly the same radius as the radius of the shell.

2.36. A bucket contains a mixture of water and ice of mass $m = 10$ kg. The bucket is brought into a room, after which the temperature of the mixture is immediately measured. The obtained T (τ) dependence is plotted in Fig. 67.

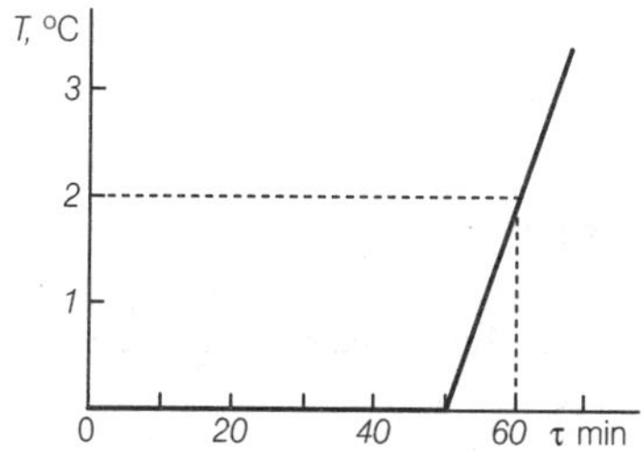

Fig. 67

The specific heat of water is $c_w = 4.2$ J/(kg · K), and the latent heat of fusion of ice is $\lambda = 340$ kJ/kg.

Determine the mass m_{ice} of ice in the bucket at the moment it is brought in the room, neglecting the heat capacity of the bucket.

2.37*. The properties of a nonlinear resistor were investigated in a series of experiments. At first, the temperature dependence of the resistor was studied. As the temperature was raised to $T_1 = 100$ °C, the resistance changed jumpwise from $R_1 = 50\ \Omega$ to $R_2 = 100\Omega$. The reverse abrupt change upon cooling took place at $T_2 = 99$ °C. Then a d.c. voltage $U_1 = 60$ V was applied to the resistor. Its temperature was found to be $T_3 = 80$ °C. Finally, when a d.c. voltage $U_2 = 80$ V was applied to the resistor, spontaneous current oscillations were observed in the circuit.

The air temperature T_0 in the laboratory was constant and equal to 20 °C. The heat transfer from the resistor was proportional to the temperature difference between the resistor and the ambient, the heat capacity of the resistor being $C = 3$ J/K.

Determine the period T of current oscillations and the maximum and minimum values of the current.

2.38. When raindrops fall on a red-brick wall after dry and hot weather, hissing sounds are produced.

Explain the phenomenon.

2.39. A thin U-tube sealed at one end consists of three bends of length $l = 250$ mm each, forming right angles. The vertical parts of the tube are filled with mercury to half the height (Fig. 68).

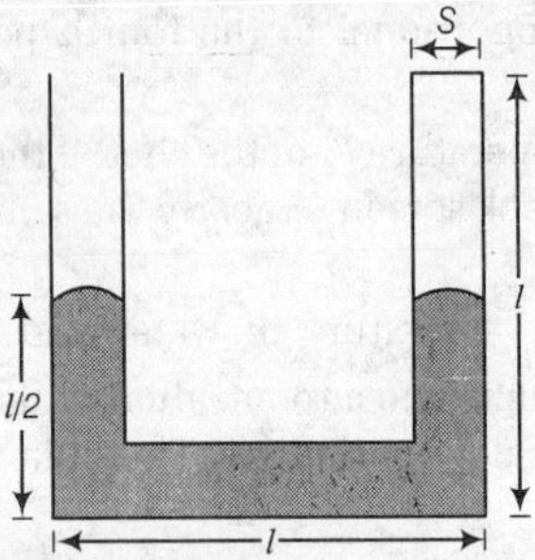

Fig. 68

All of mercury can be displaced from the tube by heating slowly the gas in the sealed end of the tube, which is separated from the atmospheric air by mercury.

Determine the work A done by the gas thereby if the atmospheric pressure is $p_0 = 10^5$ Pa, the density of mercury is $\rho_{mer} = 13.6 \times 10^3$ kg/m^3 and the cross-sectional area of the tube is $S = 1$ cm^2.

2.40. The residual deformation of an elastic rod can be roughly described by using the following model. If the elongation of the rod $\Delta l < x_0$ (where x_0 is the quantity present for the given rod), the force required to cause the elongation Δl is determined by Hooke's law; $F = k\,\Delta l$, where k is the rigidity of the rod. If $\Delta l > x_0$, the force does not depend on elongation any longer (the material of the rod starts "flowing"). If the load is then removed, the elongation of the rod will decrease along CD which for the sake of simplicity will be taken straight and parallel to the segment AB (Fig. 69).

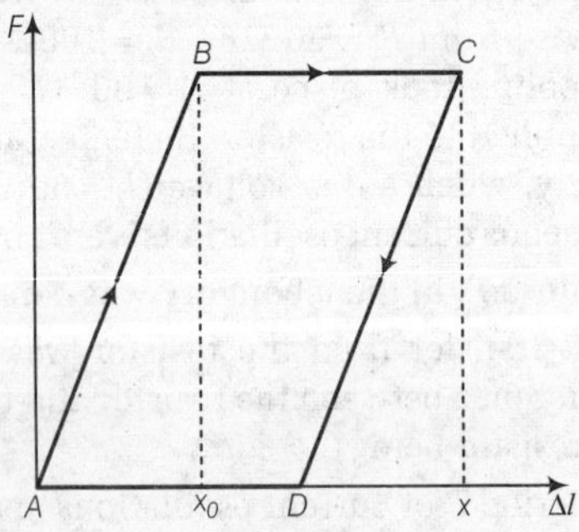

Fig. 69

Therefore, after the load has been removed completely, the rod remains deformed (point D in the figure). Let us suppose that the rod is initially stretched by $\Delta l = x > x_0$ and then the load is removed.

Determine the maximum change ΔT in the rod temperature if its heat capacity is C, and the rod is thermally insulated.

2.41. A thin-walled cylinder of mass m, height h, and cross-sectional area S is filled with a gas and floats on the surface of water (Fig. 70). As a result of leakage from the lower part of the cylinder, the depth of its submergence has increased by Δh.

Determine the initial pressure p_1 of the gas in the cylinder if the atmospheric pressure is p_0, and the temperature remains unchanged.

2.42. A shock wave is the region of an elevated pressure propagating in the positive direction of the x-axis at a high velocity v.

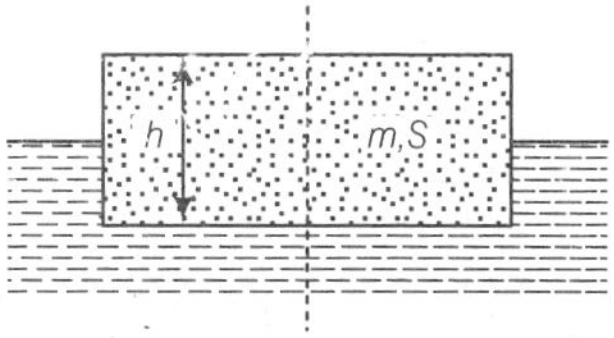

Fig. 70

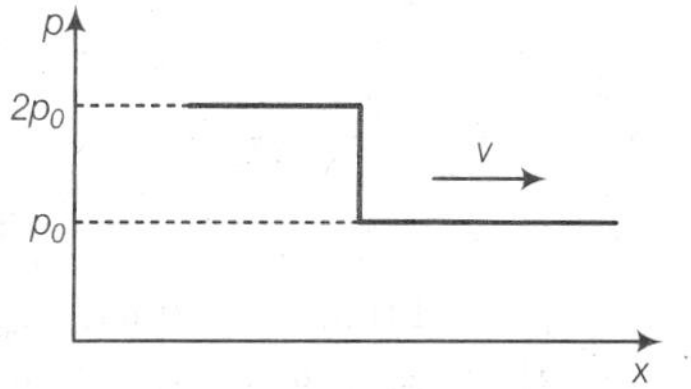

Fig. 71

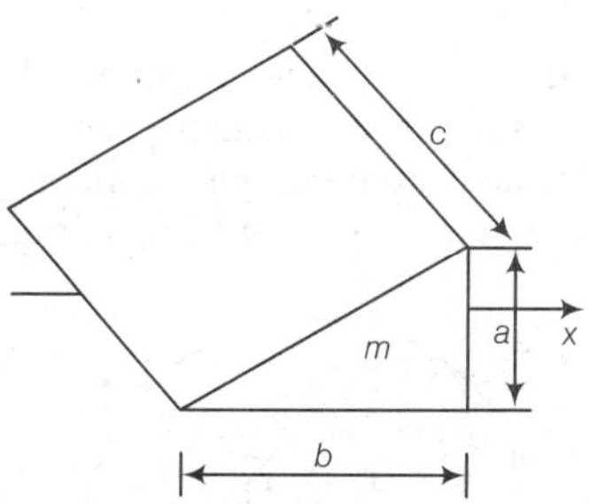

Fig. 72

At the moment of arrival of the wave, the pressure abruptly increases. This dependence is plotted in Fig. 71.

Determine the velocity u acquired by a wedge immediately after the shock front passes through it. The mass of the wedge is m, and its size is shown in Fig. 72. Friction should be neglected, and the velocity acquired by the wedge should be assumed to be much lower than the velocity of the wave ($u << v$).

3. Electricity and Magnetism

For the problems of this chapter, assume (wherever required) that the electric constant ε_0 is specified.

3.1. A thin insulator rod is placed between two unlike point charges $+q_1$ and $-q_2$. (Fig. 73).

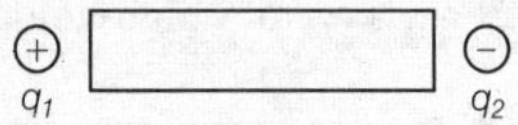

Fig. 73

How will the forces acting on the charges change?

3.2. An electric field line emerges from a positive point charge $+q_1$ at an angle α to the straight line connecting it to a negative point charge $-q_2$ (Fig. 74).

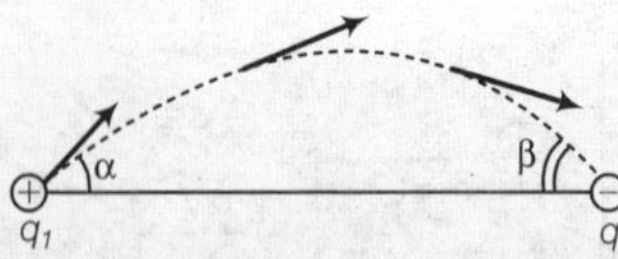

Fig. 74

At what angle β will the field line enter the charge $-q_2$?

3.3. Determine the strength E of the electric field at the centre of a hemisphere produced by charges uniformly distributed with a density σ over the surface of this hemisphere.

3.4. The strength of the electric field produced by charges uniformly distributed over the surface of a hemisphere at its centre O is E_0. A part of the surface is isolated from this hemisphere by two planes passing through the same diameter and forming an angle α with each other (Fig. 75).

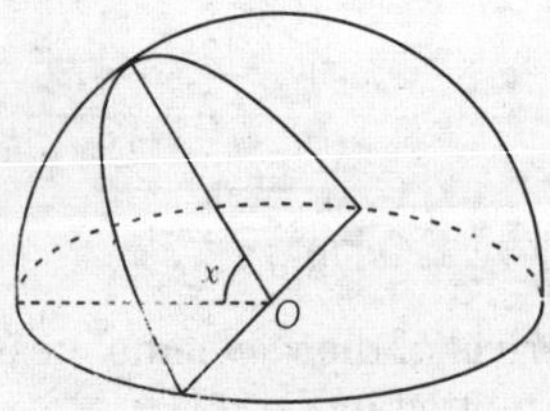

Fig. 75

Determine the electric field strength E produced at the same point O by the charges located on the isolated surface (on the "mericarp").

3.5*. Two parallel-plate capacitors are arranged perpendicular to the common axis. The separation d between the capacitors is much larger than the separation l between their plates and than their size. The capacitors are charged to q_1 and q_2 respectively (Fig. 76).

Find the force F of interaction between the capacitors.

3.6. Determine the force F of interaction between two hemispheres of radius R touching each other along the equator if one hemisphere is uniformly charged with a surface density σ_1 and the other with a surface density σ_2.

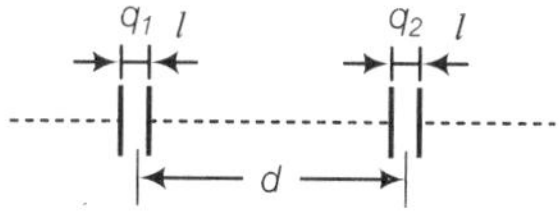

Fig. 76

3.7. The minimum strength of a uniform electric field which can tear a conducting uncharged thin-walled sphere into two parts is known to be E_0.

Determine the minimum electric field strength E_1 required to tear the sphere of twice as large radius if the thickness of its walls is the same as in the former case.

3.8. Three small identical neutral metal balls are at the vertices of an equilateral triangle. The balls are in turn connected to an isolated large conducting sphere whose centre is on the perpendicular erected from the plane of the triangle and passing through its centre. As a result, the first and second balls have acquired charges q_1 and q_2 respectively. Determine the charge q_3 of the third ball.

3.9. A metal sphere having a radius r_1 charged to a potential ϕ_1 is enveloped by a thin-walled conducting spherical shell of radius r_2 (Fig. 77).

Determine the potential ϕ_2 acquired by the sphere after it has been connected for a short time to the shell by a conductor.

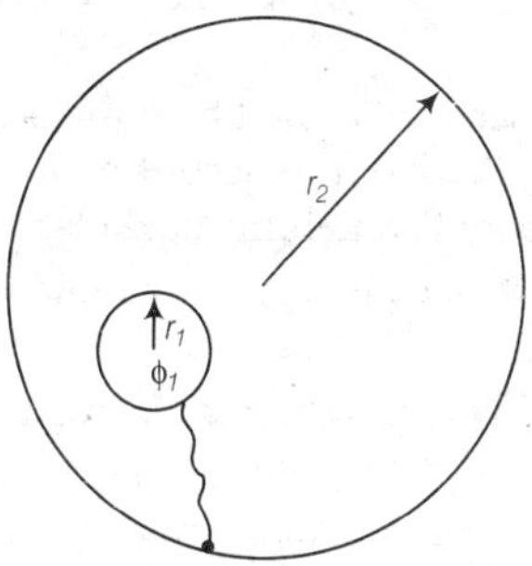

Fig. 77

3.10. A very small earthed conducting sphere is at a distance a from a point charge q_1 and at a distance b from a point charge q_2 $(a < b)$. At a certain instant, the sphere starts expanding so that its radius grows according to the law $R = vt$.

Determine the time dependence $I(t)$ of the current in the earthing conductor, assuming that the point charges and the centre of the sphere are at rest, and in due time the initial point charges get into the expanding sphere without touching it (through small holes),

3.11. Three uncharged capacitors of capacitance $C_1, C_2,$ and C_3 are connected as shown in Fig. 78 to one another and to points A, B, and D at potentials ϕ_A, ϕ_B, and ϕ_D.

Determine the potential ϕ_0 at point O.

3.12*. The thickness of a flat sheet of a metal foil is d, and its area is S. A charge q is located at a distance l from the centre of the sheet such that $d << \sqrt{S} << l$.

Determine the force F with which the sheet is attracted to the charge q, assuming that the straight line connecting the charge to the centre of the sheet is perpendicular to the surface of the sheet.

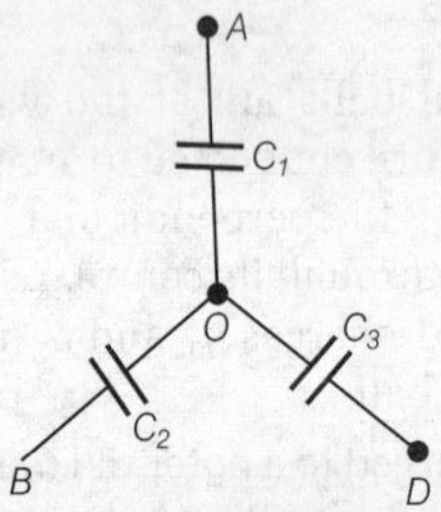

Fig. 78

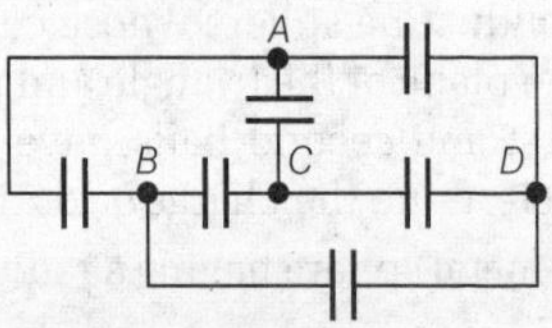

Fig. 79

3.13. Where must a current source be connected to the circuit shown in Fig. 79 in order to charge all the six capacitors having equal capacitances?

3.14. A parallel-plate capacitor is filled by a dielectric whose permittivity varies with the applied voltage according to the law $\varepsilon = \alpha U$, where $\alpha = 1\ \text{V}^{-1}$. The same (but containing no dielectric) capacitor charged to a voltage $U_0 = 156$ V is connected in parallel to the first "nonlinear" uncharged capacitor.

Determine the final voltage U across the capacitors.

3.15. Two small balls of mass m, bearing a charge q each, are connected by a nonconducting thread of length $2l$. At a certain instant, the middle of the thread starts moving at a constant velocity v perpendicular to the direction of the thread at the initial instant.

Determine the minimum distance d between the balls.

3.16. Two balls of charge q_1 and q_2 initially have a velocity of the same magnitude and direction. After a uniform electric field has been applied during a certain time, the direction of the velocity of the first ball changes by 60°, and the velocity magnitude is reduced by half. The direction of the velocity of the second ball changes thereby by 90°.

In what proportion will the velocity of the second ball change? Determine the magnitude of the charge-to-mass ratio for the second ball if it is equal to k_1 for the first ball. The electrostatic interaction between the balls should be neglected.

3.17. Small identical balls with equal charges are fixed at the vertices of a right 1977-gon with side a. At a certain instant, one of the balls is released, and a sufficiently long time interval later, the ball adjacent to the first released ball is freed. The kinetic energies of the released balls are found to differ by K at a sufficiently long distance from the polygon.

Determine the charge q of each ball.

3.18. Why do electrons and not ions cause collision ionization of atoms although both charges acquire the same kinetic energy $mv^2/2 = e\Delta\phi$ (e is the charge of the particles, and $\Delta\phi$ is the potential difference) in an accelerating field? Assume that an atom to be ionized and a particle impinging on it have approximately the same velocity after the collision.

3.19. Two small identical balls lying on a horizontal plane are connected by a weightless spring. One ball is fixed at point O and the other is free. The balls are charged identically, as a result of which the spring length increases twofold.

Determine the change in the frequency of harmonic vibrations of the system.

3.20. Two small balls having the same mass and charge and located on the same vertical at heights h_1 and h_2 are thrown in the same direction along the horizontal at the same velocity v. The first ball touches the ground at a distance l from the initial vertical.

At what height H_2 will the second ball be at this instant? The air drag and the effect of the charges induced on the ground should be neglected.

3.21. A hank of uninsulated wire consisting of seven and a half turns is stretched between two nails hammered into a board to which the ends of the wire are fixed. The resistance of the circuit between the nails is determined with the help of electrical measuring instruments.

Determine the proportion in which the resistance will change if the wire is unwound so that the ends remain to be fixed to the nails.

3.22. Five identical resistors (coils for hot plates) are connected as shown in the diagram in Fig. 80.

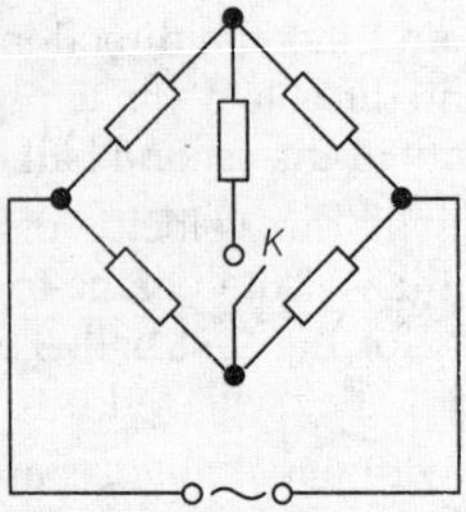

Fig. 80

What will be the change in the voltage across the right upper spiral upon closing the key K?

3.23. What will be the change in the resistance of a circuit consisting of five identical conductors if two similar conductors are added as shown by the dashed line in Fig. 81?

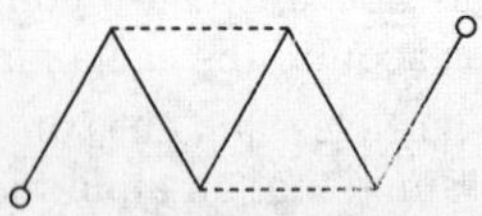

Fig. 81

3.24. A wire frame in the form of a tetrahedron $ADCB$ is connected to a d.c. source (Fig. 82). The resistances of all the edges of the tetrahedron are equal.

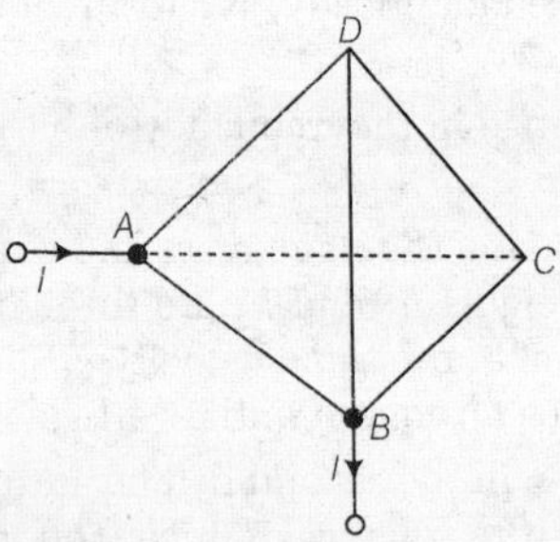

Fig. 82

Indicate the edge of the frame that should be eliminated to obtain the maximum change in the current ΔI_{max} in the circuit, neglecting the resistance of the leads.

3.25. The resistance of each resistor in the circuit diagram shown in Fig. 83 is the same and equal to R. The voltage across the terminals is U.

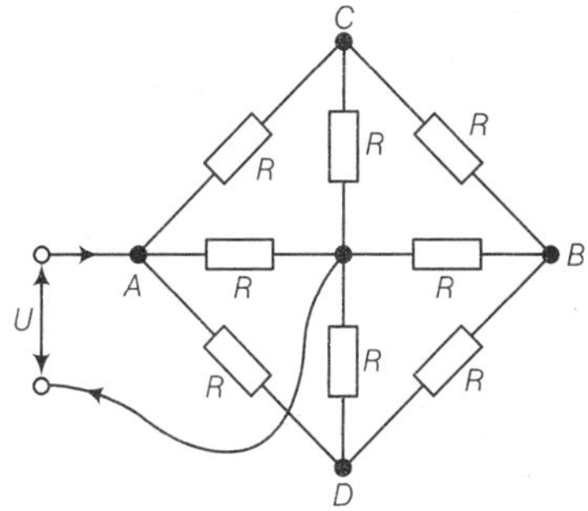

Fig. 83

Determine the current I in the leads f their resistance can be neglected.

3.26*. Determine the resistance R_{AB} between points A and B of the frame formed by nine identical wires of resistance R each (Fig. 84).

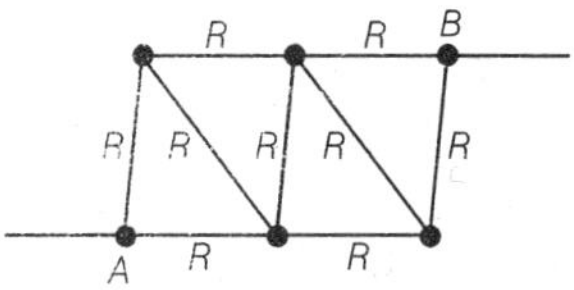

Fig. 84

3.27. Determine the resistance R_{AB} between points A and B of the frame made of thin homogeneous wire (Fig. 85), assuming that the number of successively embedded equilateral triangles (with sides decreasing by half) tends to infinity. Side AB is equal to a, and the resistance of unit length of the wire is ρ.

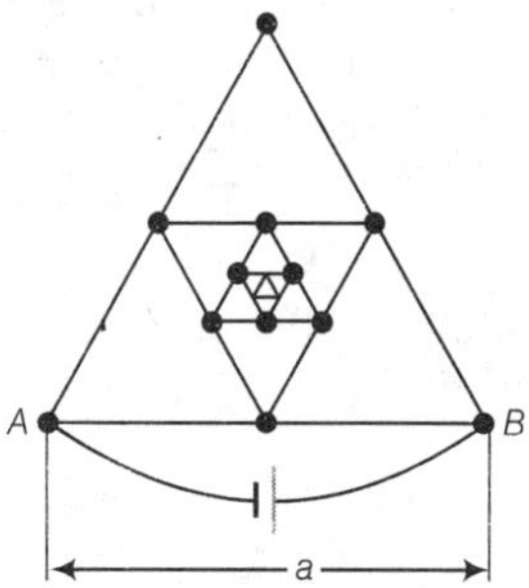

Fig. 85

3.28. The circuit diagram shown in Fig. 86 consists of a very large (infinite) number of elements.

The resistances of the resistors in each subsequent element differ by a factor of k from the resistances of the resistors in the previous elements.

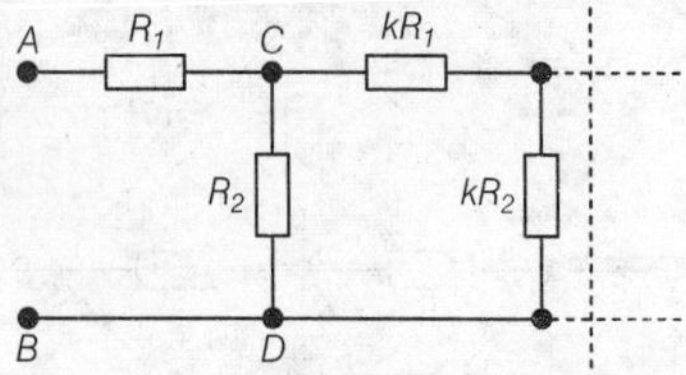

Fig. 86

Determine the resistance R_{AB} between points A and B if the resistances of the first element are R_1 and R_2.

3.29. The voltage across a load is controlled by using the circuit diagram shown in Fig. 87. The resistance of the load and of the

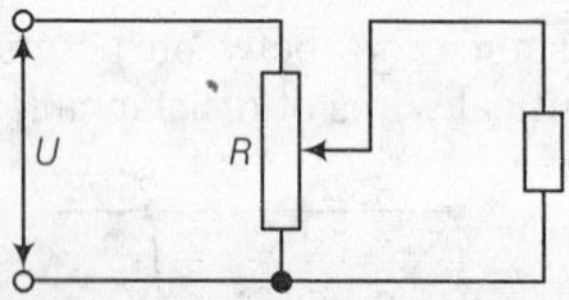

Fig. 87

potentiometer is R. The load is connected to the middle of the potentiometer. The input voltage is constant and equal to U.

Determine the change in the voltage across the load if its resistance is doubled.

3.30. Given two different ammeters in which the deflections of the pointers are proportional to current, and the scales are uniform. The first ammeter is connected to a resistor of resistance R_1 and the second to a resistor of unknown resistance R_x. At first the ammeters are connected in series between points A and B (as shown in Fig. 88).

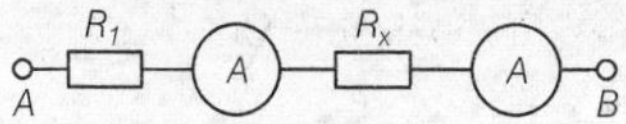

Fig. 88

In this case, the readings of the ammeters are n_1 and n_2. Then the ammeters are connected in parallel between A and B (as shown in Fig. 89) and indicate n'_1 and n'_2.

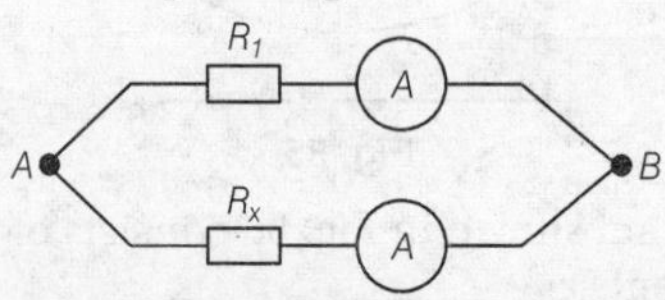

Fig. 89

Determine the unknown resistance R_x of the second resistor.

3.31. Two wires of the same length but of different square cross sections are made from the same material. The sides of the cross sections of the first and second wires are $d_1 = 1$ mm and $d_2 = 4$ mm. The current required to fuse the first wire is $I_1 = 10$ A.
Determine the current I_2 required to fuse the second wire, assuming that the amount of heat dissipated to the ambient per second obeys the law $Q = kS\,(T - T_{am})$, where S is the cross-sectional area of the wire, T is its temperature, T_{am} is the temperature of the ambient away from the wire, and k is the proportionality factor which is the same for the two wires.

3.32. The key K in circuit diagram shown in Fig. 90 can be either in position 1 or 2.

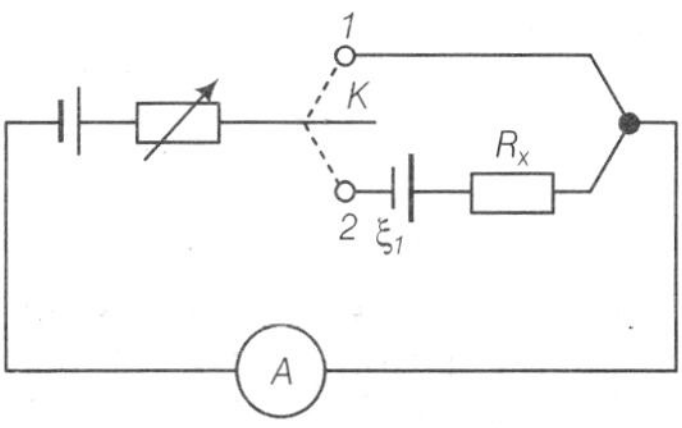

Fig. 90

The circuit includes two d.c. sources, two resistors, and an ammeter. The emf of one source is ξ_1 and of the other is unknown. The internal resistance of the sources should be taken as zero. The resistance of the resistors is also unknown. One of the resistors has a varying resistance chosen in such a way that the current through the ammeter is the same for both positions of the key. The current is measured and is found to be equal to I.
Determine the resistance denoted by R_x in the diagram.

3.33. Can a current passing through a resistor be increased by short-circuiting one of the current sources, say, the one of emf ξ_2 as

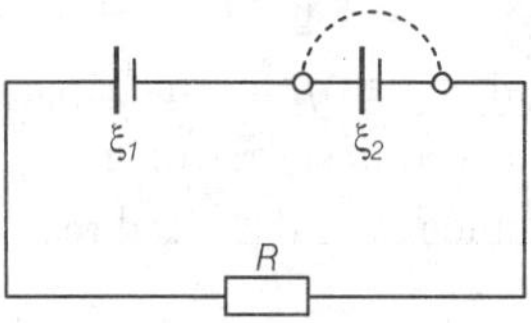

Fig. 91

shown in Fig. 91? The parameters of the elements of the circuit should be assumed to be specified.

3.34*. A concealed circuit (black box) consisting of resistors has four terminals (Fig. 92). If a voltage is applied between clamps 1 and 2

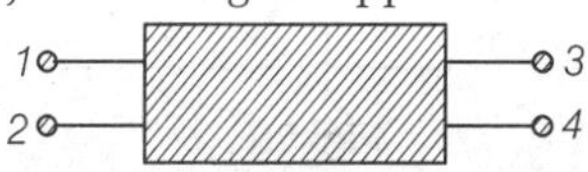

Fig. 92

when clamps 3 and 4 are disconnected, the power liberated is $N_1 = 40$ W, and when the clamps 3 and 4 are connected, the power liberated is $N_2 = 80$ W. If the same source is connected to the clamps 3 and 4, the power liberated in the circuit when the clamps 1 and 2 are disconnected is $N_3 = 20$ W. Determine the power N_4 consumed in the circuit when the clamps 1 and 2 are connected and the same voltage is applied between the clamps 3 and 4.

3.35. Determine the current through the battery in the circuit shown in Fig. 93

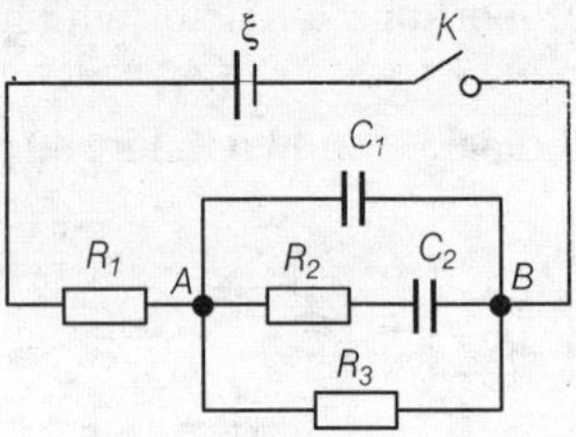

Fig. 93

(1) immediately after the key K is closed and
(2) in a long time interval, assuming that the parameters of the circuit are known.

3.36. The key K (Fig. 94) is connected in turn to each of the contacts over short identical time intervals so that the change in the charge on the capacitor over each connection is small.

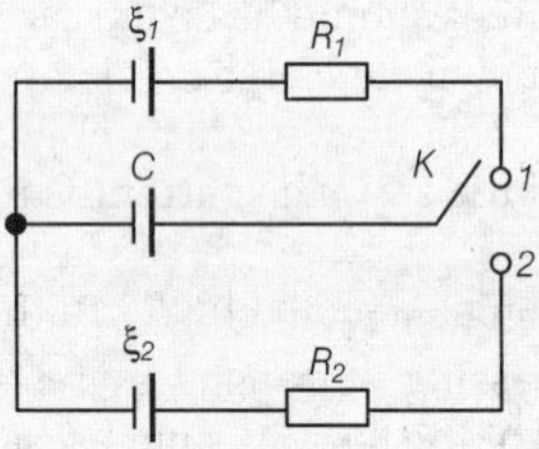

Fig. 94

What will be the final charge q_f on the capacitor?

3.37. A circuit consists of a current source of emf ξ and internal resistance r, capacitors of capacitance C_1 and C_2, and resistors of resistance R_1 and R_2 (Fig. 95).

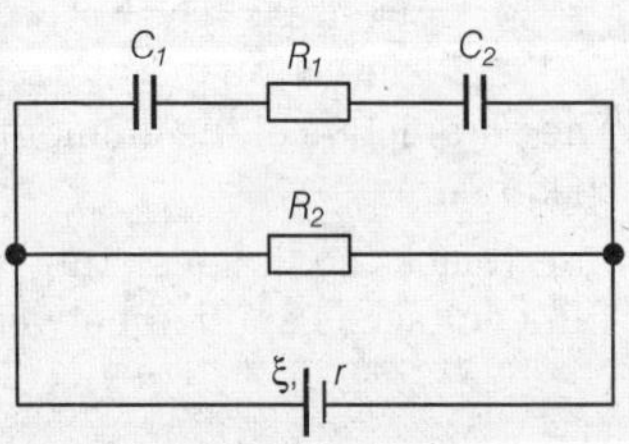

Fig. 95

Determine the voltages U_1 and U_2 across each capacitor.

3.38*. A perfect voltmeter and a perfect ammeter are connected in turn between points E and F of a circuit whose diagram is shown in Fig. 96. The readings of the instruments are U_0 and I_0.

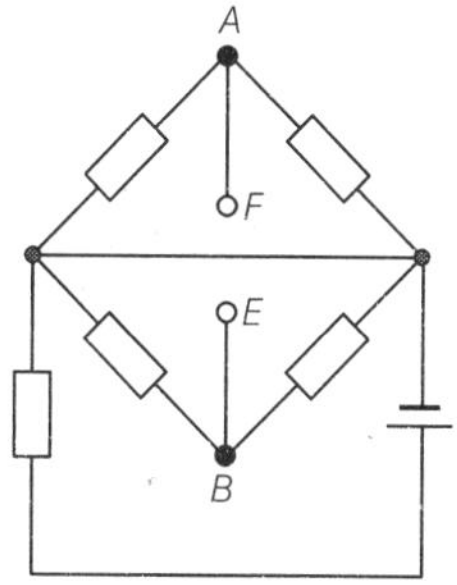

Fig. 96

Determine the current I through the resistor of resistance R connected between points E and F.

3.39. A plate A of a parallel-plate capacitor is fixed, while a plate B is attached to the wall by a spring and can move, remaining parallel to the plate A (Fig. 97). After the key K is closed, the plate B starts moving and comes to rest in a new equilibrium position. The initial equilibrium separation d between the plates decreases in this case by 10%.

What will be the decrease in the equilibrium separation between the plates if the key K is closed for such a short time that the plate B cannot be shifted noticeably?

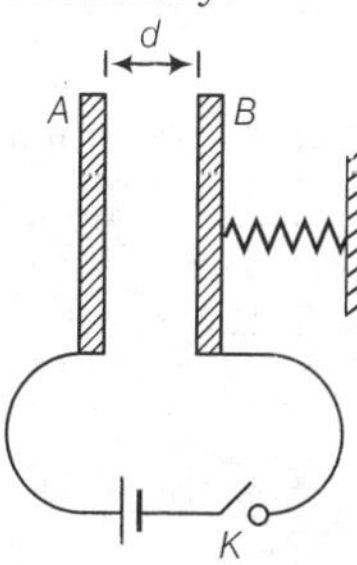

Fig. 97

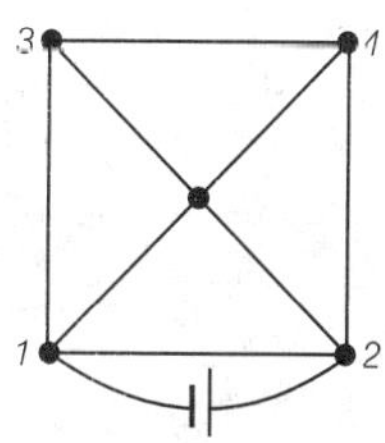

Fig. 98

3.40. The circuit shown in Fig. 98 is made of a homogeneous wire of constant cross section.

Find the ratio Q_{12} / Q_{34} of the amounts of heat liberated per unit time in conductors 1-2 and 3-4.

3.41. The voltage between the anode and the cathode of a vacuum-tube diode is U, and the anode current is I.

Determine the mean pressure p_m of electrons on the anode surface of area S.

3.42. A varying voltage is applied to the clamps AB (Fig. 99) such that the voltage across the capacitor plates varies as shown in Fig. 100.

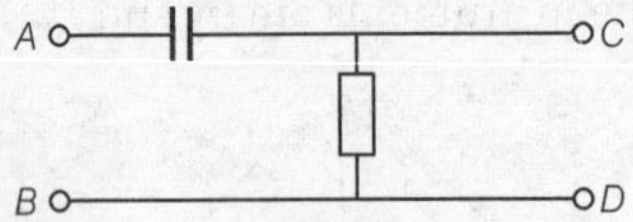

Fig. 99

Plot the time dependence of voltage across the clamps CD.

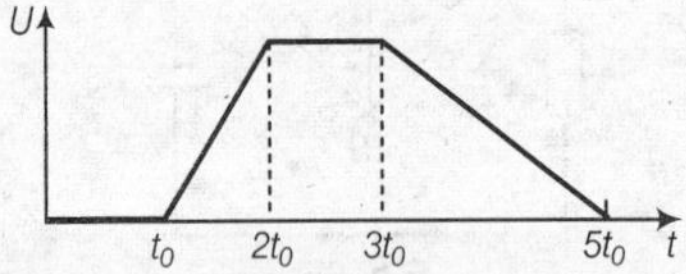

Fig. 100

3.43. Two batteries of emf ξ_1 and ξ_2, a capacitor of capacitance C, and a resistor of resistance R are connected in a circuit as shown in Fig. 101.

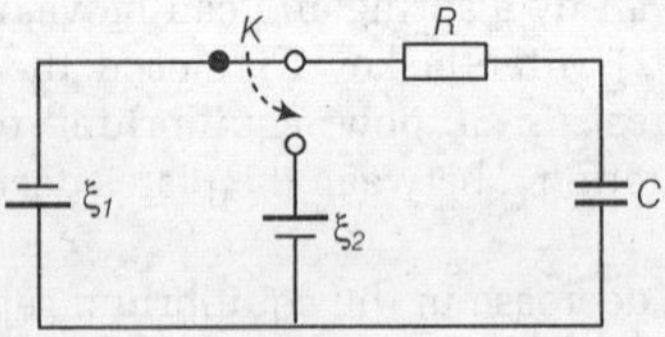

Fig. 101

Determine the amount of heat Q liberated in the resistor after switching the key K.

3.44. An electric circuit consists of a current source of emf ξ and internal resistance r, and two resistors connected in parallel to the source (Fig. 102).

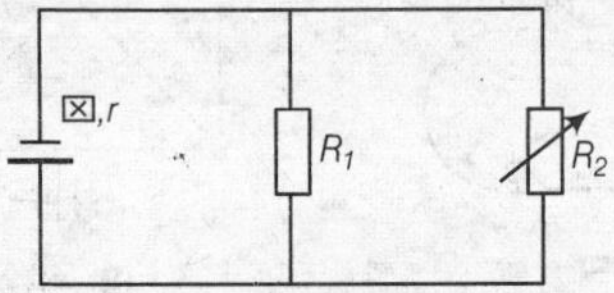

Fig. 102

The resistance R_1 of one resistor remains unchanged, while the resistance R_2 of the other resistor can be chosen so that the power liberated in this resistor is maximum.

Determine the value of R_2 corresponding to the maximum power.

3.45. A capacitor of capacitance C_1 is discharged through a resistor of resistance R.

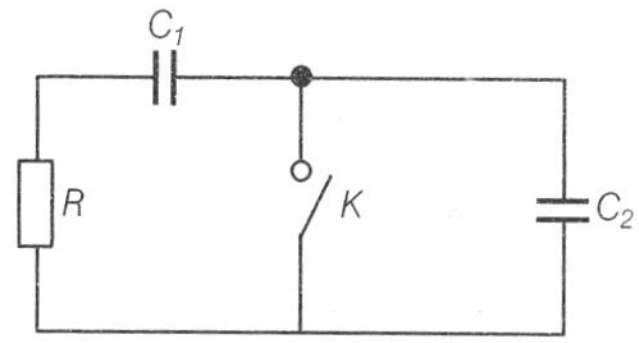

Fig. 103

When the discharge current attains the value I_0, the key K is opened (Fig. 103).

Determine the amount of heat Q liberated in the resistor starting from this moment.

3.46. A battery of emf ξ, two capacitors of capacitance C_1 and C_2, and a resistor of resistance R are connected as shown in Fig. 104.

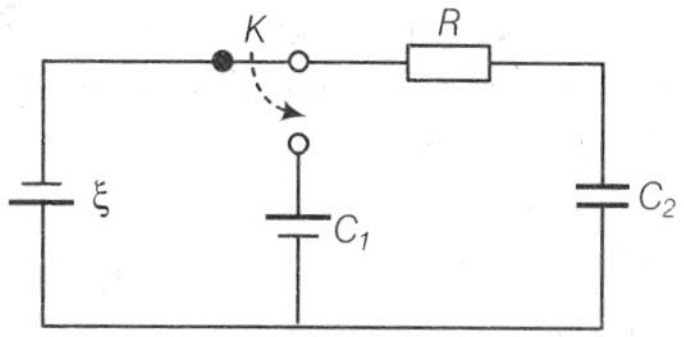

Fig. 104

Find the amount of heat Q liberated in the resistor after the key K is switched.

3.47. In the circuit diagram shown in Fig. 105, the capacitor of capacitance C

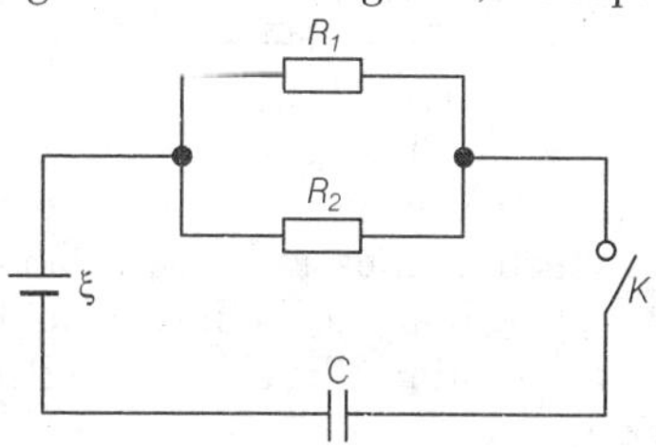

Fig. 105

is uncharged when the key K is open. The key is closed over some time during which the capacitor becomes charged to a voltage U.

Determine the amount of heat Q_2 liberated during this time in the resistor of resistance R_2 if the emf of the source is ξ, and its internal resistance can be neglected.

3.48. A jumper of mass m can slide without friction along parallel horizontal rails separated by a distance d. The rails are connected to a resistor of

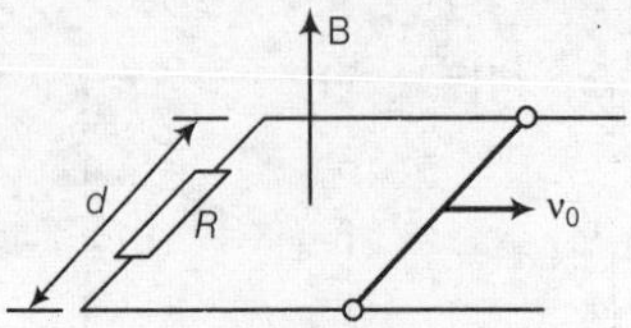

Fig. 106

resistance R and placed in a vertically uniform magnetic field of induction **B**. The jumper is pushed at a velocity $\mathbf{v}_0$ (Fig. 106).

Determine the distance s covered by the jumper before it comes to rest. How does the direction of induction **B** affect the answer?

3.49. What will be the time dependence of the reading of a galvanometer connected to the circuit of a horizontal circular loop when a charged ball falls along the axis of the loop?

3.50. A small charged ball suspended on an inextensible thread of length l moves in a uniform time-independent upward magnetic field of induction **B**. The mass of the ball is m, the charge is q, and the period of revolution is T.

Determine the radius r of the circle in which the ball moves if the thread is always stretched.

3.51. A metal ball of radius r moves at a constant velocity **v** in a uniform magnetic field of induction **B**.

Indicate the points on the ball the potential difference between which has the maximum value $\Delta\phi_{max}$. Find this value, assuming that the direction of velocity forms an angle α with the direction of the magnetic induction.

3.52. A direct current flowing through the winding of a long cylindrical solenoid of radius R produces in it a uniform magnetic field of induction **B**. An electron flies into the solenoid along the radius between its turns (at right angles to the solenoid axis) at a velocity **v** (Fig. 107). After a certain time, the electron deflected by the magnetic field leaves the solenoid.

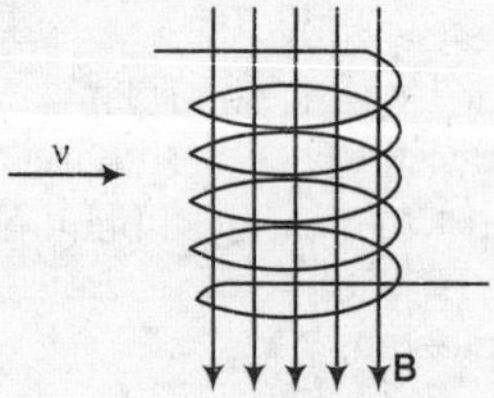

Fig. 107

Determine the time t during which the electron moves in the solenoid.

3.53. A metal jumper of mass m can slide without friction along two parallel metal guides directed at an angle α to the horizontal and separated by a distance b.

The guides are connected at the bottom through an uncharged capacitor of capacitance C, and the entire system is placed in an upward magnetic field of induction **B**.

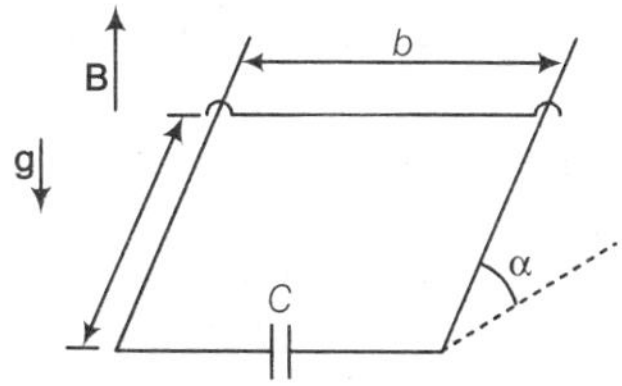

Fig. 108

At the initial moment, the jumper is held at a distance l from the foot of the "hump" (Fig. 108).

Determine the time t in which the released jumper reaches the foot of the hump. What will be its velocity v_f at the foot? The resistance of the guides and the jumper should be neglected.

3.54*. A quadratic undeformable superconducting loop of mass m and side a lies in a horizontal plane in a nonuniform magnetic field whose induction varies in space according to the law $B_x = -\alpha x$, $B_y = 0$, $B_z = \alpha z + B_0$ (Fig. 109).

The inductance of the loop is L. At the initial moment, the centre of the loop coincides with the origin O, and its sides are parallel to the x-and y-axes. The current in the loop is zero, and it is released.

How will it move and where will it be in time t after the beginning of motion?

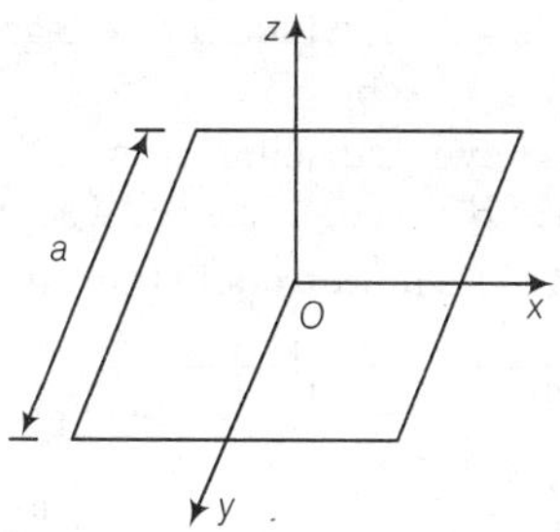

Fig. 109

3.55. A long cylindrical coil of inductance L_1 is wound on a bobbin of diameter D_1. The magnetic induction in the coil connected to a current source is B_1. After rewinding the coil on a bobbin of diameter D_2, its inductance becomes L_2.

Determine the magnetic induction B_2 of the field in the new coil connected to the same current source, assuming that the length of the wire is much larger than that of the coil.

3.56*. Two long cylindrical coils with uniform windings of the same length and nearly the same radius have inductances L_1 and L_2.

The coils are coaxially inserted into each other and connected to a current source as shown in Fig. 110. The directions of the current in the circuit and in the turns are shown by arrows.

Determine the inductance L of such a composite coil.

3.57. A winch is driven by an electric motor with a separate excitation and fed from a battery of emf $\xi = 300$ V. The rope and the hook of the winch rise at a velocity $v_1 = 4$ m/s without a load and at a velocity $v_2 = 1$ m/s with a load of mass $m = 10$ kg.

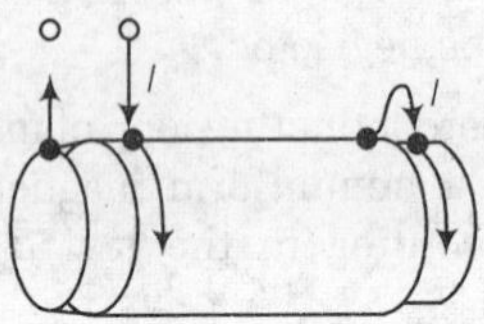

Fig. 110

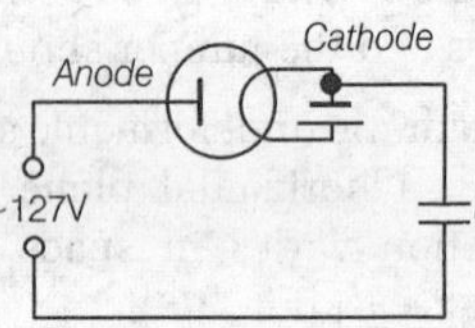

Fig. 111

Determine the velocity v' of the load and its mass m' for which the winch has the maximum power, neglecting the mass of the rope and the hook.

3.58. A perfect diode is connected to an a.c. circuit (Fig.111).

Determine the limits within which the voltage between the anode and the cathode varies.

3.59. A capacitor of unknown capacitance, a coil of inductance L, and a resistor of resistance R are connected to a source of a.c. voltage $\xi = \xi_0 \cos \omega t$ (Fig. 112). The current in the circuit is $I = (\xi_0 / R) \cos \omega t$.

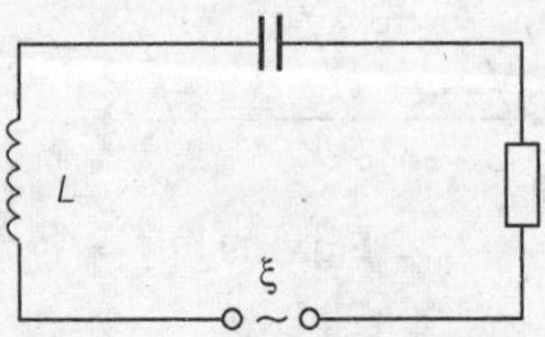

Fig. 112

Determine the amplitude U_0 of the voltage across the capacitor plates.

3.60. Under the action of a constant voltage U, a capacitor of capacitance $C = 10^{-11}$ **F** included in the circuit shown in Fig. 113 is charged to $q_1 = 10^{-9}$ C.

The inductance of the coil is $L = 10^{-5}$ H, and the resistance of the resistor is $R = 100\ \Omega$.

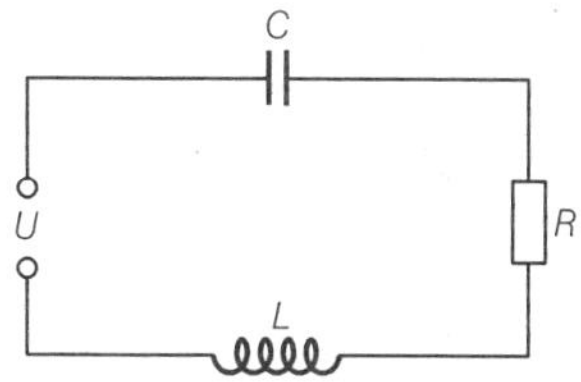

Fig. 113

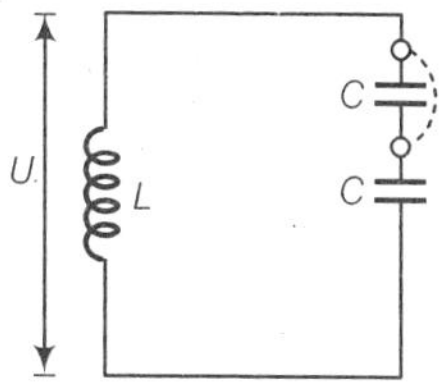

Fig. 114

Determine the amplitude q_0 of steady-state oscillations of the charge on the capacitor at resonance if the amplitude of the external sinusoidal voltage is $U_0 = U$.

3.61. A bank of two series-connected capacitors of capacitance C each is charged to a voltage U and is connected to a coil of inductance L so that an oscillatory circuit (Fig. 114) is formed at the initial moment. After a time τ, a breakdown occurs in one of the capacitors, and the resistance between its plates becomes zero.

Determine the amplitude q_0 of charge oscillations on the undamaged capacitor.

3.62. How can the damage due to overheating the coil of a superconducting solenoid be avoided?

4. Optics

4.1. A point light source S is on the axis of a hollow cone with a mirror inner surface (Fig. 115). A converging lens produces on a screen

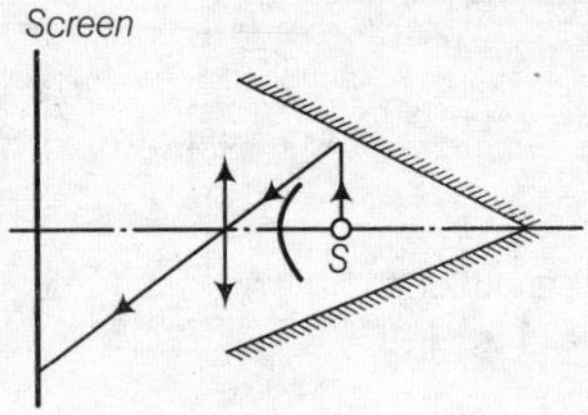

Fig. 115

the image of the source formed by the rays undergoing a single reflection at the inner surface (direct rays from the source do not fall on the lens).

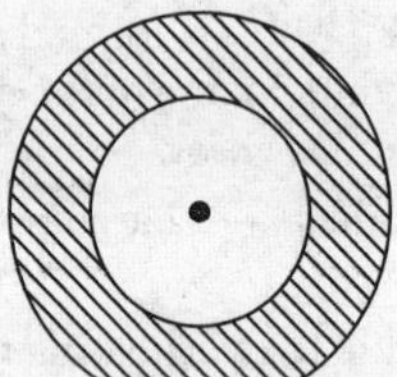

Fig. 116

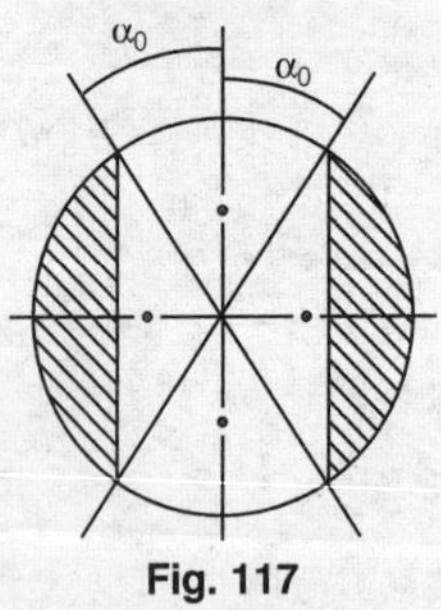

Fig. 117

What will happen to the image if the lens is covered by diaphragms like those shown in Figs. 116 and 117?

4.2. Remote objects are viewed through a converging lens with a focal length $F = 9$ cm placed at a distance $a = 36$ cm in front of the eye.

Estimate the minimum size of the screen that should be placed behind the lens so that the entire field of view is covered. Where should the screen be placed? Assume that the radius r of the pupil is approximately 1.5 mm.

4.3*. A cylindrical transparent vessel of height h ($h << R_{ves}$), where R_{ves} is the radius of the vessel, is filled with an ideal gas of molar mass μ at a temperature T and a pressure p_0. The dependence of the refractive index n of the gas on its density ρ obeys the law $n = 1 + \alpha\rho$. The vessel is rotated at an angular velocity ω about its axis. A narrow parallel beam of light of radius r_{beam} is incident along the axis of the vessel. Determine the radius R of the spot on the screen placed at right angles to the vessel axis at a distance L behind the vessel, assuming that the change in the gas pressure at each point of the vessel due to rotation is small as compared with p_0. The effect of the end faces of the vessel on the path of the rays should be neglected.

4.4. A telescope with an angular magnification $k = 20$ consists of two converging thin lenses, viz. an objective with a focal length $F = 0.5$ m and an eyepiece which can be adjusted to the eye within the limits between $D_- = -7$D and $D_+ = +10$ D (during the adjustment, the eyepiece is displaced relative to the objective).

What is the smallest possible distance a from the objective starting from which remote objects can be viewed by an unstrained normal eye through this telescope?

4.5. Can a diverging lens be used to increase the illuminance of some regions on the surface of a screen?

4.6. A point light source is exactly above a pencil erected vertically over the water surface. The umbra of the pencil can be seen at the bottom of the vessel with water. If the pencil is immersed in water, the size of the dark spot at the bottom increases. When the pencil is drawn out of water, a bright spot appears instead of the dark one.
Explain the described phenomena.

4.7. If an illuminated surface is viewed through the wide hole in the body of a ballpoint pen, several concentric dark and bright rings are seen around the narrow hole in the body.

Explain why these rings are observed.

4.8. A point light source S is at a distance $l = 1$ m from a screen. A hole of diameter $d = 1$ cm, which lets the light through, is made in the screen in front of the light source. A transparent cylinder is arranged between the source and the screen (Fig. 118). The refractive index of the cylinder material is $n = 1.5$, the cylinder length is $l = 1$ m, and the diameter is the same as that of the hole.

What will be the change in the luminous flux through the hole? Neglect the absorption of light in the substance.

4.9. The objective and the eyepiece of a telescope are double-convex symmetrical lenses made of glass with a refractive index $n_{gl} = 1.5$.

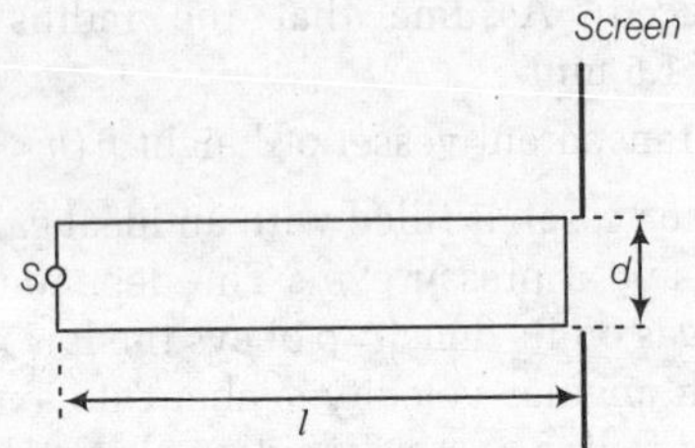

Fig. 118

The telescope is adjusted to infinity when the separation between the objective and the eyepiece is $L_0 = 16$ cm.

Determine the distance L separating the objective and the eyepiece of the telescope adjusted to infinity with water poured in the space between the objective and the eyepiece ($n_w = 1.3$).

4.10. A spider and a fly are on the surface of a glass sphere. Where must the fly be for the spider to be able to see it? Assume that the radius of the sphere is much larger than the sizes of the spider and the fly. The refractive index of glass is $n_{gl} = 1.43$.

4.11. A point light source S is outside a cylinder on its axis near the end face (base).

Determine the minimum refractive index n of the cylinder material for which none of the rays entering the base will emerge from the lateral surface.

4.12. Two converging lenses are mounted at the ends of a tube with a blackened inner lateral surface. The diameters of the lenses are equal to the diameter of the tube. The focal length of one lens is twice that of the other lens. The lenses are at such a distance from each other that parallel light rays incident along the axis of the tube on one lens emerge from the other lens in a parallel beam. When a wide light beam is incident on the lens with the larger focal length, a bright spot of illuminance E_1 is formed on the screen. When the tube is turned through 180°, the bright spot formed on the screen has an illuminance E_2.

Determine the ratio of illuminances on the screen.

4.13. An amateur photographer (who is an expert in geometrical optics) photographs the facade of a building from a distance of 100 m with a certain exposure. Then he decides to make a photograph from a distance of 50 m (to obtain a picture on a larger scale). Knowing that the area of the image will increase by a factor of four, he decides to increase accordingly the exposure in the same proportion. After developing the film, he finds out that the first picture is good, while the exposure for the second photograph has been chosen incorrectly.

Determine the factor by which the exposure had to be changed for obtaining a good picture and explain why.

4.14*. A fisherman lives on the shore of a bay forming a wedge with angle α in a house located at point A (Fig. 119). The distance from point A to the nearest point C of the bay is h, and the distance from point D to point A is l. A friend of the fisherman lives across the bay in a house located at point B. Point B is symmetric (relative to the bay) to point A. The fisherman has a boat.

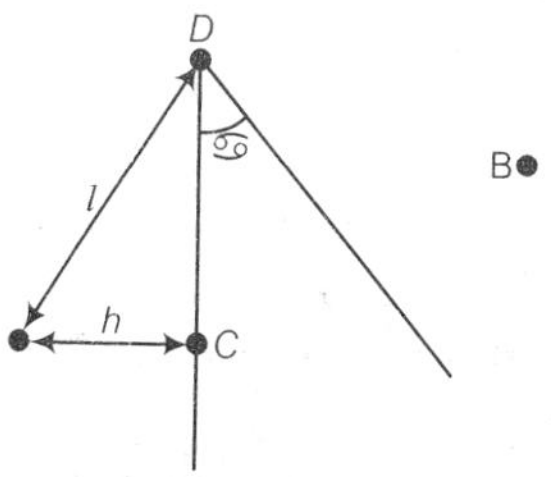

Fig. 119

Determine the minimum time t required for the fisherman to get to his friend from the house provided that he can move along the shore at a velocity v and row the boat at half that velocity ($n = 2$).

4.15. The image of a point source S' lying at a distance b from a transparent sphere is formed by a small diaphragm only by rays close to the optical axis (Fig. 120).

Where will the image be after the sphere is cut into two parts perpendicular to the horizontal axis, and the plane surface of the left half is silvered?

4.16. A glass porthole is made at the bottom of a ship for observing sealife. The hole diameter $D = 40$ cm is much larger than the thickness of the glass.

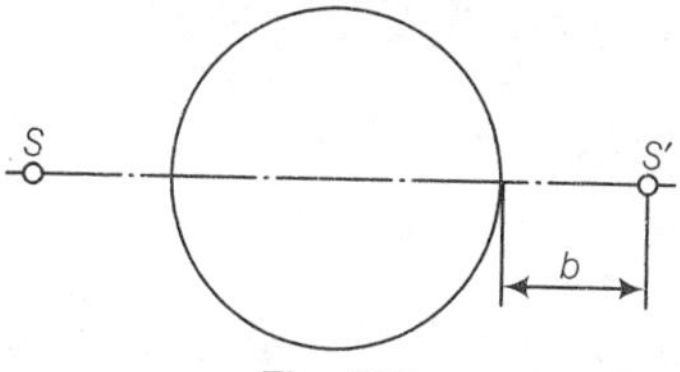

Fig. 120

Determine the area S of the field of vision at the sea bottom for the porthole if the refractive index of water is $n_w = 1.4$, and the sea depth is $h = 5$ m.

4.17*. Let us suppose that a person seating opposite to you at the table wears glasses.

Can you determine whether he is short-sighted or long-sighted? Naturally, being a polite person, you would not ask him to let you try his glasses and in general would make no mention of them.

4.18. A person walks at a velocity v in a straight line forming an angle α with the plane of a mirror.

Determine the velocity v_{rel} at which he approaches his image, assuming that the object and its image are symmetric relative to the plane of the mirror.

4.19. Two rays are incident on a spherical mirror of radius $R = 5$ cm parallel to its optical axis at distances $h_1 = 0.5$ cm and $h_2 = 3$ cm.

Determine the distance Δx between the points at which these rays intersect the optical axis after being reflected at the mirror.

4.20. The inner surface of a cone coated by a reflecting layer forms a conical mirror. A thin incandescent filament is stretched in the cone along its axis.

Determine the minimum angle α of the cone for which the rays emitted by the filament will be reflected from the conical surface not more than once.

Solutions

1. Mechanics

1.1. Let us first assume that there is no friction. Then according to the energy conservation law, the velocity v of the body sliding down the inclined plane from the height h at the foot is equal to the velocity which must be imparted to the body for its ascent to the same height h. Since for a body moving up and down an inclined plane the magnitude of acceleration is the same, the time of ascent will be equal to the time of descent.

If, however, friction is taken into consideration, the velocity v_1 of the body at the end of the descent is smaller than the velocity v (due to the work done against friction), while the velocity v_2 that has to be imparted to the body for raising it along the inclined plane is larger than v for the same reason. Since the descent and ascent occur with constant (although different) accelerations, and the traversed path is the same, the time t_1 of descent and the time t_2 of ascent can be found from the formulas

$$s = \frac{v_1 t_1}{2}, \qquad s = \frac{v_2 t_2}{2},$$

where s is the distance covered along the inclined plane. Since the inequality $v_1 < v_2$ is satisfied, it follows that $t_1 > t_2$. Thus, in the presence of sliding friction, the time of descent from the height h is longer than the time of ascent to the same height.

While solving the problem, we neglected an air drag. Nevertheless, it can easily be shown that if an air drag is present in addition to the force of gravity and the normal reaction of the inclined plane, the time of descent is always longer than the time of ascent irrespective of the type of this force.

Indeed, if in the process of ascent the body attains an intermediate height h', its velocity v' at this point, required to reach the height h in the presence of drag, must be higher than the velocity in the absence of drag since a fraction of the kinetic energy will be transformed into heat during the subsequent ascent. The body sliding down from the height h and reaching the height h' will have (due to the work done by the drag force) a velocity v'' which is lower than the velocity of the body moving down without a drag. Thus, while passing by the same point on the inclined plane, the ascending body has a higher velocity than the descending body.

For this reason, the ascending body will cover a small distance in the vicinity of point h' in a shorter time than the descending body.

Dividing the entire path into small regions, we see that each region will be traversed by the ascending body in a shorter time than by the descending body. Consequently, the total time of ascent will be shorter than the time of descent.

1.2. Since the locomotive moves with a constant deceleration after the application of brakes, it will come to rest in $t = v / a = 50$ s, during which it will cover a distance $s = v^2 / (2a) = 375$ m. Thus, in 1 min after the application of brakes, the locomotive will be at a distance $l = L - s = 25$ m from the traffic light.

1.3. At the moment the pilot switches off the engine, the helicopter is at an altitude $h = at_1^2 / 2$. Since the sound can no longer be heard on the ground after a time t_2, we obtain the equation

$$t_2 = t_1 + \frac{at_1^2}{2c},$$

where on the right-hand side we have the time of ascent of the helicopter to the altitude h and the time taken for the sound to reach the ground from the altitude h. Solving the obtained quadratic equation, we find that

$$t_1 = \sqrt{\left(\frac{c}{a}\right)^2 + 2\frac{c}{a}t_2} - \frac{c}{a}.$$

We discard the second root of the equation since it has no physical meaning.

The velocity v of the helicopter at the instant when the engine is switched off can be found from the relation

$$v = at_1 = a\left[\sqrt{\left(\frac{c}{a}\right)^2 + 2\frac{c}{a}t_2} - \frac{c}{a}\right]$$

$$= \sqrt{c^2 + 2act_2} - c = 80\,\text{m/s}.$$

1.4. During a time t_1, the point mass moving with an acceleration a will cover a distance $s = at_1^2 / 2$ and will have a velocity $v = at_1$. Let us choose the x-axis as shown in Fig. 121. Here point O marks

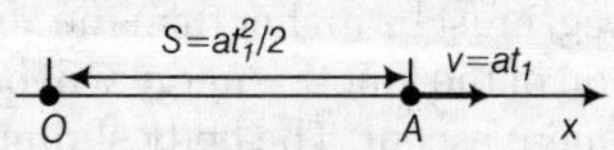

Fig. 121

the beginning of motion, and A is the point at which the body is at the moment t_1. Taking into account the sign reversal of the acceleration and applying the formula for the path length in uniformly varying motion, we determine the time t_2 in which the body will return from point A to point O:

$$0 = \frac{at_1^2}{2} + at_1t_2 - \frac{at_2^2}{2}, \text{ whence } t_2 = t_1(1 + \sqrt{2}).$$

The time elapsed from the beginning of motion to the moment of return to the initial position can be determined from the formula

$$t = t_1 + t_2 = t_1(2 + \sqrt{2}).$$

1.5. We shall consider the relative motion of the bodies from the viewpoint of the first body. Then at the initial moment, the first body is at rest (it can be at rest at the subsequent instants as well), while the second body moves towards it at a velocity $v_1 + v_2$. Its acceleration is constant, equal in magnitude to $a_1 + a_2$, and is directed against the initial velocity. The condition that the bodies meet indicates that the distance over which the velocity of the second body vanishes must be longer than the separation between the bodies at the beginning of motion; hence we obtain

$$l_{max} = \frac{(v_1 + v_2)^2}{2(a_1 + a_2)}.$$

1.6. Since the balls move along the vertical, we direct the coordinate axis vertically upwards. We plot the time dependence of the projections of the velocities of the balls on this axis. Figures 122 and 123 show the dependences $v_1(t)$ and $v_2(t)$ respectively

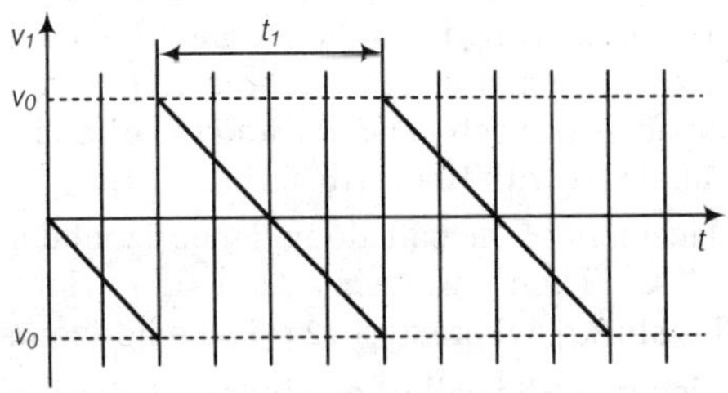

Fig. 122

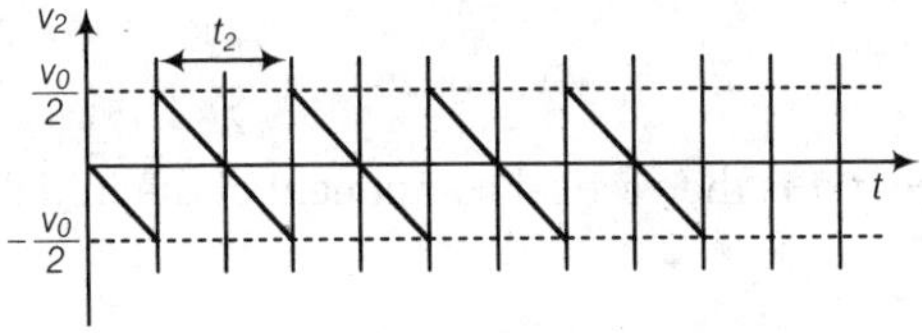

Fig. 123

(the moments of the beginning of motion are not matched so far).

These graphs present infinite sets of straight line segments with equal slopes (since the acceleration is the same). These segments are equidistant on the time axis, their separations being $t_1 = 2\sqrt{2h_1/g}$ for the first ball and $t_2 = 2\sqrt{2h_2/g}$ for the second ball. Since $h_1 = 4h_2$ by hypothesis, $t_1 = 2t_2$, i.e. the frequency of motion of the second ball is twice as high as that of the first ball. It follows from the ratio of the initial heights that the maximum velocities attained by the balls will also differ by a factor of two (see Figs. 122 and 123):

$$v_{1\,max} = 2v_{2\,max} = \sqrt{2h_1 g} = v_0 .$$

There are two possibilities for the coincidence of the velocities of the balls in magnitude and direction. The velocities of the balls may coincide for the first time $\tau = nt_1$ s after the beginning of motion (where $n = 0, 1, 2, \ldots$) during the time interval $t_1/4$, then they coincide $3t_1/4$ s after the beginning of motion during the time interval $t_1/2$. Subsequently, the velocities will coincide with a period t_1 during the time interval $t_1/2$. The other possibility consists in that the second ball starts moving $\tau = t_1/2 + nt_1$s (where $n = 0, 1, 2, \ldots$) after the first ball. After $t_1/4$ s, the velocities of the balls coincide for the first time and remain identical during the time interval $t_1/2$. Subsequently, the situation is repeated with a period t_1.

For other starting instants for the second ball, the velocity graphs will have no common points upon superposition because of the multiplicity of the periods of motion of the balls, and the problem will have no solution.

1.7*. Let us consider the motion of a ball falling freely from a height H near the symmetry axis starting from the moment it strikes the surface. At the moment of impact, the ball has the initial velocity $v_0 = \sqrt{2gH}$ (since the impact is perfectly elastic), and the direction of the velocity v_0 forms an angle 2α with the vertical (Fig. 124).

Let the displacement of the ball along the horizontal in time t after the impact be s. Then $v_0 \sin 2\alpha \cdot t = s$. Hence we obtain $t = s/(\sqrt{2gH} \times \sin 2\alpha)$, where $v_0 \sin 2\alpha$ is the horizontal component of the initial velocity of the ball (the ball does not strike the surface any more during the time t). The height at which the ball will be in time t is

$$\Delta h = h_0 + v_0 \cos 2\alpha \cdot t - \frac{gt^2}{2},$$

where $v_0 \cos 2\alpha$ is the vertical component of the initial velocity of the ball.

Since, the ball starts falling from the height H near the symmetry axis (the angle α is small),
we can assume that $h_0 \simeq 0$, $\sin 2\alpha \simeq 2\alpha$, $\cos 2\alpha \simeq 1$, and $s \approx R\alpha$.

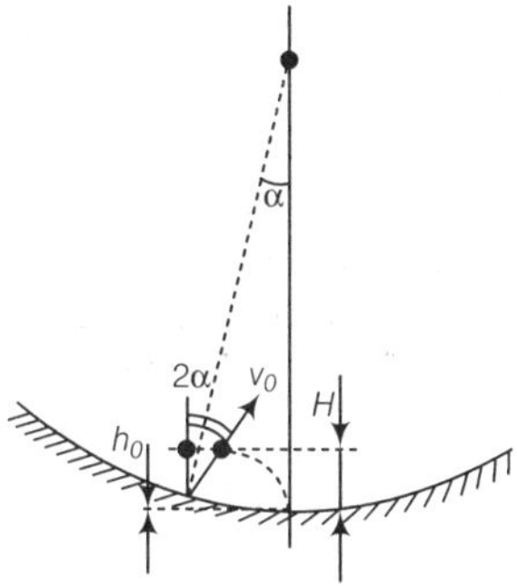

Fig. 124

Taking into account these and other relations obtained above, we find the condition for the ball to get at the lowest point on the spherical surface:

$$t = \frac{s}{\sqrt{2gH}\,\sin 2\alpha} = \frac{R}{2\sqrt{2gH}},$$

$$\Delta h \approx v_0 t - \frac{gt^2}{2} = \frac{R}{2} - \frac{R^2}{16\,H} = 0,$$

Hence, $H = R/8$.

1.8. Since the wall is smooth, the impact against the wall does not alter the vertical component of the ball velocity. Therefore, the total time t_1 of motion of the ball is the total time of the ascent and descent of the body thrown upwards at a velocity $v_0 \sin\alpha$ in the gravitational field. Consequently, $t_1 = 2v_0 \sin\alpha / g$. The motion of the ball along the horizontal is the sum of two motions. Before the collision with the wall, it moves at a velocity $v_0 \cos\alpha$. After the collision, it traverses the same distance backwards, but at a different velocity. In order to calculate the velocity of the backward motion of the ball, it should be noted that the velocity at which the ball approaches the wall (along the horizontal) is $v_0 \cos\alpha + v$. Since the impact is perfectly elastic, the ball moves away from the wall after the collision at a velocity $v_0 \cos\alpha + v$. Therefore, the ball has the following horizontal velocity relative to the ground:

$$(v_0 \cos\alpha + v) + v = v_0 \cos\alpha + 2v.$$

If the time of motion before the impact is t, by equating the distances covered by the ball before and after the collision, we obtain the following equation:

$$v_0 \cos\alpha \cdot t = (t_1 - t)\,(v_0 \cos\alpha + 2v).$$

Since the total time of motion of the ball is $t_1 = 2v_0 \sin\alpha / g$,

we find that $t = \dfrac{v_0 \sin\alpha (v_0 \cos\alpha + 2v)}{g(v_0 \cos\alpha + v)}$.

1.9*. Figure 125 shows the top view of the trajectory of the ball. Since the collisions of the ball with the wall and the bottom of the well are elastic, the magnitude of the horizontal component of the ball velocity remains unchanged and equal to v. The horizontal distances between points of two successive collisions are

$A A_1 = A_1 A_2 = A_2 A_3 = \ldots = 2r \cos\alpha$. The time between two successive collisions of the ball with the wall of the well is $t_1 = 2r \cos\alpha / v$.

The vertical component of the ball velocity does not change upon a collision with the wall and reverses its sign upon a collision with the bottom. The magnitude of the vertical velocity component for the first impact against the bottom is $\sqrt{2gH}$, and the time of motion from the top to the bottom of the well is $t_2 = \sqrt{2H/g}$.

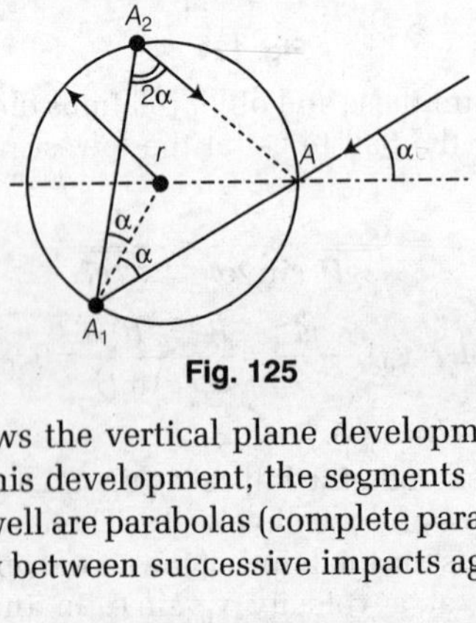

Fig. 125

Figure 126 shows the vertical plane development of the polyhedron $A_1 A_2 A_3$ ... On this development, the segments of the trajectory of the ball inside the well are parabolas (complete parabolas are the segments of the trajectory between successive impacts against the bottom).

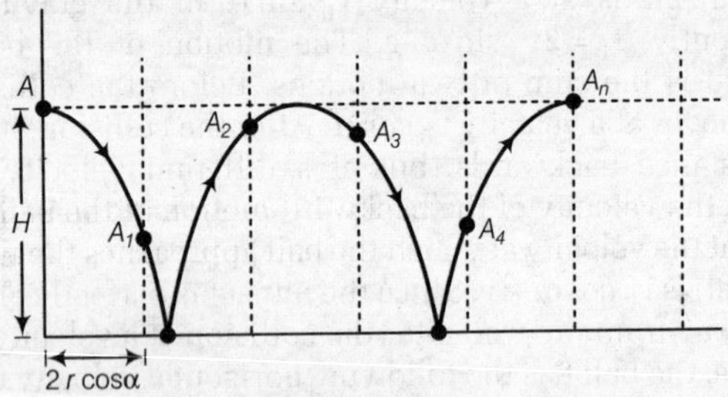

Fig. 126

The ball can "get out" of the well if the moment of the maximum ascent along the parabola coincides with the moment of an impact against the wall (i.e. at the moment of maximum ascent, the ball is at point A_n of the well edge). The time t_1 is connected to the time t_2 through the following relation:

$$nt_1 = 2kt_2,$$

where n and k are integral and mutually prime numbers. Substituting the values of t_1 and t_2, we obtain the relation between v, H, r, and α for which the ball can "get out" of the well:

$$\frac{nr\cos\alpha}{v} = k\sqrt{\frac{2H}{g}}.$$

1.10. From all possible trajectories of the shell, we choose the one that touches the shelter. Let us analyze the motion of the shell in the coordinate system with the axes directed as shown in Fig. 127.

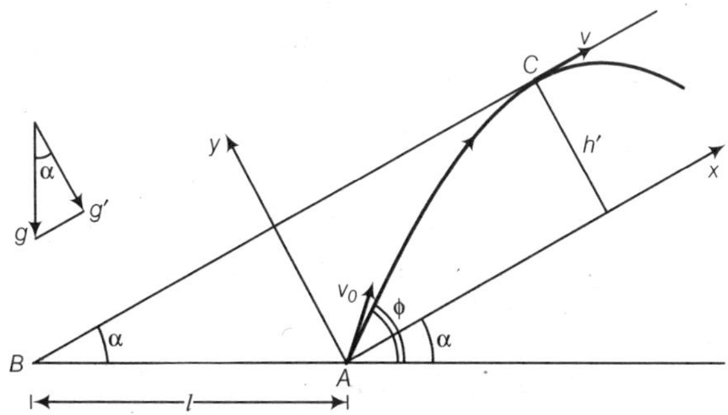

Fig. 127

The "horizontal" component (along the axis Ax) of the initial velocity of the shell in this system is $v_{0x} = v_0 \cos(\phi - \alpha)$, and the "vertical" component (along the axis Ay) is $v_{0y} = v_0 \sin(\phi - \alpha)$, where ϕ is the angle formed by the direction of the initial velocity of the shell and the horizontal.

Point C at which the trajectory of the shell touches the shelter determines the maximum altitude h' of the shell above the horizontal. Figure 127 shows that $h' = l\sin\alpha$. The projection of the total velocity v of the shell on the axis Ay is zero at this point, and

$$h' = \frac{v_{0y}^2}{2g'},$$

where $g' = g\cos\alpha$ is the "free-fall" acceleration in the coordinate system xAy. Thus,

$$v_0^2 \sin^2(\phi - \alpha) = 2gl\cos\alpha\sin\alpha.$$

Hence it follows, in particular, that if

$$v_0^2 < 2gl\cos\alpha\sin\alpha = gl\sin 2\alpha$$

by hypothesis, none of the shell trajectories will touch the shelter, and the maximum range L_{max} will correspond to the shell fired at an angle $\phi = \pi/4$ to the horizontal. Here $L_{max} = v_0^2/g$

If $$v_0^2 \geq gl\sin 2\alpha$$

by hypothesis, the angle at which the shell should be fired to touch the shelter will be

$$\phi = \phi_t = \alpha + \arcsin \frac{\sqrt{gl \sin 2\alpha}}{v_0}.$$

If, moreover, the inequality $\frac{v_0^2}{v_0^2 + 2gl} \le \sin 2\alpha$

is satisfied by hypothesis, which means that the condition $\phi_t \ge \pi / 4$ holds (prove this!), the angle ϕ at which the shell having the maximum range should be fired will be equal to $\pi / 4$, and $L_{max} = v_0^2 / g$. If, however, the inverse inequality

$$\frac{v_0^2}{v_0^2 + 2gl} > \sin 2\alpha$$

is known to be valid, which in turn means that $\phi_t < \pi / 4$, we have

$$\phi = \phi_t = \alpha + \arcsin \frac{\sqrt{gl \sin 2\alpha}}{v_0},$$

$$L_{max} = \frac{v_0^2}{g} \sin 2\phi = \frac{v_0^2}{g} \sin 2\left(\alpha + \arcsin \frac{\sqrt{gl \sin 2\alpha}}{v_0}\right).$$

1.11. Let us suppose that hail falls along the vertical at a velocity **v**. In the reference frame fixed to the motorcar, the angle of incidence of hailstones on the windscreen is equal to the angle of reflection. The velocity of a hailstone before it strikes the windscreen is v − v_1 (Fig. 128).

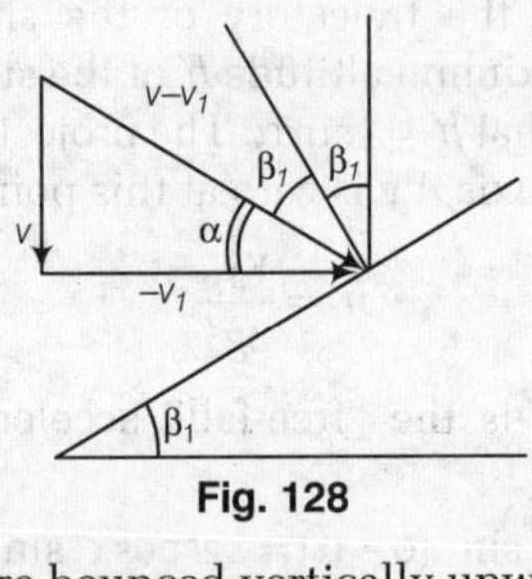

Fig. 128

Since hailstones are bounced vertically upwards (from the viewpoint of the driver) after the reflection, the angle of reflection, and hence the angle of incidence, is equal to β_1 (β_1 is the slope of the windscreen of the motorcar). Consequently, $\alpha + 2\beta_1 = \pi / 2$, and $\tan \alpha = v / v_1$. Hence $\tan \alpha \;\; \tan(\pi / 2 - 2\beta_1) = \cot 2\beta_1$, and $v / v_1 = \cot 2\beta_1$. Therefore, we obtain the following ratio of the velocities of the two motorcars: $\frac{v_1}{v_2} = \frac{\cot 2\beta_2}{\cot 2\beta_1} = 3.$

1.12. Let us go over to a reference frame moving with points A and B. In this system, the velocities of points A and B are zero. Since, the distances AC and BC are constant, point C, on the one hand, can move in a circle of radius AC with the centre at point A, and on the other hand, in a circle of radius BC with the centre at point B. Therefore, the direction of velocity of point C must be perpendicular both to the straight line AC and the straight line BC. Since points A, B, and C do not lie on the same straight line, the direction of velocity at point C would be perpendicular to two intersecting straight lines AC and BC, which is impossible. Consequently, in the moving reference frame, the velocity of point C is zero, while in the initial system (fixed to the ground), the velocity of point C is equal to the velocity of points A and B.

If point C lay on the straight line AB (in the reference frame fixed to the sheet of plywood) and its velocity differed from zero, after a certain small time interval either the distance AC or the distance BC would increase, which is impossible.

Therefore, in the motion of the sheet of plywood under consideration, the velocities of all the points are identical.

1.13. Let a car get in a small gap between two other cars. It is parked relative to the pavement as shown in Fig. 129.

Is it easier for the car to be

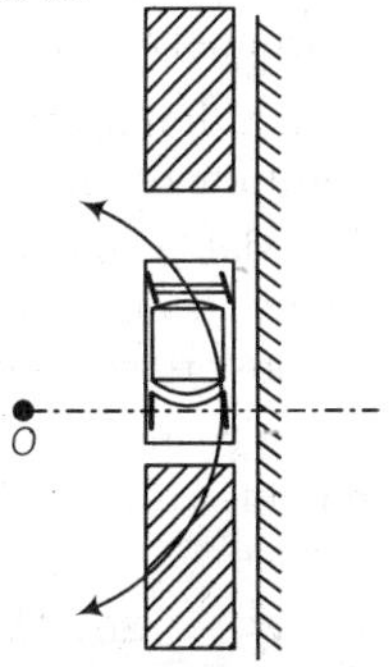

Fig. 129

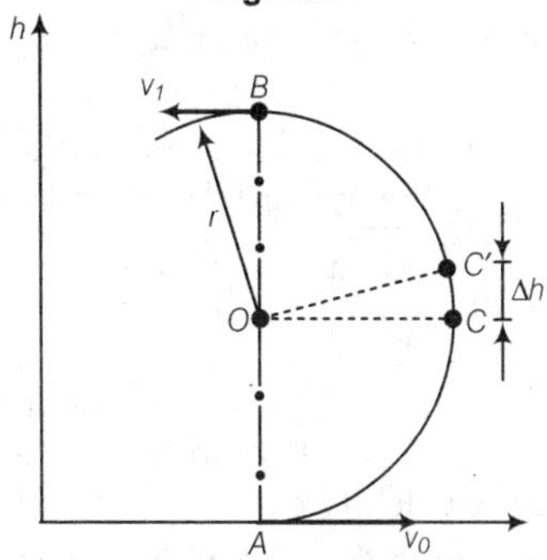

Fig. 130

driven out of the gap by forward or backward motion? Since, only the front wheels can be turned, the centre O of the circle along which the car is driven out for any manoeuvre (forward or backward) always lies on the straight line passing through the centres of the rear wheels of the car. Consequently, the car being driven out is more likely to touch the hind car during backward motion than the front car during forward motion (the centre of the corresponding circle is shifted backwards relative to the middle of the car). Obviously, a driving out is a driving in inversed in time. Therefore, the car should be driven in a small gap by backward motion.

1.14*. Let us consider the motion of the plane starting from the moment it goes over to the circular path (Fig. 130). By hypothesis, at the upper point B of the path, the velocity of the plane is $v_1 = v_0/2$, and hence the radius r of the circle described by the plane can be found from the relation

$$\frac{v_0^2}{4} = v_0^2 - 2a_0 \cdot 2r,$$

which is obtained from the law of motion of the plane for $h = 2r$. At point C of the path where the velocity of the plane is directed upwards, the total acceleration will be the sum of the centripetal acceleration $a_c = v_C^2 / r$ ($v_C^2 = v_o^2\ 2a_0 r$, where v_C is the velocity of the plane at point C) and the tangential acceleration a_t (this acceleration is responsible for the change in the magnitude of the velocity).

In order to find the tangential acceleration, let us consider a small displacement of the plane from point C to point C'. Then, $v_{C'}^2 = v_0^2 - 2a_0(r + \Delta h)$. Therefore, $v_{C'}^2 - v_C^2 = -2a_0\,\Delta h$, where Δh is the change in the altitude of the plane as it goes over to point C'. Let us divide both sides of the obtained relation by the time interval Δt during which this change takes place:

$$\frac{v_{C'}^2 - v_C^2}{\Delta t} = -\frac{2a_0\,\Delta h}{\Delta t}.$$

Then, making point C' tend to C and Δt to zero, we obtain

$$2a_t v_C = -2a_0 v_C.$$

Hence, $a_t = -a_0$. The total acceleration of the plane at the moment when the velocity has the upward direction is then

$$a = \sqrt{a_0^2 + \left(\frac{v_C^2}{r}\right)^2} = \frac{a_0\sqrt{109}}{3}.$$

1.15. Let the velocity of the drops above the person relative to the merry-go-round be at an angle α to the vertical. This angle can be determined from the velocity triangle shown in Fig. 131.

Since in accordance with the velocity composion rule

$$\mathrm{v}_0 = \mathrm{v}_{rel} + \mathrm{v}_{m \cdot g \cdot r},$$

where $v_{m \cdot g \cdot r}$ is the velocity of the merry-go-round in the region of location of the person, $v_{rel} = v_0 - v_{m \cdot g \cdot r}$ $V = v_{m \cdot g \cdot r}$

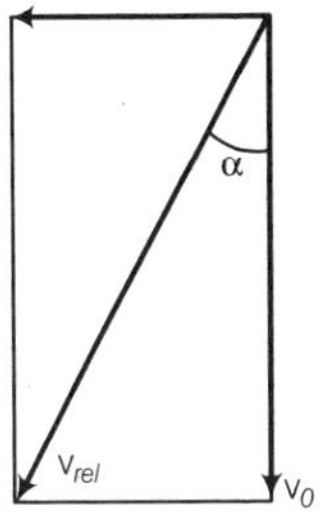

Fig. 131

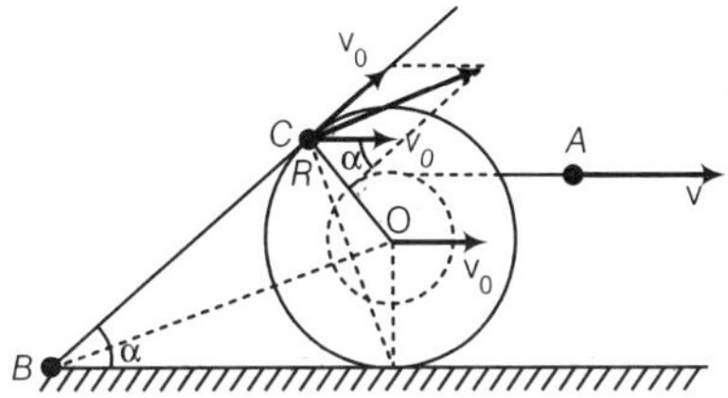

Fig. 132

The velocity of the merry-go-round is $v_{m \cdot g \cdot r} = \omega r$.

Consequently $\cot \alpha = v_0 / (\omega r)$.

Therefore, the axis of the umbrella should be tilted at the angle $\alpha = \text{arc cot}\,[v_0 / (\omega r)]$ to the vertical in the direction of motion of the merry-go-round and perpendicular to the radius of the latter.

1.16*. Let the board touch the bobbin at point C at a certain instant of time. The velocity of point C is the sum of the velocity v_0 of the axis O of the bobbin and the velocity of point C (relative to point O), which is tangent to the circle at point C and equal in magnitude to v_0 (since there is no slipping). If the angular velocity of the board at this instant is ω, the linear velocity of the point of the board touching the bobbin will be $\omega R \tan^{-1} (\alpha / 2)$ (Fig. 132). Since the board remains in contact with the bobbin all the time, the velocity of point C relative to the board is directed along the board, whence $\omega R \tan^{-1} (\alpha / 2) = v_0 \sin \alpha$. Since there is no slipping of the bobbin over the horizontal surface, we can write

$$\frac{v_0}{R} = \frac{v}{R + r}.$$

Therefore, we obtain the following expression for the angular velocity ω:

$$\omega = \frac{v}{R + r} \sin \alpha \cdot \tan \frac{\alpha}{2} = \frac{2v \sin^2 (\alpha / 2)}{(R + r) \cos (\alpha / 2)}.$$

1.17. The area of the spool occupied by the wound thick tape is $S_1 = \pi (r_f^2 - r_i^2) = 8\pi r_i^2$. Then the length of the wound tape is $l = S_1 / d = 8\pi (r_i^2 / d)$, where d is the thickness of the thick tape.

The area of the spool occupied by the wound thin tape is $S_2 = \pi (r_f'^2 - r_i^2)$, where r_f' is the final radius of the wound part in the latter case. Since the lengths of the tapes are equal, and the tape thickness in the latter case is half that in the former case, we can write

$$l = \frac{2\pi (r'^2_f - r_i^2)}{d}, \; r'^2_f - r_i^2 = 4r_i^2.$$

Consequently, the final radius r'_f of the wound part in the latter case is $r'_f = \sqrt{5}r_1$.

The numbers of turns N_1 and N_2 of the spool for the former and latter winding can be written as

$$N_1 = \frac{2r_1}{d}, \qquad N_2 = \frac{(\sqrt{5}-1)\,r_1}{d/2},$$

whence $t_2 = (\sqrt{5}-1)\,t_1$.

1.18. Let the initial winding radius be $4r$, Then the decrease in the winding area as a result of the reduction of the radius by half (to $2r$) will be

$$S = \pi\,(16r^2 - 4r^2) = 12\pi r^2,$$

which is equal to the product of the length l_1 of the wound tape and its thickness d. The velocity v of the tape is constant during the operation of the tape-recorder; hence $l_1 = vt_1$, and we can write

$$12\pi r^2 = vt_1 d. \qquad (1)$$

When the winding radius of the tape on the cassette is reduced by half again (from $2r$ to r), the winding area is reduced by $\pi\,(4r^2 - r^2) = 3\pi r^2$, i.e.

$$3\pi r^2 = vt_2\, d, \qquad (2)$$

where t_2 is the time during which the winding radius will be reduced in the latter case. Dividing Eqs. (1) and (2) termwise, we obtain

$$t_2 = \frac{t_1}{4} = 5 \text{ min}.$$

1.19. Let us go over to the reference frame fixed to ring O'. In this system, the velocity of ring O is $v_1/\cos\alpha$ and is directed upwards since the thread is inextensible, and is pulled at a constant velocity v_1 relative to ring O'. Therefore, the velocity of ring O relative to the straight line AA' (which is stationary with respect to the ground) is

$$v_2 = \frac{v_1}{\cos\alpha} - v_1 = v_1\frac{2\sin^2(\alpha/2)}{\cos\alpha}$$

and is directed upwards.

1.20. By the moment of time t from the beginning of motion, the wedge covers a distance $s = at^2/2$ and acquires a velocity $v_{wed} = at$. During this time, the load will move along the wedge over the same distance s, and its velocity relative to the wedge is $v_{rel} = at$ and directed upwards along the wedge. The velocity of the load relative to the ground is $\mathbf{v}_1 = \mathbf{v}_{rel} + \mathbf{v}_{wed}$, i.e. (Fig. 133)

$$v_1 = 2v_{wed}\sin\frac{\alpha}{2} = \left(2a\sin\frac{\alpha}{2}\right)t,$$

and the angle formed by the velocity v_1 with the horizontal is

$$\beta = \frac{\pi - \alpha}{2} = \text{const.}$$

Thus, the load moves in the straight line forming the angle $\beta = (\pi - \alpha)/2$ with the horizontal.

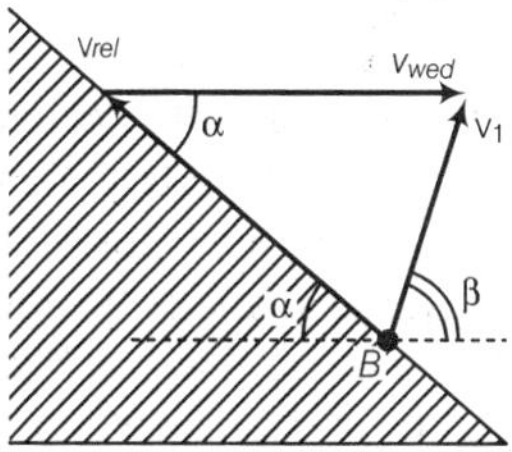

Fig. 133

The acceleration of the load on the wedge relative to the ground is

$$a_1 = 2a\sin\frac{\alpha}{2}.$$

1.21. The velocity of the ant varies with time according to a nonlinear law. Therefore, the mean velocity on different segments of the path will not be the same, and the well-known formulas for mean velocity cannot be used here.

Let us divide the path of the ant from point A to point B into small segments traversed in equal time intervals Δt. Then $\Delta t = \Delta l / v_m(\Delta l)$, where $v_m(\Delta l)$ is the mean velocity over a given segment Δl. This formula suggests the idea of the solution of the problem: we plot the dependence of $1/v_m(\Delta l$ on l for the path between points A and B. The graph is a segment of a straight line (Fig. 134). The hatched area S under this segment is numerically equal to the sought time.

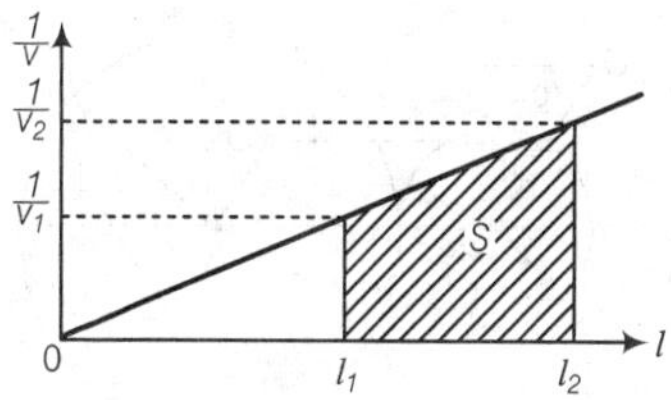

Fig. 134

Let us calculate this area:

$$S = \frac{1/v_1 + 1/v_2}{2}(l_2 - l_1) = \left(\frac{1}{2v_1} + \frac{1}{2v_1}\frac{l_2}{l_1}\right)(l_2 - l_1) = \frac{l_2^2 - l_1^2}{2v_1 l_1}$$

since $1/v_2 = (1/v_1)\, l_2/l_1$. Thus, the ant reaches point B in the time

$$t = \frac{4\text{m}^2 - 1\text{m}^2}{2 \times 2\,\text{m/s} \times 10^{-2} \times 1\text{m}} = 75\text{ s}.$$

1.22. Obviously, all the segments of the smoke trace move in the horizontal direction with the velocity of wind. Let us consider the path of the locomotive in the reference frame moving with the wind (Fig. 135).

Points A' and B' of the smoke trace correspond to the smoke ejected by the locomotive at points A and B of its circular path relative to the ground. Obviously, $AA' \parallel BB'$. It can easily be seen that the path of the locomotive relative to the reference frame moving with the wind is the path of the point of a wheel of radius R rotating at a velocity v_{loc} and moving against the wind (to the left) at a velocity v_{wind}.

This trajectory is known as a cycloid. Depending on the ratio of velocities v_{loc} and v_{wind}, the shape of the lower part of the path will be different. It is a loop (when $v_{loc} > v_{wind}$, Fig. 136), or a parabola (when $v_{loc} < v_{wind}$, Fig. 137), or a "beak" (when $v_{loc} = v_{wind}$, Fig. 138). The latter case corresponds to the condition of our problem.

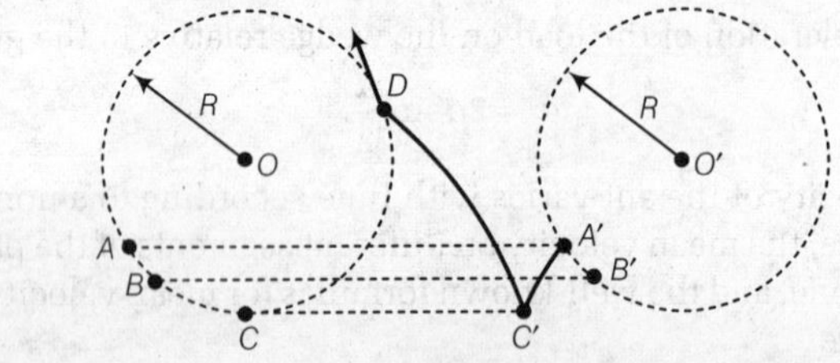

Fig. 135

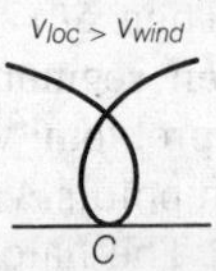

Fig. 136

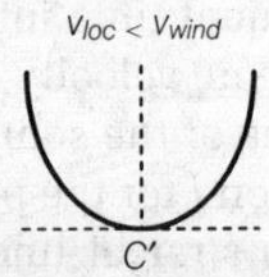

Fig. 137

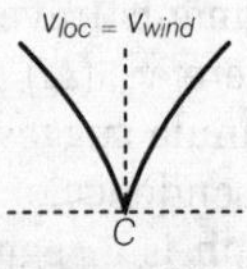

Fig. 138

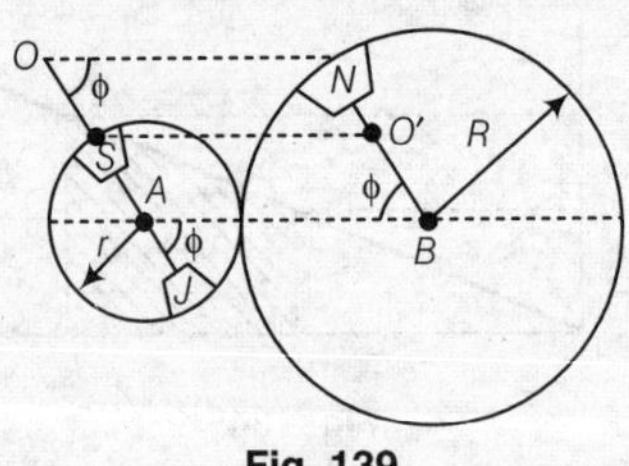

Fig. 139

Thus, the velocity of the wind is $v_{wind} = v_{loc} = 10$ m/s, and in order to find its direction, we draw the tangent CC' from the point of the "beak" to the path of the locomotive (viz. the circle) relative to the ground.

1.23*. Let the merry-go-round turn through a certain angle ϕ (Fig. 139). We construct a point O ($OA = R$) such that points O, S, A, and J lie on the same straight line. Then it is clear that $ON = R + r$ at any instant of time. Besides, point O is at rest relative to John (Sam is always opposite to John). Therefore, from John's point of view, Nick translates in a circle of radius $R + r$ with the centre at point O which moves relative to the ground in a circle of radius R with the centre at point A. From Nick's point of view, Sam translates in a circle of radius $R + r$ with the centre at point O which is at rest relative to Nick. However, point O moves relative to the ground in a circle of radius r with the centre at point B.

1.24. Since the hoop with the centre at point O_1 is at rest, the velocity v_A of the upper point A of "intersection" of the hoops must be directed along the tangent to the circle with centre O_1 at any instant

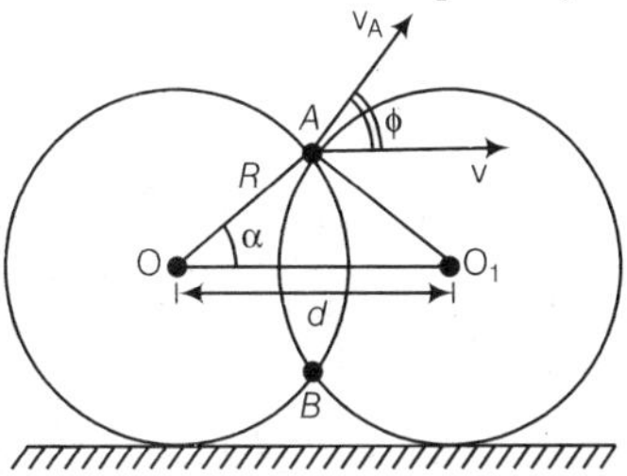

Fig. 140

of time (Fig. 140). At any instant of time, the segment AB divides the distance $d = OO_1$ between the centres of the hoops into two equal parts, and hence the horizontal projection of the velocity v_A is always equal to $v/2$. Consequently, the velocity v_A forms an angle $\phi = \pi/2 - \alpha$ with the horizontal and is given by

$$v_A = \frac{v}{2\cos\phi} = \frac{v}{2\sin\alpha}$$

Since $\sin\alpha = \sqrt{1-\cos^2\alpha} = \sqrt{1-(d/2R)^2}$, the velocity of the upper point of "intersection" of the hoops is $v_A = \dfrac{v}{2\sqrt{1-(d/2R)^2}}$.

1.25. By hypothesis, the following proportion is preserved between the lengths l_1, l_2, and l_3 of segments A_0A_1, A_0A_2, and A_0A_3 during the motion:

$$l_1 : l_2 : l_3 = 3:5:6.$$

Therefore, the velocities of points A_1, A_2, and A_3 are to one another as

$$v_{A_1} : v_{A_2} : v_{A_3} = 3:5:6,$$

and hence (Fig. 141)

$$v_{A_1} = \frac{v}{2},\ v_{A_2} = \frac{5v}{6}.$$

Let us now consider the velocity of the middle link $(A_1B_2A_2C_2)$ at the instant when the angles of the construction are equal to 90°.

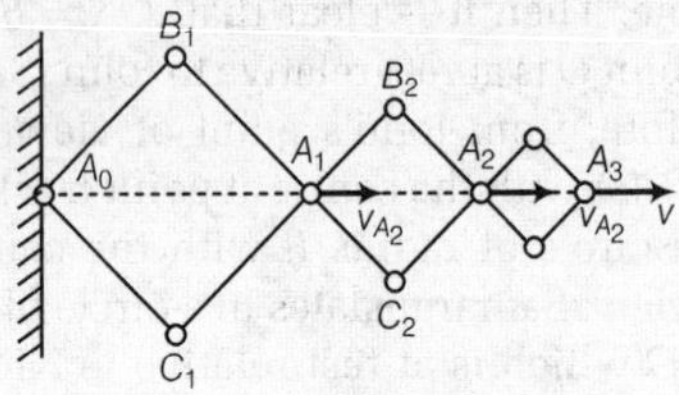

Fig. 141

In the reference frame moving at a velocity v_{A_1}, the velocity v'_{B_2} of point B_2 is directed at this instant along B_2A_2. The velocity of point A_2 is directed along the horizontal and is given by

$$v'_{A_2} = v_{A_2} - v_{A_1} = \frac{v}{3}.$$

From the condition of inextensibilit of the rod B_2A_2, it follows that

$$v'_{B_1} = v_{A_2} \sin\frac{\pi}{4} = \frac{v\sqrt{2}}{6}.$$

We can find the velocity of point B_2 relative to a stationary reference frame by using the cosine law:

$$v^2_{B_2} = v^2_{A_1} + v^2_{B_2} + \left(\frac{2\sqrt{2}}{2}\right) v_{A_1} v'_{B_2} = \frac{17}{36} v^2,$$

$$v_{B_2} = \frac{\sqrt{17}}{6} v.$$

1.26. If the thread is pulled as shown in Fig. 142, the bobbin rolls to the right, rotating clockwise about its axis.

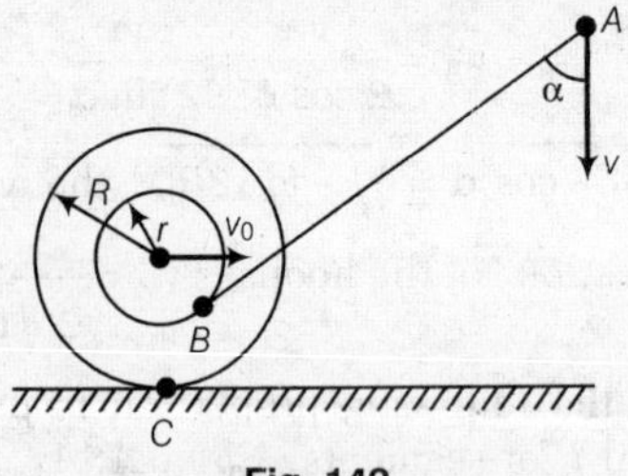

Fig. 142

For point B, the sum of the projections of velocity v_0 of translatory motion and the linear velocity of rotary motion (with an angular velocity ω) on the direction of the thread is equal to v:

$$v = v_0 \sin\alpha - \omega r.$$

Since the bobbin is known to move over the horizontal surface without slipping, the sum of the projections of the corresponding velocities for point C is equal to zero:

$$v_0 - \omega R = 0.$$

Solving the obtained equations, we find that the velocity v_0 is

$$v_0 = \frac{vR}{R \sin \alpha - r}.$$

It can be seen that for $R \sin \alpha = r$ (which corresponds to the case when points A, B, and C lie on the same straight line), the expression for v_0 becomes meaningless. It should also be noted that the obtained expression describes the motion of the bobbin to the right (when point B is above the straight line AC and $R \sin \alpha > r$) as well as to the left (when point B is below the straight line AC and $R \sin \alpha < r$).

1.27. The velocities of the points of the ingot lying on a segment AB at a given instant uniformly vary from v_1 at point A to v_2 at point B.

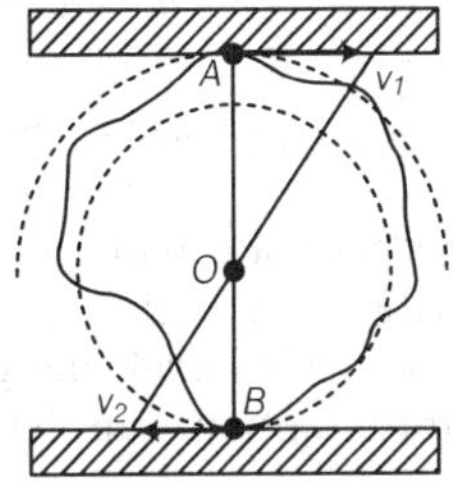

Fig. 143

Consequently, the velocity of point O (Fig. 143) at a given instant is zero. Hence point O is an instantaneous centre of rotation. (Since the ingot is three-dimensional, point O lies on the instantaneous rotational axis which is perpendicular to the plane of the figure.) Clearly, at a given instant, the velocity v_1 corresponds to the points of the ingot lying on the circle of radius OA, while the velocity v_2 to points lying on the circle of radius OB.

(In a three-dimensional ingot, the points having such velocities lie on cylindrical surfaces with radii OA and OB respectively.)

1.28. In order to describe the motion of the block, we choose a reference frame fixed to the conveyer belt. Then the velocity of the block at the initial moment is $v_{bl} = v_0 + v$, and the block moves with a constant acceleration $a = -\mu g$.

For the instant of time t when the velocity of the block vanishes, we obtain the equation $0 = v_0 + v - \mu g t$. Hence the velocity of the conveyer belt is $v = \mu g t - v_0 = 3$ m/s.

1.29. Let us write the equation of motion for the body over the inclined plane. Let the instantaneous coordinate (the displacement of the top of the inclined plane) be x; then

$$ma = mg \sin\alpha - mg \cos\alpha \cdot bx,$$

where m is the mass of the body, and a is its acceleration. The form of the obtained equation of motion resembles that of the equation of vibratory motion for a body suspended on a spring of rigidity $k = mg \cos\alpha \cdot b$ in the field of the "force of gravity" $mg \sin\alpha$. This analogy with the vibratory motion helps solve the problem.

Let us determine the position x_0 of the body for which the sum of the forces acting on it is zero. It will be the "equilibrium position" for the vibratory motion of the body. Obviously, $mg \sin\alpha - mg \cos\alpha \cdot bx_0 = 0$. Hence we obtain $x_0 = (1/b)\tan\alpha$. At this moment, the body will have the velocity v_0 which can be obtained from the law of conservation of the mechanical energy of the body:

$$\frac{mv_0^2}{2} = mg \sin\alpha \cdot x_0 - \frac{k\,x_0^2}{2} = mg \sin\alpha \cdot x_0 - \frac{mgb \cos\alpha}{2}\,x_0^2,$$

$$v_0^2 = 2g\,x_0 \sin\alpha - gb\,x_0^2 \cos\alpha = \frac{g \sin^2\alpha}{b \cos\alpha}.$$

In its further motion, the body will be displaced again by x_0 (the "amplitude" value of vibrations, which can easily be obtained from the law of conservation of mechanical energy). The frequency of the corresponding vibratory motion can be found from the relation $k/m = gb \cos\alpha = \omega_0^2$.

Therefore, having covered the distance $x_0 = (1/b)\tan\alpha$ after passing the "equilibrium position", the body comes to rest. At this moment, the restoring force "vanishes" since it is just the force of sliding friction. As soon as the body stops, sliding friction changes the direction and becomes static friction equal to $mg \sin\alpha$. The coefficient of friction between the body and the inclined plane at the point where the body stops is $\mu_{st} = b \cdot 2x_0 = 2\tan\alpha$, i.e. is more than enough for the body to remain at rest.

Using the vibrational approach to the description of this motion, we find that the total time of motion of the body is equal to half the "period of vibrations". Therefore,

$$t = \frac{T}{2} = \frac{2\pi}{2\omega_0} = \frac{\pi}{\sqrt{gb \cos\alpha}}.$$

1.30. The friction $F_{fr}(x)$ of the loaded sledge is directly proportional to the length x of the part of the sledge stuck in the sand. We write the equation of motion for the sledge decelerated in the sand in the first case:

$$ma = -\,mg\,\frac{x}{l}\,\mu,$$

where m is the mass, a the acceleration, l the length, and μ the coefficient of friction of the sledge against the sand. As in the solution of Problem 1.29, we obtained an "equation of vibrations". Therefore, the deceleration of the sledge stuck in the sand corresponds to the motion of a load on a spring (of rigidity $k = (mg / l)\mu$) having acquired the velocity v_0 in the equilibrium position. Then the time dependence $x(t)$ of the part of the sledge stuck in the sand and its velocity $v(t)$ can be written as

$$x(t) = x_0 \sin \omega_0 t,\ v(t) = v_0 \cos \omega_0 t,$$

where
$$x_0 = \frac{v_0}{\omega_0},\ \omega_0 = \sqrt{\frac{k}{m}} = \sqrt{\frac{g}{l}\mu}.$$

It can easily be seen that the time before the sledge comes to rest is equal to quarter the "period of vibrations". Therefore,

$$t_1 = \frac{\pi}{2\omega_0} = \frac{\pi / 2}{\sqrt{l/(\mu g)}}.$$

In the second case (after the jerk), the motion can be regarded as if the sledge stuck in the sand had a velocity $v_1 > v_0$ and having traversed the distance x_0 were decelerated to the velocity v_0 (starting from this moment, the second case is observed). The motion of the sledge after the jerk can be represented as a part of the total vibratory motion according to the law

$$x(t) = x_1 \sin \omega_0 t,\ v(t) = v_1 \cos \omega_0 t$$

starting from the instant t_2 when the velocity of the sledge becomes equal to v_0. As before, $x_1 = v_1 / \omega_0$. Besides,

$$\frac{mg}{2l}\mu x_0^2 = \frac{mv_1^2}{2} - \frac{mv_0^2}{2},$$

whence $v_1 = x_0\omega_0\sqrt{2}$.

The distance covered by the sledge after the jerk is

$$x_1 - x_0 = \frac{v_1}{\omega_0} - \frac{v_0}{\omega_0} = \frac{1}{\omega_0}(v_1 - v_0) = x_0(\sqrt{2} - 1).$$

Consequently, the ratio of the braking lengths is $\dfrac{x_1 - x_0}{x_0} = \sqrt{2} - 1.$

In order to determine the time of motion of the sledge after the jerk, we must find the time of motion of the sledge from point x_0 to point x_1 by using the formula $x(t) = x_1 \sin \omega_0 t$. For this purpose, we determine t_2 from the formula

$$x_0 = x_1 \sin \omega_0 t_2.$$

Since $x_1 = \sqrt{2}x_0$, $\omega_0 t_2 = \pi / 4$. Consequently, $t_2 = \pi/(4\omega_0) = t_1 / 2$. Since $t_3 = t_1 - t_2$, where t_3 is the time of motion of the sledge after the jerk, we obtain the required ratio of the braking times $\dfrac{t_3}{t_1} = \dfrac{1}{2}$.

1.31. The force of gravity $mg = 60$ N acting on the load is considerably stronger than the force with which the rope should be pulled to keep the load. This is due to considerable friction of the rope against the log.

At first, the friction prevents the load from slipping under the action of the force of gravity. The complete analysis of the distribution of friction acting on the rope is rather complex since the tension of the rope at points of its contact with the log varies from F_1 to mg. In turn, the force of pressure exerted by the rope on the log also varies, being proportional at each point to the corresponding local tension of the rope. Accordingly, the friction acting on the rope is determined just by the force of pressure mentioned above. In order to solve the problem, it should be noted, however, that the total friction F_{fr} (whose components are proportional to the reaction of the log at each point) will be proportional (with the corresponding proportionality factors) to the tensions of the rope at the ends. In particular, for a certain coefficient k, it is equal to the maximum tension: $F_{fr} = kmg$. This means that the ratio of the maximum tension to the minimum tension is constant for a given arrangement of the rope and the log:

$$mg / T_1 = 1/(1-k) \text{ since } T_1 = mg - kmg.$$

When we want to lift the load, the ends of the rope as if change places. The friction is now directed against the force T_2 and plays a harmful role. The ratio of the maximum tension (which is now equal to T_2) to the minimum tension (mg) is obviously the same as in the former case:

$$T_2/(mg) = 1/(1-k) = mg/T_1. \text{ Hence we obtain } T_2 = \frac{(mg)^2}{T_1} = 90 \text{ N}.$$

1.32. Let us see what happens when the driver turns the front wheels of a stationary car (we shall consider only one tyre). At the initial moment, the wheel is undeformed (from the point of view of torsion), and the area of the tyre region in contact with the ground is S. By turning the steering wheel, the driver deforms the stationary tyre until the moment of force M_S applied to the wheel and tending to turn it becomes larger than the maximum possible moment of static friction acting on the tyre of contact area S. In this case, the forces of friction are perpendicular to the contact plane between the tyre and the ground.

Let now the motorcar move. Static frictional forces are applied to the same region of the tyre of area S. They almost attain the maximum values and lie in the plane of the tyre. A small moment of force M_S applied to the wheel is sufficient to turn the wheel since it is now counteracted by the total moment of "oblique" forces of static friction which is considerably smaller than for the stationary car. In fact, in the case of the moving car, the component of the static friction responsible for the torque preventing the wheel from being turned is similar to liquid friction since stagnation is not observed for turning wheels of a moving car. Thus, a small torque can easily turn a moving wheel, and the higher the velocity (the closer the static friction to the limiting value), the more easily can the wheel be turned.

1.33. Let us choose the reference frame as shown in Fig. 144. Suppose that vector $\overrightarrow{OA}$ is the vector of the initial velocity **v**. Then vector $\overrightarrow{AB}$ is the change in velocity during the time interval Δt. Since the force acting on the body is constant, vector $\overrightarrow{BC}$ equal to vector $\overrightarrow{AB}$ is the change in velocity during the next time interval Δt. Therefore, in the time

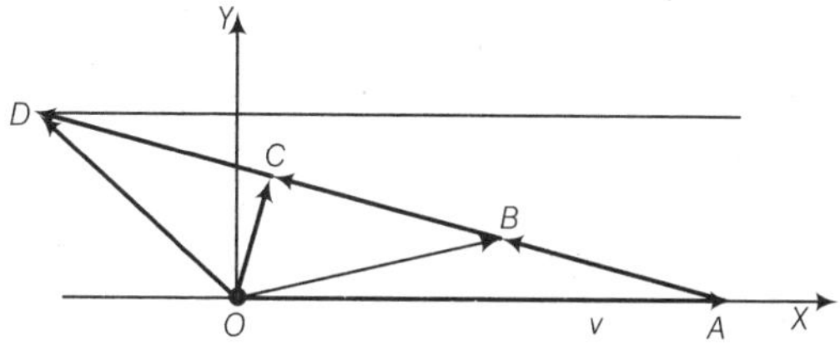

Fig. 144

interval $3\Delta t$ after the beginning of action of the force, the direction of velocity will be represented by vector $\overrightarrow{OD}$, and $\overrightarrow{AB} = \overrightarrow{BC} = \overrightarrow{CD}$. Let the projections of vector $\overrightarrow{AB}$ on the
x-and y-axes be Δv_x and Δv_y. Then we obtain two equations :

$$(v + \Delta v_x)^2 + \Delta v_y^2 = \frac{v^2}{4},$$

$$(v + 2\Delta v_x)^2 + (2\Delta v_y)^2 = \frac{v^2}{16}.$$

Since the final velocity satisfies the relation

$$v_f^2 = (v + 3\Delta v_x)^2 + (3\Delta v_y)^2,$$

using the previous equations, we obtain $v_f = \frac{\sqrt{7}}{4} v$.

1.34. Since the motion occurs in the horizontal plane, the vertical component of the force acting on the load is mg, and the horizontal component is given by $F^2 - (mg)^2 = mg\sqrt{\alpha^2 - 1}$, where $\alpha = 1.25$ (Fig. 145). The horizontal acceleration of the load (and the carriage) is determined by this horizontal force: $ma = mg\sqrt{\alpha^2 - 1}$.

Consequently, $a = g\sqrt{\alpha^2 - 1} = (3/4)g = 7.5 \text{ m/s}^2$.

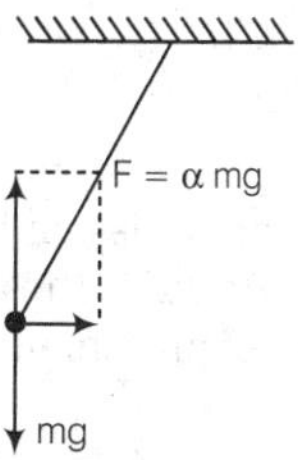

Fig. 145

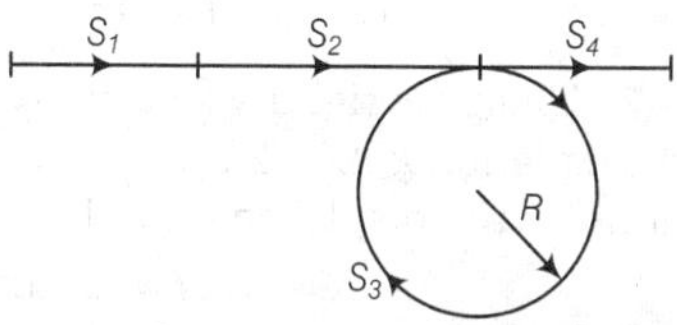

Fig. 146

On the first segment of the path, the carriage is accelerated to the velocity $v = at_1 = (3/4)\,gt_1 = 30$ m/s and covers the distance s_1 in the forward direction in the straight line:

$$s_1 = \frac{at_1^2}{2} = \frac{3}{8}\,gt_1^2 = 60 \text{ m.}$$

Further, it moves at a constant velocity v during the time interval $t_2 = 3$ s and traverses the path of length

$$s_2 = vt_2 = 90 \text{ m.}$$

Thus, seven seconds after the beginning of motion, the carriage is at a distance $s_1 + s_2 = 150$ m in front of the initial position.

On the third segment, the carriage moves round a bend to the right. Since the velocity of the carriage moving on the rails is always directed *along* the carriage, the constant (during the time interval ($t_3 = 25.12$ s) transverse acceleration $a = (3/4)\,g$ is a *centripetal* acceleration, i.e. the carriage moves in a circle at a constant velocity $v : a = v^2/R$, the radius of the circle being $R = v^2/a = 120$ m. The path traversed by the carriage in the circle is $s_3 = R\varphi = vt_3$,

whence the angle of rotation of the carriage about the centre of the circle is $\phi = vt_3 / R = 6.28 = 2\pi$ rad, i.e. the carriage describes a complete circumference.

On the last segment, the carriage brakes and comes to a halt since the acceleration along the carriage is equal to the initial acceleration and acts during the same time interval. Therefore, $s_4 = s_1 = 60$ m. The carriage stops at a distance $s = 2s_1 + s_2 = 210$ m in front of the initial position (Fig. 146).

1.35. Let the hinge be displaced downwards by a small distance Δx as a result of application of the force F, and let the rods be elongated by Δl

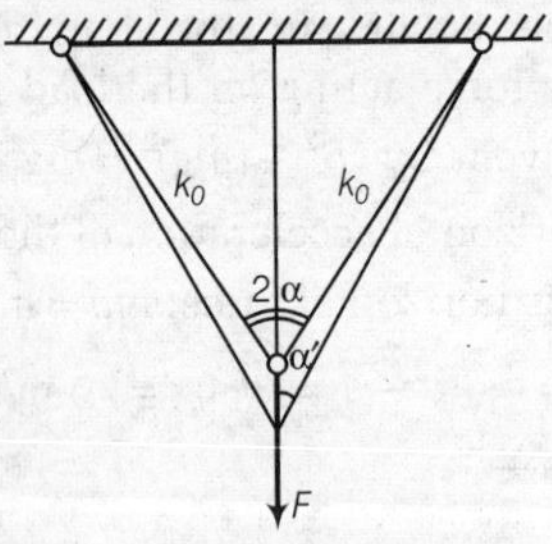

Fig. 147

(Fig. 147). Then the rigidity k of the system of rods can be determined from the equation $k\,\Delta x = 2k_0\,\Delta l \cos\alpha'$, where $2\alpha'$ is the angle between the rods after the displacement. Since the displacement is small

$$\alpha' \approx \alpha, \Delta l \approx \Delta x \cos\alpha,$$

and hence

$$k \approx 2k_0 \cos^2\alpha.$$

1.36. Let us first suppose that the air drag is absent. Then the balls will meet if the vertical component of the initial velocity of the second ball is equal to that of the first ball:

$$v_1 = v_2 \sin\alpha,$$

whence $\sin\alpha = v_1/v_2 = 10/20 = 1/2$, $\alpha = 30°$. Then the time of motion of the balls before collision is $t = s/(v_2 \cos\alpha) \simeq 0.6$ s.

Since the balls are heavy, the role of the air drag can easily be estimated. The nature of motion of the first ball will not change significantly since the acceleration due to the air drag is $a_{max} = 1$ m/s^2 even if the mass of each ball is 10 g, and the maximum velocity of the first ball is $v_1 = 10$ m/s. This acceleration does not change the total time of motion of the first ball by more than 1%. Since the air drag is directed against the velocity of the ball, we can make the balls collide by imparting the same vertical velocity component to the second ball as that of the first ball provided that in subsequent instants the vertical projections of the accelerations of the balls are identical at any instant of time. For this purpose, the angle α formed by the velocity vector of the second ball with the horizontal at the moment it is shot off must be equal to 30°.

1.37. Let us write the equation of motion for the ball at the moment when the spring is compressed by Δx:

$$ma = mg - k\,\Delta x.$$

As long as the acceleration of the ball is positive, its velocity increases. At the moment when the acceleration vanishes, the velocity of the ball attains the maximum value. The spring is compressed thereby by Δl such that

$$mg - k\,\Delta l = 0,$$

whence

$$\Delta l = \frac{mg}{k}.$$

Thus, when the velocity of the ball attains the maximum value, the ball is at a height

$$h = l - \frac{mg}{k}$$

from the surface of the table.

1.38*. It can easily be seen that the ball attains the equilibrium position at an angle α of deflection of the thread from the vertical, which is determined from the condition

$$\tan\alpha = \frac{\mu v}{mg}.$$

During the oscillatory motion of the ball, it will experience the action of a constant large force $F = \sqrt{(mg)^2 + (\mu v)^2}$ and a small drag force (Fig. 148).

Consequently, the motion of the ball will be equivalent to a weakly

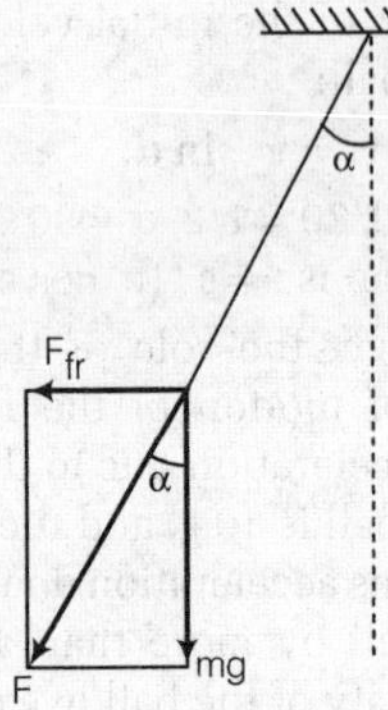

Fig. 148

attenuating motion of a simple pendulum with a free-fall acceleration g' given by

$$g' = \frac{g}{\cos\alpha} = g\,\frac{\sqrt{(mg)^2 + (\mu v)^2}}{mg} = g\,\sqrt{1 + \left(\frac{\mu v}{mg}\right)^2}$$

The period of small (but still damped) oscillations of the ball can be determined from the relation

$$T = \frac{2\pi}{\sqrt{g'/l - \mu^2/(4m^2)}} = \frac{2\pi}{\sqrt{(g/l)\sqrt{1 + (\mu v/mg)^2} - \mu^2/(4m^2)}}.$$

1.39. We write the equilibrium condition for a small segment of the string which had the length

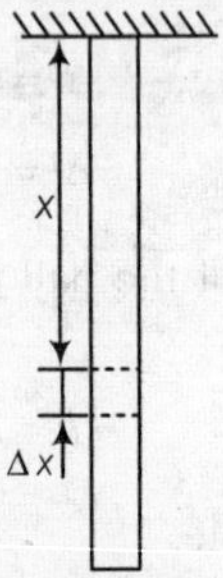

Fig. 149

Δx before suspension and was at a distance x from the point of suspension (Fig. 149):

$$\frac{m}{L}\,\Delta x g + T\,(x + \Delta x) = T\,(x),$$

where L is the length of the rubber string in the unstretched state. Thus, it is clear that after the suspension the tension will uniformly decrease along the string from mg to zero.

Therefore, the elongations per unit length for small equal segments of the string in the unstressed state after the suspension will also linearly decrease from the maximum value to zero. For this reason, the half-sum of the elongations of two segments of the string symmetric about its middle will be equal to the elongation of the central segment which experiences the tension $mg/2$. Consequently, the elongation Δl of the string will be such as if it were acted upon by the force $mg/2$ at the point of suspension and at the lower end, and the string were weightless; hence

$$\Delta l = \frac{mg}{2k}.$$

1.40. We assume that the condition $m_1 + m_2 > m_3 + m_4$ is satisfied, otherwise the equilibrium is impossible. The left spring was stretched with the force T_1 balancing the force of gravity m_2g of the load: $T_1 = m_2g$. The equilibrium condition for the load m_3 was

$$m_3g + T_2 - F_{\text{ten}} = 0,$$

where T_2 is the tension of the right spring, and F_{ten} is the tension of the rope passed through the pulley (see Fig. 14). This rope holds the loads of mass m_1 and m_2, whence

$$F_{\text{ten}} = (m_1 + m_2)g.$$

We can express the tension T_2 in the following way:

$$T_2 = (m_1 + m_2 - m_3)\,g.$$

After cutting the lower thread, the equations of motion for all the loads can be written as follows:

$$m_1a_1 = m_1g + T_1 - F_{\text{ten}}, \qquad m_2a_2 = m_2g - T_1,$$
$$m_3a_3 = T_2 + m_3g - F_{\text{ten}}, \qquad -m_4a_4 = m_4g - T_2.$$

Using the expressions for the forces T_1, T_2, and F_{ten} obtained above, we find that

$$a_1 = a_2 = a_3 = 0, \; a_4 = \frac{(m_3 + m_4 - m_1 - m_2)\,g}{m_4}.$$

1.41 Immediately after releasing the upper pulley, the left load has a velocity v directed upwards, while the right pulley remains at rest. The accelerations of the loads will be as if the free end of the rope were fixed instead of moving at a constant velocity. They can be found from the following equations:

$$ma_1 = T_1 - mg, \quad ma_2 = T_2 - mg, \quad 2T_1 = T_2, \quad a_1 = -2a_2,$$

where m is the mass of each load, and T_1 and T_2 are the tensions of the ropes acting on the left and right loads. Solving the system of equations, we obtain $a_1 = -(2/5)\,g$ and $a_2 = (1/5)\,g$. Thus, the acceleration of the left load is directed downwards, while that of the right load upwards.

The time of fall of the left load can be found from the equation

$$h - vt - \frac{0.4gt^2}{2} = 0,$$

whence
$$t = \frac{2.5v}{g} + \sqrt{\frac{6.25v^2}{g^2} + \frac{5h}{g}}$$

During this time, the right load will move upwards. Consequently, the left load will be the first to touch the floor.

1.42. Each time the block will move along the inclined plane with a constant acceleration; the magnitudes of the accelerations for the downward and upward motion and the motion along the horizontal guide will be respectively

$$a_1 = \mu g \cos \alpha - g \sin \alpha,$$
$$a_2 = \mu g \cos \alpha + g \sin \alpha,$$
$$a = \mu g \cos \alpha$$

(Fig. 150). Here α is the slope of the inclined plane and the horizontal, and μ is the coefficient of friction. Hence we obtain

$$a = \frac{a_1 + a_2}{2}.$$

The distances traversed by the block in uniformly varying motion at the initial velocity v before it stops can be written in the form

$$l_1 = \frac{v^2}{2a_1},\ l_2 = \frac{v^2}{2a_2},\ l = \frac{v^2}{2a}.$$

Taking into account the relations for the accelerations a_1, a_2 and a, we

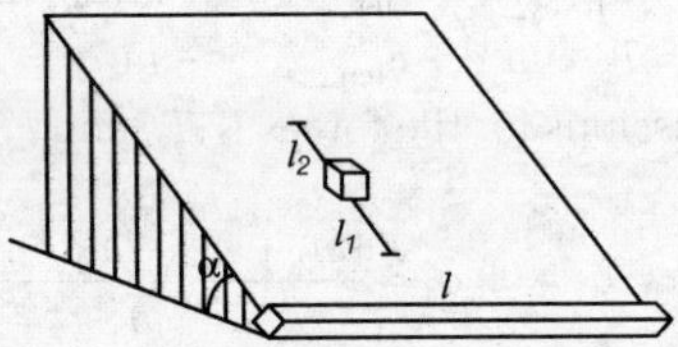

Fig. 150

can find the distance l traversed by the block along the horizontal guide: $l = \dfrac{2l_1l_2}{l_1 + l_2}$.

1.43. We shall write the equations of motion for the block in terms of projections on the axis directed downwards along the inclined plane.

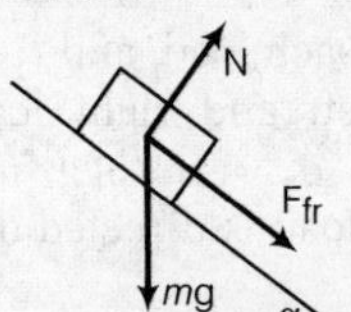

Fig. 151

For the upward motion of the block, we take into account all the forces acting on it: the force of gravity mg the normal reaction N, and friction F_{fr} (Fig. 151) and obtain the following equation:

$$mg \sin \alpha + \mu mg \cos \alpha = ma_1.$$

The corresponding equation for the downward motion is

$$mg \sin \alpha - \mu mg \cos \alpha = ma_2.$$

Let the distance traversed by the block in the upward and downward motion be s. Then the time of ascent t_1 and descent t_2 can be determined from the equations

$$s = \frac{a_1 t_1^2}{2}, \; s = \frac{a_2 t_2^2}{2}.$$

By hypothesis, $2t_1 = t_2$, whence $4a_2 = a_1$. consequently,

$g \sin \alpha + \mu g \cos \alpha = 4(g \sin \alpha - \mu g \cos \alpha)$, and finally $\mu = 0.6 \tan \alpha$.

1.44. If the lower ball is very light, it starts climbing the support. We shall find its minimum mass m_2 for which it has not yet started climbing,

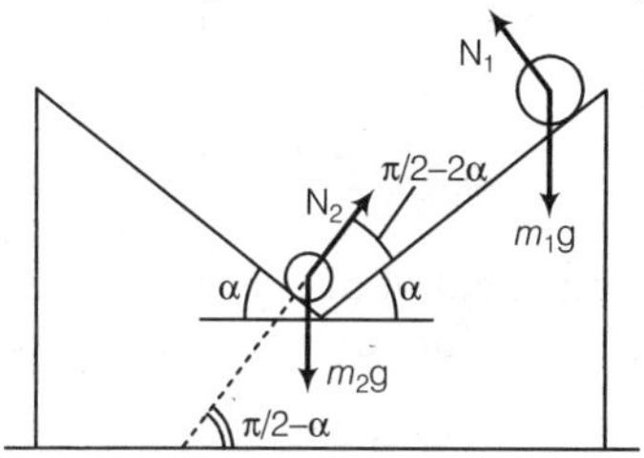

Fig. 152

but has stopped pressing against the right inclined plane. Since the support is weightless, the horizontal components of the forces of pressure (equal in magnitude to the normal reactions) exerted by the balls on the support must be equal (Fig. 152): otherwise, the "support" would acquire an infinitely large acceleration:

$$N_1 \sin \alpha = N_2 \sin \alpha, \; N_1 = N_2.$$

Moreover, since the lower ball does not ascend, the normal components of the accelerations of the balls relative to the right inclined plane must be equal (there is no relative displacement in this direction). Figure 152 shows that the angle between the direction of the normal reaction N_2 of the support and the right inclined plane is $\pi / 2 - 2\alpha$, and hence the latter condition can be written in the form

$$\frac{m_1 g \cos \alpha - N_1}{m_1} = \frac{m_2 g \cos \alpha - N_2 \cos 2\alpha}{m_2},$$

whence $m_2 = m_1 \cos 2\alpha$. Thus, the lower ball will "climb" up if the following condition is satisfied:

$$m_2 < m_1 \cos 2\alpha.$$

perpendicular to the radius $OA = r$ at any instant of time. Consequently, all points of the axis move with a centripetal acceleration $a_c = u^2 / r$.

We shall write the equation of motion for point O in terms of projections on the "centripetal" axis:

$$mg \cos \alpha - N = ma_c = \frac{mu^2}{r}, \tag{1}$$

where N is the normal reaction of the stationary support. The condition that the separation between the supports is $r\sqrt{2}$ implies that the normal reaction of the movable support gives no contribution to the projections on the "centripetal" axis. According to Newton's third law, the cylinder exerts the force of the same magnitude on the stationary support. From Eq. (1), we obtain

$$N = mg \cos \alpha - \frac{mu^2}{r}.$$

At the moment when the distance between points A and B of the supports (see Fig. 18) is $AB = r\sqrt{2}$, we have

$$\cos \alpha = \frac{r\sqrt{2}}{2r} = \frac{1}{\sqrt{2}}.$$

The horizontal component of the velocity of point O is $u \cos \alpha = v/2$, whence $u = v\sqrt{2}$. Thus, for $AB = r\sqrt{2}$, the force of normal pressure exerted by the cylinder is $N = \dfrac{mg}{\sqrt{2}} - \dfrac{mv^2}{2r}$.

For the cylinder to remain in contact with the supports until AB becomes equal to $r\sqrt{2}$, the condition $g/\sqrt{2} > v^2/(2r)$ must be satisfied, i.e. $v < \sqrt{gr\sqrt{2}}$.

1.46. The cylinder is acted upon by the force of gravity m_1g, the normal reaction N_1 of the left inclined plane, and the normal reaction N_3 of the wedge (force N_3 has the horizontal direction).

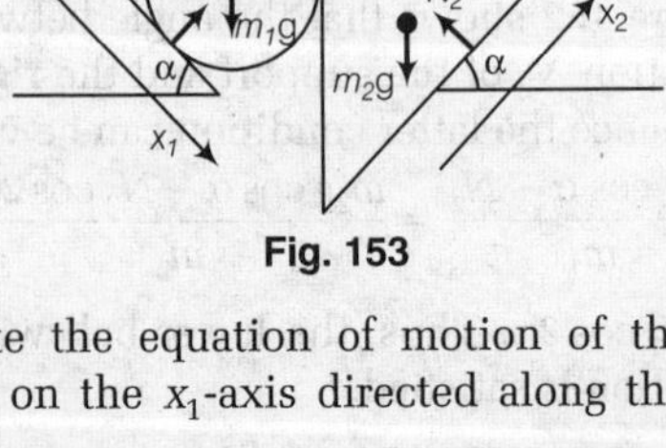

Fig. 153

We shall write the equation of motion of the cylinder in terms of projections on the x_1-axis directed along the left inclined plane (Fig. 153):

$$m_1 a_1 = m_1 g \sin\alpha - N_3 \cos\alpha, \tag{1}$$

We shall write the equation of motion of the cylinder in terms of projections on the x_1-axis directed along the left inclined plane (Fig. 153):

$$m_1 a_1 = m_1 g \sin\alpha - N_3 \cos\alpha, \quad (1)$$

where a_1 is the projection of the acceleration of the cylinder on the x_1-axis.

The wedge is acted upon by the force of gravity $m_2 g$, the normal reaction N_2 of the right inclined plane, and the normal reaction of the cylinder, which, according to Newton's third law, is equal to $-N_3$.

We shall write the equation of motion of the wedge in terms of projections on the x_2-axis directed along the right inclined plane:

$$m_2 a_2 = - m_2 g \sin\alpha + N_3 \cos\alpha. \quad (2)$$

During its motion, the wedge is in contact with the cylinder. Therefore, if the displacement of the wedge along the x_2-axis is Δx, the centre of the cylinder (together with the vertical face of the wedge) will be displaced along the horizontal by $\Delta x \cos\alpha$.

The centre of the cylinder will be thereby displaced along the left inclined plane (x_1-axis) by Δx. This means that in the process of motion of the wedge and the cylinder, the relation

$$a_1 = a_2 \quad (3)$$

is satisfied.

Solving Eqs. (1)-(3) simultaneously, we determine the force of normal pressure $N = N_3$ exerted by the wedge on the cylinder:

$$N_3 = \frac{2m_1 m_2}{m_1 + m_2} \tan\alpha.$$

1.47. As long as the load touches the body, the velocity of the latter is equal to the horizontal component of the velocity of the load, and the acceleration of the body is equal to the horizontal component of the acceleration of the load.

Let a be the total acceleration of the load. Then we can write $a = a_t + a_c$, where a_c is the centripetal acceleration of the load moving in the circle of radius l, i.e. $a_c = v^2/l$, where v is the velocity of the load (Fig. 154). The horizontal component of the acceleration is

$$a_h = a_t \sin\alpha - \frac{v^2}{l}\cos\alpha.$$

The body also has the same acceleration. We can write the equation of motion for the body:

$$N = Ma_h = Ma_t \sin\alpha - M\frac{v^2}{l}\cos\alpha,$$

where N is the force of normal pressure exerted

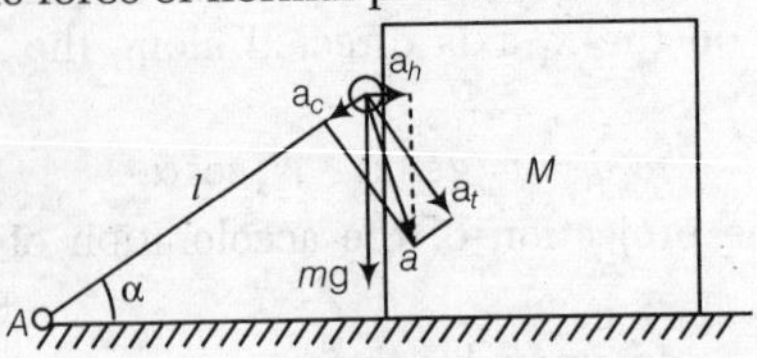

Fig. 154

by the load on the body. At the moment of separation of the load, $N = 0$ and $a_t \sin\alpha = \frac{v^2}{l}\cos\alpha$.

The acceleration component a_t at the moment of separation of the load ia only due to the force of gravity:

$$a_t = g\cos\alpha.$$

Thus, the velocity of the load at the moment of separation is

$$v = \sqrt{gl\sin\alpha},$$

and the velocity of the body at the same moment is

$$u = v\sin\alpha = \sin\alpha\sqrt{gl\sin\alpha}.$$

According to the energy conservation law, we have

$$mgl = mgl\sin\alpha + \frac{mv^2}{2} + Mv^2\sin^2\frac{\alpha}{2}.$$

Substituting the obtained expression for v at the moment of separation and the value of $\sin\alpha = \sin\pi/6 = 1/2$ into this equation, we obtain the ratio: $\frac{M}{m} = \frac{2 - 3\sin\alpha}{\sin^3\alpha} = 4$.

The velocity of the body at the moment of separation is

$$u = v\sin\alpha = \frac{1}{2}\sqrt{\frac{gl}{2}}$$

1.48. The rod is under the action of three forces: the tension **T** of the string, the force of gravity mg, and the reaction of the wall $\mathbf{R} = \mathbf{N} + \mathbf{F}_{fr}$ (**N** is the normal reaction of the wall, and $\mathbf{F}_{fr}$ is friction, $F_{fr} \le \mu N$). When the rod is in equilibrium, the sum of the moments of these forces about any point is zero. For this condition to be satisfied, the line of action of the force R must pass through the point of intersection of the lines of action of T and mg (the moments of the forces T and mg about this point are zero).

Depending on the relation between the angles α and β, the point of intersection of the lines of action of T and mg may lie (1) above the perpendicular AM_0 to the wall (point M_1 in Fig. 155); (2) below this perpendicular (point M_2); (3) on the perpendicular (point M_0). Accordingly, the friction is either directed upwards along AC (F_{fr1}), or downwards along AC(F_{fr2}), or is equal to zero. Let us consider each case separately.

(1) The equilibrium conditions for the rod are

$$T\cos\alpha + F_{fr1} - mg = 0,\ N - T\sin\alpha = 0 \tag{1}$$

(the sums of the projections of all the forces on the x-and y-axes respectively must be zero), and the moments of forces about point A must also be zero:

$$mgd_1 = Td_2,\ \frac{mgl}{2}\sin\beta = \frac{Tl}{3}\sin(\alpha+\beta), \tag{2}$$

where d_1 and d_2 are the arms of the forces mg and T respectively. From Eqs. (1) and (2), we obtain

$$\mu_1 \geq \frac{F_{fr1}}{N} = \frac{2}{3}\frac{\sin(\alpha+\beta)}{\sin\alpha\sin\beta} - \frac{1}{\tan\alpha} = \frac{1}{3}\left(\frac{2}{\tan\beta} - \frac{1}{\tan\alpha}\right).$$

This case is realized when $2\tan\alpha > \tan\beta$.

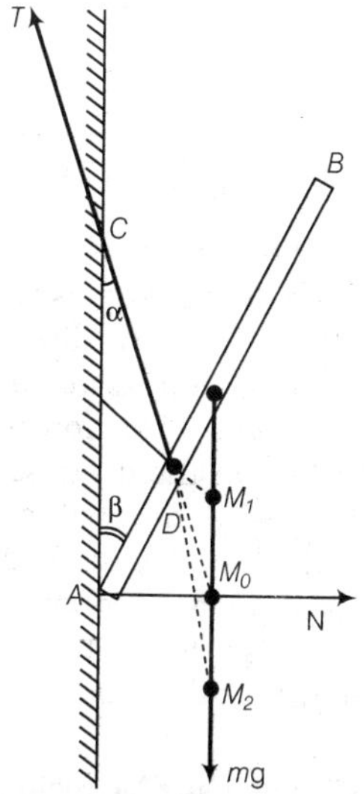

Fig. 155

(2) After writing the equilibrium conditions, we obtain

$$\mu_2 \geq \frac{1}{3}\left(\frac{1}{\tan\alpha} - \frac{2}{\tan\beta}\right).$$

This case corresponds to the condition $2\tan\alpha < \tan\beta$.

(3) In this case, the rod is in equilibrium for any value of $\mu_3 : 2\tan\alpha = \tan\beta$.

Thus, for an arbitrary relation between the angles α and β, the rod is in equilibrium if

$$\mu \geq \frac{1}{3}\left|\frac{1}{\tan\alpha} - \frac{2}{\tan\beta}\right|.$$

1.49*. Let us analyze the motion of the smaller disc immediately after it comes in contact with the larger disc.

We choose two equal small regions of the smaller disc lying on the same diameter symmetrically about the centre O' of this disc. In Fig. 156,

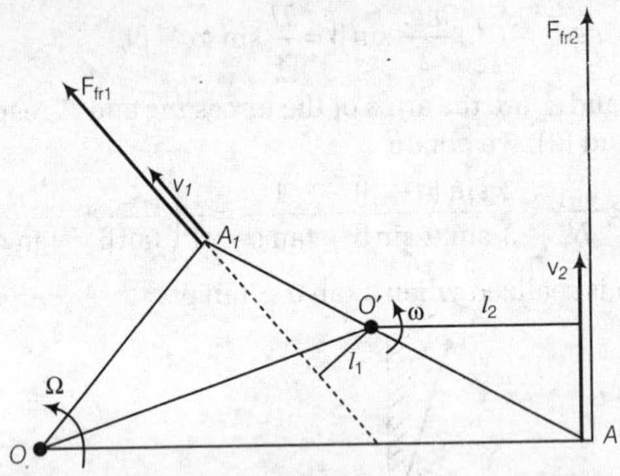

Fig. 156

points A_1 and A_2 are the centres of mass of these regions. At the moment of contact (when the smaller disc is still at rest), the velocities v_1 and v_2 of the points of the larger disc which are in contact with points A_1 and A_2 of the smaller disc are directed as shown in Fig. 156 ($v_1 = \Omega.OA_1$ and $v_2 = \Omega \cdot OA_2$). The forces of friction F_{fr1} and F_{fr2} exerted by the larger disc on the centres of mass A_1 and A_2 of the selected regions of the smaller disc will obviously be directed at the moment of contact along the velocities v_1 and v_2($F_{fr1} = F_{fr2}$). Since the arm l_1 of the force F_{fr1} about the axis of the smaller disc is smaller than the arm l_2 of the force F_{fr2} (see Fig. 156), the total torque of the couple $F_{fr1}$and F_{fr2} will rotate the smaller disc in the direction of rotation of the larger disc.

Having considered similar pairs of regions of the smaller disc, we arrive at the conclusion that immediately after coming in contact, the smaller disc will be rotated in the direction of rotation of the larger disc.

Let the angular velocity of the smaller disc at a certain moment of time become ω. The velocities of the regions with the centres of mass at points $A_1$and A_2 will be $v_1' = v_2' = \omega r$, where $r = O'A_1 = O'A_2$ (Fig. 157). The forces of friction F'_{fr1} and F'_{fr2} acting on these regions will be directed along vectors $\mathbf{v_1} - \mathbf{v_1}'$ (the relative velocity of the point of the larger disc touching point A_1) and $\mathbf{v}_2 - \mathbf{v}_1'$ (the relative velocity of the point of the larger disc touching point A_2).

Obviously, the torque of the couple F'_{fr1} and F'_{fr2} will accelerate the smaller disc (i.e. the angular velocity of the disc will vary) if $v_1' = v_2' < B_1B_2/2 = \Omega r$ (see Fig. 157; for the sake of convenience, the vectors "pertaining" to point A_2 are translated to point A_1).

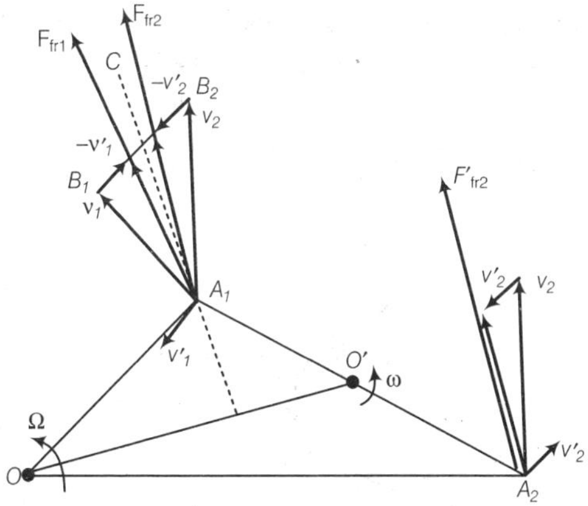

Fig. 157

Thus, as long as $\omega < \Omega$, there exists a nonzero frictional torque which sets the smaller disc into rotation. When $\omega = \Omega$, the relative velocities of the regions with the centres of mass at points A_1 and A_2 are perpendicular to the segment OO' (directed along the segment A_1C in Fig. 157), and the frictional torque about the axis of the smaller disc is zero. Consequently, the smaller disc will rotate at the steady-state angular velocity Ω.

For $\omega = \Omega$, all the forces of friction acting on similar pairs of regions of the smaller disc will be equal in magnitude and have the same direction, viz. perpendicular to the segment OO'. According to Newton's third law, the resultant of all the forces of friction acting on the larger disc will be applied at the point of the larger disc touching the centre O' of the smaller disc and will be equal to μmg. In order to balance the decelerating torque of this force, the moment of force

$$M = \mu mgd$$

must be applied to the axis of the larger disc.

1.50. After the translatory motion of the system has been established, the ratio of the forces of friction F_{fr1} and F_{fr2} acting on the first and second rods will be equal to the ratio of the forces of pressure of the corresponding regions: $F_{fr1}/F_{fr2} = N_1/N_2$. Since each force of pressure is proportional to the mass ($N_1 = m_1g$ and $N_2 = m_2g$), the ratio of the forces of friction can be written in the form

$$\frac{F_{fr1}}{F_{fr2}} = \frac{m_1}{m_2}. \qquad (1)$$

On the other hand, from the equality of the moments of these forces about the vertex of the right angle (Fig. 158, top view), we obtain

$$lF_{fr1}\cos\varphi = lF_{fr2}\sin\varphi, \qquad (2)$$

where l is the distance from the vertex to the centres of mass of the rods. From Eqs. (1) and (2), we obtain $\tan\phi = m_1/m_2$, where $\phi = \alpha - \pi/2$. Consequently, $\alpha = \pi/2 + \arctan((m_1/m_2)$.

1.51. If the foot of the football player moves at a velocity u at the moment of kick, the velocity of the ball is $v + u$ (the axis of motion is directed along the motion of the ball) in the reference frame fixed to the foot of the player. After the perfectly elastic impact, the velocity of the ball in the

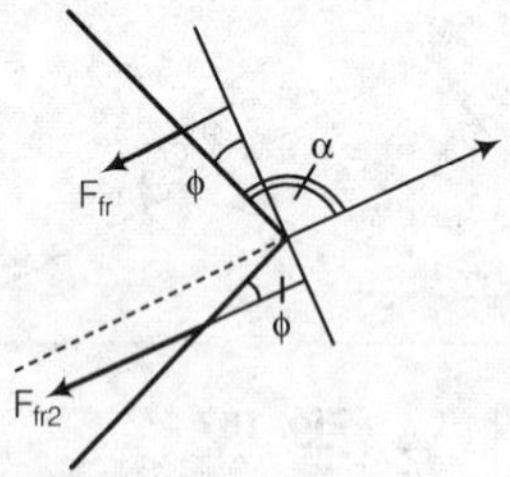

Fig. 158

same reference frame will be $-(v + u)$, and its velocity relative to the ground will be $-(v + u) - u$. If the ball comes to a halt after the impact, $v + 2u = 0$, where $u = -v/2 = -5$ m/s. The minus sign indicates that the foot of the sportsman must move in the same direction as that of the ball before the impact.

1.52. Since in accordance with the momentum conservation law, the vertical component of the velocity of the body-bullet system decreases after the bullet has hit the body, the time of fall of the body to the ground will increase.

In order to determine this time, we shall find the time t_1 of fall of the body before the bullet hits it and the time t_2 of the motion of the body with the bullet. Let t_0 be the time of free fall of the body from the height h. Then the time in which the body falls without a bullet is $t_1 = \sqrt{h/g} = t_0/\sqrt{2}$. At the moment the bullet of mass M hits the body of mass m, the momentum of the body is directed vertically downwards and is

$$mv = \frac{mgt_0}{\sqrt{2}}.$$

The horizontally flying bullet hitting the body will not change the vertical component of the momentum of the formed system, and hence the vertical component of the velocity of the body-bullet system will be

$$u = \frac{m}{m+M}v = \frac{m}{m+M}g\frac{t_0}{\sqrt{2}}.$$

The time t_2 required for the body-bullet system to traverse the remaining half the distance can be determined from the equation

$$\frac{h}{2} = ut_2 + \frac{gt_2^2}{2}.$$

This gives $t \frac{t_0}{\sqrt{2}} \frac{\sqrt{m^2 + (m + M)^2} - m}{m + M}$.

Thus, the total time of fall of the body to the ground ($M >> m$) will be

$$t = \frac{t_0}{\sqrt{2}} \frac{\sqrt{m^2 + (m + M)^2} + M}{m + M} \approx t_0\sqrt{2}.$$

1.53. In order to solve the problem, we shall use the momentum conservation law for the system. We choose the coordinate system as shown in Fig. 159: the x-axis is directed along the velocity v_1 of the body of mass m_1, and the y-axis is directed along the velocity v_2 of the body of mass m_2. After the collision, the bodies will stick together and fly at a velocity u. Therefore,

$$m_1 v_1 = (m_1 + m_2) u_x,$$
$$m_2 v_2 = (m_1 + m_2) u_y.$$

The kinetic energy of the system before the collision was

$$W'_k = \frac{m_1 v_1^2}{2} + \frac{m_2 v_2^2}{2}.$$

The kinetic energy of the system after the collision (sticking together) of the bodies will become

$$W''_k = \frac{m_1 + m_2}{2}(u_x^2 + u_y^2) = \frac{m_1 v_1^2 + m_2 v_2^2}{2(m_1 + m_2)}.$$

Thus, the amount of heat liberated as a result of collision will be

$$Q = W'_k - W''_k = \frac{m_1 m_2}{2(m_1 + m_2)}(v_1^2 + v_2^2) \simeq 4.3 \text{ J}.$$

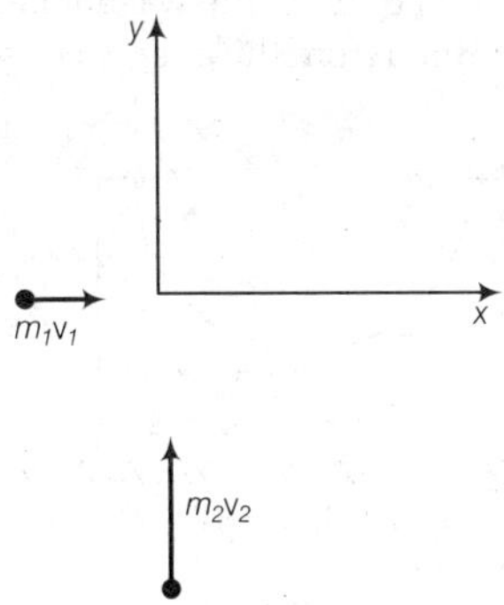

Fig. 159

1.54. Since there is no friction, external forces do not act on the system under consideration in the horizontal direction (Fig. 160).

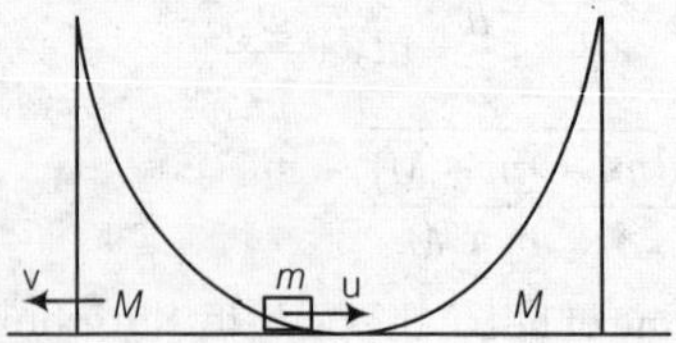

Fig. 160

In order to determine the velocity v of the left wedge and the velocity u of the washer immediately after the descent, we can use the energy and momentum conservation laws:

$$\frac{Mv^2}{2} + \frac{mu^2}{2} = mgh, \ Mv = mu.$$

Since at the moment of maximum ascent h_{max} of the washer along the right wedge, the velocities of the washer and the wedge will be equal, the momentum conservation law can be written in the form

$mu = (M + m)V,$

where V is the total velocity of the washer and the right wedge. Let us also use the energy conservation law:

$$\frac{mu^2}{2} = \frac{M + m}{2}V^2 + mgh_{max}.$$

The joint solution of the last two equations leads to the expression for the maximum height h_{max} of the ascent of the washer along the right wedge:

$$h_{max} = h\frac{M^2}{(M + m)^2}.$$

1.55. The block will touch the wall until the washer comes to the lowest position. By this instant of time, the washer has acquired the velocity v which can be determined from the energy conservation law: $v^2 = 2gr$.

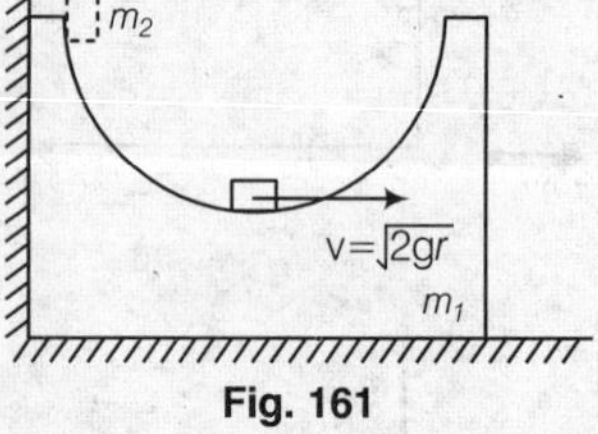

Fig. 161

During the subsequent motion of the system, the washer will "climb" the right-hand side of the block, accelerating it all the time in the rightward direction (Fig. 161) until the velocities of the washer and the block become equal.

Then the washer will slide down the block, the block being accelerated until the washer passes through the lowest position. Thus, the block will have the maximum velocity at the instants at which the washer passes through the lowest position during its backward motion relative to the block.

In order to calculate the maximum velocity of the block, we shall write the momentum conservation law for the instant at which the block is separated from the wall:

$$m_2\sqrt{2gr} = m_1v_1 + m_2v_2,$$

and the energy conservation law for the instants at which the washer passes through the lowest position:

$$m_2gr = \frac{m_1v_1^2}{2} + \frac{m_2v_2^2}{2}.$$

This system of equations has two solutions:

1. $v_1 = 0, \; v_2 = \sqrt{2gr}$,

2. $v_1 = \dfrac{2m_2}{m_1 + m_2}\sqrt{2gr}, \qquad v_2 = \dfrac{m_2 - m_1}{m_1 + m_2}\sqrt{2gr}.$

Solution (1) corresponds to the instants at which the washer moves and the block is at rest. We are interested in solution (2) corresponding to the instants when the block has the maximum velocity:

$$v_{1\,\max} = \frac{2m_2\sqrt{2gr}}{m_1 + m_2}.$$

1.56. Let us go over to a reference frame fixed to the box. Since the impacts of the washer against the box are perfectly elastic, the velocity of the washer relative to the box will periodically reverse its direction, its magnitude remaining equal to v.

It can easily be seen that the motion of the washer will be repeated with period $2\Delta t$, where $\Delta t = (D - 2r)/v$ is the time of flight of the washer between two successive collisions with the box (every time the centre of the washer covers a distance $D - 2r$ at a velocity v).

Returning to the reference frame fixed to the ground, we can plot the time dependence $v_{\text{wash}}(t)$ of the velocity of the centre of the washer.

Knowing the velocity graph $v_{wash}(t)$, we can easily plot the time dependence of the displacement $x_{wash}(t)$ of the centre of the washer (Fig. 162.)

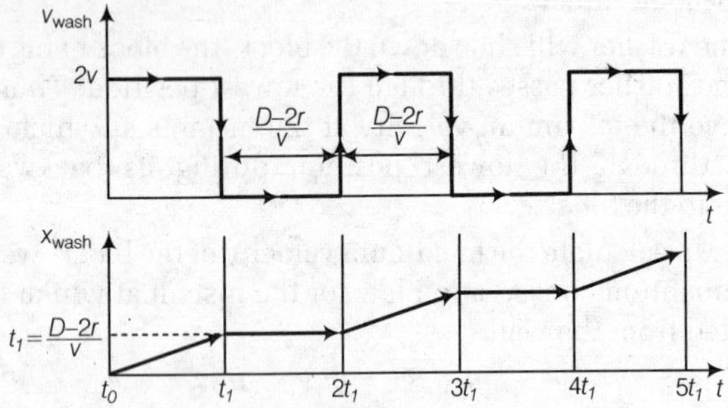

Fig.162

1.57. The forces acting on the hoop-washer system are the force of gravity and the normal reaction of the plane. These forces are directed along the vertical. Consequently, the centre of mass of the system does not move in the horizontal direction.

Since there is no friction between the hoop and the plane, the motion of the hoop is translatory. According to the momentum conservation law, at any instant of time we have

$$Mu + mv_x = 0, \qquad (1)$$

where u and v_x are the horizontal components of the velocities of the centre of the hoop and the washer. Since v_x periodically changes its sign, u also changes sign "synchronously". The general nature of motion of the hoop is as follows: the centre of the hoop moves to the right when the washer is on segments BC and BE, and to the left when the washer is on segments CD and DE (Fig. 163).

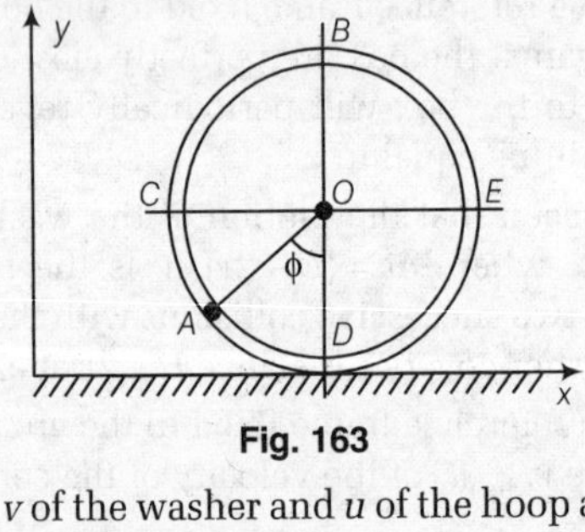

Fig. 163

The velocities v of the washer and u of the hoop are connected through the energy conservation law:

$$mgr(1 + \cos\phi) = \frac{mv^2}{2} + \frac{Mu^2}{2}. \qquad (2)$$

The motion of the washer relative to a stationary observer can be represented at any instant as the superposition of two motions: the motion relative to the centre of the hoop at a velocity v_t directed along the tangent to the hoop, and the motion together with the hoop at its velocity u having the horizontal direction (Fig. 164). The figure shows that

$$\frac{v_y}{v_x + v_y} = \tan\phi \quad (3)$$

Solving Eqs. (1)-(3) together, we determine the velocity of the centre of the hoop at the instant when the radius vector of the point of location of the washer forms an angle ϕ with the vertical

$$u = m\cos\phi\sqrt{\frac{2gr\,(1+\cos\phi)}{(M+m)(M+m\sin\phi)}}.$$

1.58. At the moment of snapping of the right string, the rod is acted upon by the tension T of the left string and the forces N_1 and N_2 of normal pressure of the loads of mass m_1 and m_2 (Fig. 165).

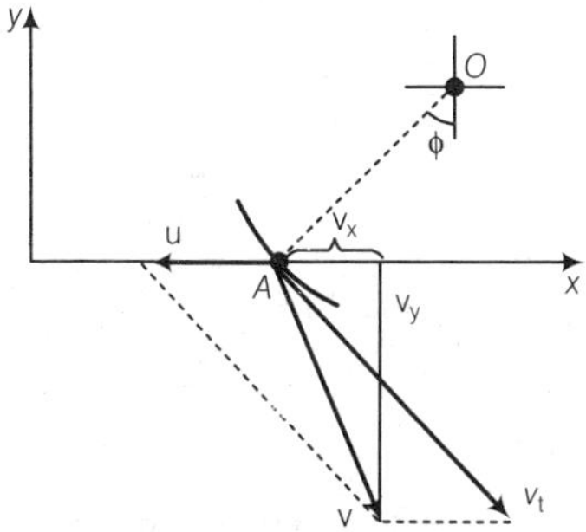

Fig. 164

Since the rod is weightless (its mass is zero), the equations of its

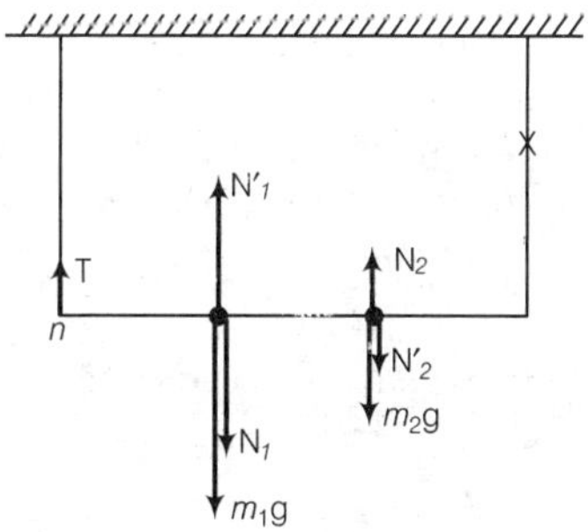

Fig. 165

translatory and rotary motions will have the form

$$-T + N_1 - N_2 = 0, N_1 l = 2N_2 l.$$

The second equation (the condition of equality to zero of the sum of all moments of force about point O) implies that

$$N_1 = 2N_2. \quad (1)$$

Combining these conditions, we get (see Fig. 165)

$$T = N_1 - N_2 = N_2. \tag{2}$$

At the moment of snapping of the right string, the accelerations of the loads of mass m_1 and m_2 will be vertical (point O is stationary, and the rod is inextensible) and connected through the relation

$$a_2 = 2a_1. \tag{3}$$

Let us write the equations of motion for the loads at this instant:

$$m_1 g - N'_1 = m_1 a_1, \quad m_2 g + N'_2 = m_2 a_2,$$

where N'_1 and N'_2 are the normal reactions of the rod on the loads of mass m_1 and m_2. Since $N'_1 = N_1$ and $N'_2 = N_2$, we have

$$m_1 g - 2N_2 = m_1 a_1, \; m_2 g + N_2 = 2m_2 a_1.$$

Hence we can find N_2, and consequently (see Eq. (2)) the tension of the string

$$T = N_2 = \frac{m_1 m_2}{m_1 + 4m_2} g.$$

1.59. Let the ring move down from point A by a distance Δx during a small time interval Δt elapsed after the beginning of motion of the system

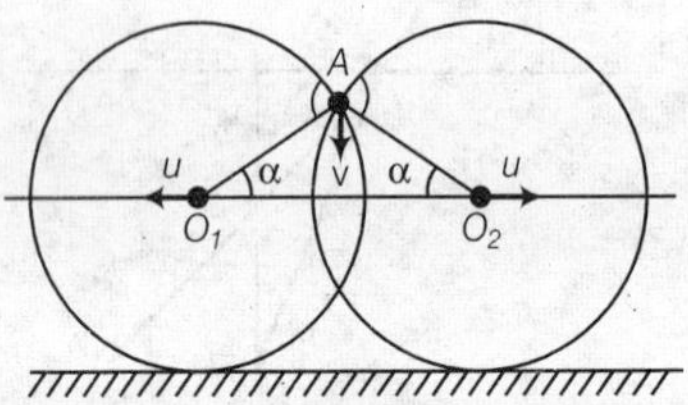

Fig. 166

and acquire a velocity v (Fig. 166). The velocity of translatory motion of the hoops at this moment must be equal to $u = v \tan\alpha$ (Δt is so small that the angle α practically remains unchanged). Consequently, the linear velocity of all points of the hoops must have the same magnitude. According to the energy conservation law, we have

$$mg\,\Delta x = 2Mu^2 + \frac{mv^2}{2} = 2Mv^2 \tan^2\alpha + \frac{mv^2}{2},$$

where Mu^2 is the kinetic energy of each hoop at a given instant. From this equality, we obtain

$$\frac{v^2}{2\Delta x} = \frac{m}{4M\tan^2\alpha + m} g = \frac{1}{1 + 4(M/m)\tan^2\alpha} g.$$

As $\Delta x \to 0$, we can assume that $v^2 = 2a\,\Delta x$, where a is the acceleration of the ring at the initial instant of time. Consequently,

$$a = \frac{1}{1 + 4(M/m)\tan^2\alpha} g.$$

1.60. Let the rope move over a distance Δl during a small time interval Δt after the beginning of motion and acquire a velocity v. Since Δt is small, we can assume that

$$v^2 = 2a\,\Delta l, \tag{1}$$

where a is the acceleration of all points of the rope at the initial instant. From the energy conservation law (friction is absent), it follows that

$$\frac{Mv^2}{2} = \Delta W_p, \tag{2}$$

where M is the mass of the rope, and ΔW_P is the change in the potential energy of the rope during the time interval Δt. Obviously, ΔW_P corresponds to the redistribution of the mass of the rope, as a result of which a piece of the rope of length Δl "passes" from point A to point B (see Fig. 31).

Therefore, $\Delta W_p = \left(\frac{M}{l}\right) gh\,\Delta l$ (3)

From Eqs. (1)-(3), we find the condition of motion for the rope at the initial instant of time:

$$a = \frac{gh}{l}.$$

1.61. It is clear that at the moment of impact, only the extreme blocks come in contact with the washer. The force acting on each such block is perpendicular to the contact surface between the washer and a block and passes through its centre (the diameter of the washer is equal to the edge of the block!). Therefore, the middle block remains at rest as a result of the impact. For the extreme blocks and the washer, we can write the conservation law for the momentum in the direction of the velocity v of the washer:

$$mv = \frac{2mu\sqrt{2}}{2} + mv'.$$

Here m is the mass of each block and the washer, v' is the velocity of the washer after the impact, and u is the velocity of each extreme block. The energy conservation law implies that $v^2 = 2u^2 + v'^2$.

As a result, we find that $u = v\sqrt{2}$ and $v' = 0$. Consequently, the velocities of the extreme blocks after the impact form the angles of 45° with the velocity v, the washer stops, and the middle block remains at rest.

1.62. In this case, the momentum conservation law can be applied in a peculiar form. As a result of explosion, the momentum component of the ball along the pipe remains equal to zero since there is no friction, and the reaction forces are directed at right angles to the velocities of the fragments. Inelastic collisions do not change the longitudinal momentum component either. Consequently, the final velocity of the body formed after all collisions is zero.

1.63. For the liberated amount of heat to be maximum, the following conditions must be satisfied:

(1) the potential energy of the bodies must be maximum at the initial moment;

(2) the bodies must collide simultaneously at the lowest point of the cup;

(3) the velocity of the bodies must be zero immediately after the collision.

If these conditions are satisfied, the whole of the initial potential energy of the bodies will be transformed into heat. Consequently, at the initial instant the bodies must be arranged on the brim of the cup at a height r above the lowest point. The arrangement of the bodies must be such that their total momentum before the collision is zero (in this case, the body formed as a result of collision from the bodies stuck together will remain at rest at the bottom of the cup). Since the values of the momenta of the bodies at any instant are to one another as 3 : 4 : 5, the arrangement of the

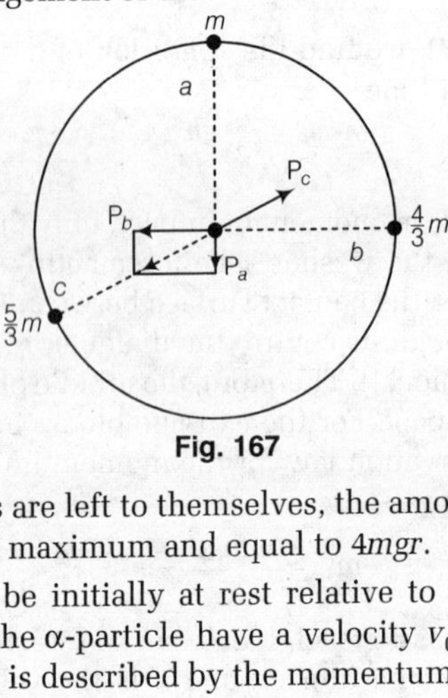

Fig. 167

After the bodies are left to themselves, the amount of heat Q liberated in the system is maximum and equal to $4mgr$.

1.64. Let the proton be initially at rest relative to a stationary reference frame, and let the α-particle have a velocity v_0. The process of their elastic collision is described by the momentum conservation law

$$4mv_0 = mv_1 + 4mv_2$$

and by the energy conservation law $\dfrac{4mv_0^2}{2} = \dfrac{mv_1^2}{2} + \dfrac{4mv_2^2}{2}$,

where v_1 and v_2, are the velocities of the proton and the α-particle in the stationary reference frame after the collision, and m and 4 m are the masses of the proton and the α-particle respectively.

Let us consider the collision of these particles in the centre-of-mass system, i.e. in an inertial reference frame moving relative to the stationary reference frame at a velocity

$$v' = \frac{4mv_0}{m + 4m} = \frac{4}{5}v_0$$

(the numerator of the first fraction contains the total momentum of the system, and the denominator contains its total mass).

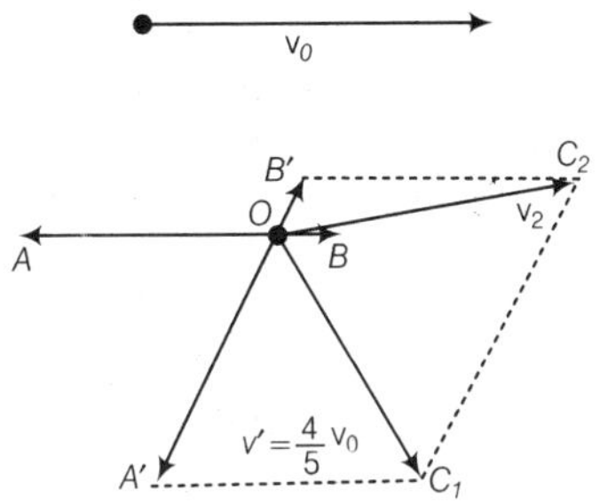

Fig. 168

Figure 168 shows the velocity v_0 and the velocities of the α-particle (vector $\overrightarrow{OB}$) and the proton (vector $\overrightarrow{OA}$) in the centre-of-mass system before the collision: $OB = (1/5)v_0$ and $OA = (4/5)v_0$. According to the momentum conservation law, after the collision, the velocity vectors $\overrightarrow{OB}$ and $\overrightarrow{OA}$ of the α-particle and the proton must lie on the same straight line, and the relation $OB' : OA' = 1:4$ (see Fig. 168) must be satisfied. According to the energy conservation law, $OB' = OB$ and $OA' = OA$ (prove this!).

In the stationary reference frame, the velocities of the α-particle and the proton are represented in the figure by vectors $\overrightarrow{OC_2} = \overrightarrow{OB'} + \mathbf{v}'$ and $\overrightarrow{OC_1} = \overrightarrow{OA'} + \mathbf{v}'$.

In order to solve the problem, we must determine the maximum possible length of vector $\overrightarrow{OC_1}$, i.e. in the isosceles triangle $OA'C_1$, we must determine the maximum possible length of the base for constant values of the lateral sides. Obviously, the maximum magnitude of $\overrightarrow{OC_1}$ is equal to $2 \times (4/5)v_0 = 1.6v_0$. This situation corresponds to a central collision.

1.65. The tyres of a motorcar leave a trace in the sand. The higher the pressure on the sand, the deeper the trace, and the higher the probability that the car gets stuck. If the tyres are deflated considerably, the area of contact between the tyres and the sand increases. In this case, the pressure on the sand decreases, and the track becomes more shallow.

1.66. At any instant of time, the complex motion of the body in the pipe can be represented as the superposition of two independent motions: the motion along the axis of the pipe and the motion in the circle in a plane perpendicular to the pipe axis (Fig. 169). The separation of the body from the pipe surface will affect only the latter motion (the body will not move in a circle). Therefore, we shall consider only this motion.

The body moving in a circle experiences the action of the normal reaction N of the pipe walls (vector **N** lies in the plane perpendicular to the pipe axis) and the "force of gravity" $mg' = mg\cos\alpha$. We shall write the condition of motion for the body in a circle:

$$mg'\cos\beta + N = \frac{mv^2}{r}, \tag{1}$$

where β is the angle formed by the radius vector of the point of location of the body at a given instant and the "vertical" y' (Fig. 170). For the body to remain in contact with the surface of the pipe the condition $N = mv^2/r - mg'\cos\beta \geq 0$ must be fulfilled, whence

$$v^2 \geq g'r\cos\beta. \tag{2}$$

The relation between the velocity v at which the body moves in a circle

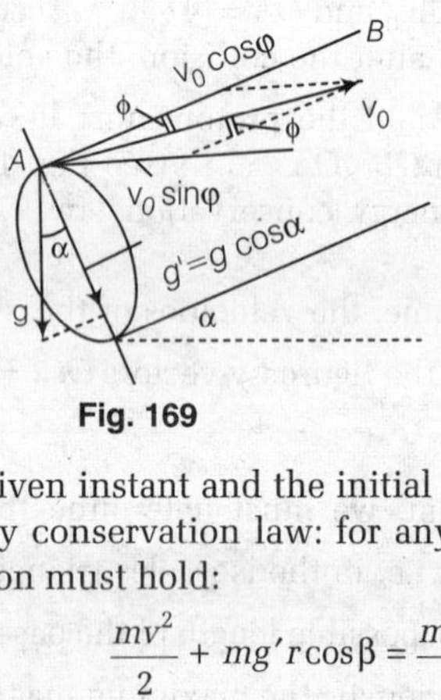

Fig. 169

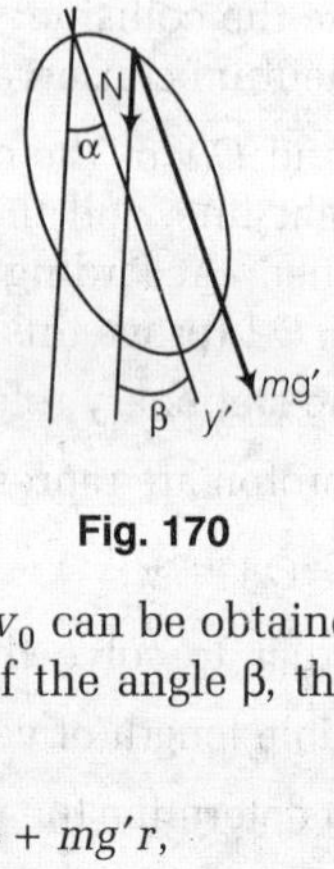

Fig. 170

at a given instant and the initial velocity v_0 can be obtained from the energy conservation law: for any value of the angle β, the following relation must hold:

$$\frac{mv^2}{2} + mg'r\cos\beta = \frac{m(v_0\sin\phi)^2}{2} + mg'r,$$

whence

$$v^2 = v_0^2\sin^2\phi + 2g'r - 2g'r\cos\beta. \tag{3}$$

Substituting Eq. (3) into Eq. (2), we obtain the values of v_0 for which the body remains in contact with the pipe:

$$v_0^2 \geq \frac{3g'r\cos\beta}{\sin^2\phi} - \frac{2g'r}{\sin^2\phi}.$$

Since this condition must be satisfied for any value of $\beta \in [0, 2\pi]$, we finally obtain

$$v_0^2 \geq \frac{g'r}{\sin^2\phi} = \frac{gr\cos\alpha}{\sin^2\phi}$$

1.67*. Let us suppose that at a certain instant, the wheel is in one of the positions such that its centre of mass is above a rod, and its velocity is v. At the moment of the impact against the next rod (Fig. 171), the centre of mass of the wheel has a certain velocity v' perpendicular to

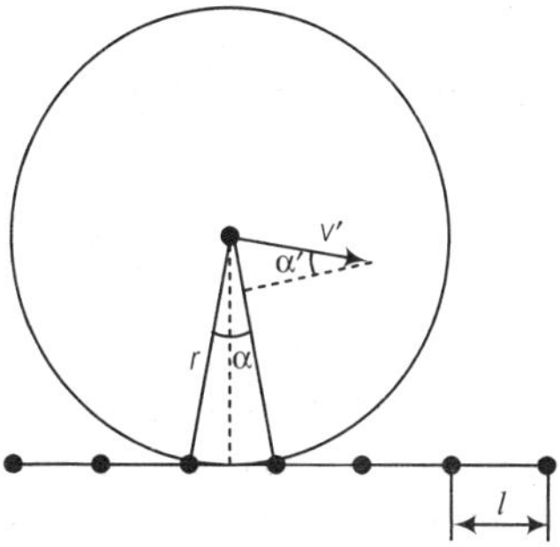

Fig. 171

the line connecting it to the previous rod. This velocity can be obtained from the energy conservation law:

$$mgh + \frac{mv^2}{2} = \frac{mv'^2}{2}.$$

Here $h = r - \sqrt{r^2 - l^2/4} \approx l^2/(8r)$. Therefore,

$$v' = v\sqrt{1 + \frac{gl^2}{4rv^2}}.$$

By hypothesis (the motion is without jumps), the impact of the wheel against the rod is perfectly inelastic. This means that during the impact, the projection of the momentum of the wheel on the straight line connecting the centre of the wheel to the rod vanishes. Thus, during each collision, the energy

$$\Delta W = \frac{m(v'\sin\alpha)^2}{2},$$

where $\sin\alpha \approx l/r$, is lost (converted into heat). For the velocity v to remain constant, the work done by the tension T of the rope over the path l must compensate for this energy loss. Therefore,

$$Tl = \frac{mv^2}{2}\left(1 + \frac{gl^2}{4rv^2}\right)\frac{l^2}{r^2},$$

whence

$$T = \frac{mv^2 l}{2r^2}\left(1 + \frac{gl^2}{4rv^2}\right) \approx \frac{mv^2 l}{2r^2}.$$

1.68. Since the wheels move without slipping, the axle of the coupled wheels rotates about point O while passing through the boundary

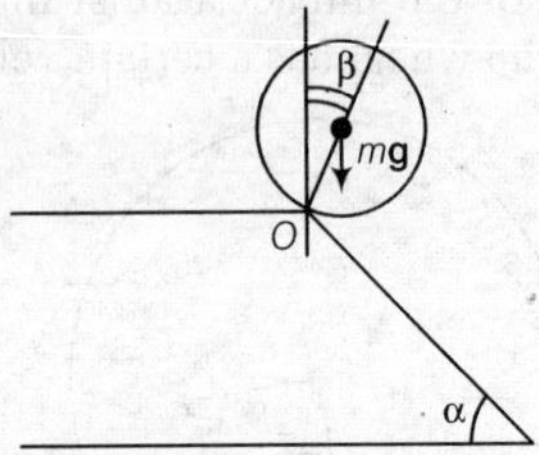

Fig. 172

between the planes (Fig. 172). At the moment of separation, the force of pressure of the coupled wheels on the plane and the force of friction are equal to zero, and hence the angle β at which the separation takes place can be found from the condition

$$mg\cos\beta = \frac{mv_1^2}{r}.$$

From the energy conservation law, we obtain

$$\frac{mv^2}{2} - \frac{mv_1^2}{2} - mgr\,(1 - \cos\beta).$$

No separation occurs if the angle β determined from these equations is not smaller than α, and hence

$$\cos\beta \le \cos\alpha.$$

Therefore, we find that the condition

$$v \le \sqrt{gr\,(3\cos\alpha - 2)}$$

is a condition of crossing the boundary between the planes by the wheels without separation. If $3\cos\alpha - 2 < 0$, i.e. $a > \arccos\,(2/3)$, the separation will take place at any velocity v.

1.69. At the initial moment, the potential energy of the system is the sum of the potential energy $mg\,(r + h)$ of the rim and the potential energy $\rho g h^2 / (2\sin\alpha)$ of the part of the ribbon lying on the inclined plane.

The total energy of the system in the final state will also be a purely potential energy equal to the initial energy in view of the absence of friction. The final energy is the sum of the energy mgr of the rim and the energy of the ribbon wound on it.

The centre of mass of the latter will be assumed to coincide with the centre of mass of the rim. This assumption is justified if the length of the wound ribbon is much larger than the length of the circumference of the rim. Then the potential energy of the wound ribbon is

$$\rho\left(\frac{h}{\sin\alpha} + s\right)gr,$$

the length of the ribbon being $h/\sin\alpha + s$, where s is the required distance traversed by the rim from the foot of the inclined plane to the point at which it comes to rest.

From the energy conservation law, we obtain

$$mg(r + h) + \rho g \frac{h^2}{2\sin\alpha} = mgr + \rho gr\left(\frac{h}{\sin\alpha} + s\right),$$

whence

$$s = \frac{mg + \rho(h/\sin\alpha)(r - h/2)}{\rho r}.$$

1.70. The steady-state motion of the system in air will be the falling of the balls along the vertical at a constant velocity. The air drag F acting on the lower (heavier) and the upper ball is the same since the balls have the same velocity and size. Therefore, the equations of motion for the balls can be written in the form

$$m_1 g - T - F = 0, \; m_2 g + T - F = 0.$$

Solving this system of equations, we obtain the tension of the thread:

$$T = \frac{(m_1 - m_2)g}{2}.$$

1.71*. At each instant of time, the instantaneous axis of rotation of the ball passes through the point of contact between the thread and the cylinder. This means that the tension of the thread is perpendicular to the velocity of the ball, and hence it does no work. Therefore, the kinetic energy of the ball does not change, and the magnitude of its velocity remains equal to v.

In order to determine the dependence $l(t)$, we mentally divide the segment of the thread unwound by the instant t into a very large number N of small equal pieces of length $\Delta l = l/N$ each. Let the time during which the nth piece is unwound be Δt_n. During this time, the end of the thread has been displaced by a distance $v\Delta t_n$, and the thread has turned through an angle $\Delta\phi_n = v\Delta t_n/(n\Delta l)$ (Fig. 173). The radius drawn to the point of contact between the thread and the cylinder has turned through the same angle, i.e.

$$\Delta\phi_n = \Delta\phi = \frac{\Delta l}{r},$$

whence

$$\Delta t_n = \frac{n(\Delta l)^2}{vr}.$$

Then

$$t = \Delta t_1 + \Delta t_2 + \ldots + \Delta t_N = \frac{1(\Delta l)^2}{vr} + \frac{2(\Delta l)^2}{vr} + \ldots + \frac{N(\Delta l)^2}{vr} = \frac{(\Delta l)^2}{vr}\frac{N(N+1)}{2}.$$

Since N is large, we have

$$t = \frac{(\Delta l)^2 N^2}{2vr} = \frac{l^2}{2vr}$$

$$l = \sqrt{2vrt}.$$

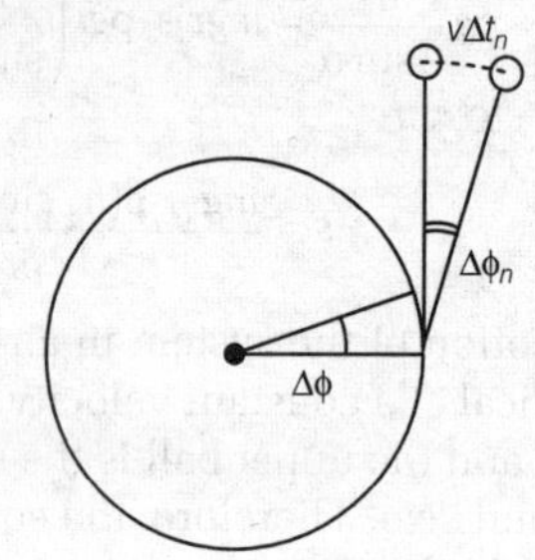

Fig. 173

1.72. During the time T, the distance covered by the blue ball is $\omega(l/\sqrt{3})T = 2\pi l/\sqrt{3}$ (Fig. 174), where $\omega = 2\pi/T$ is the rotational frequency. During the same time, the centre of mass of the green

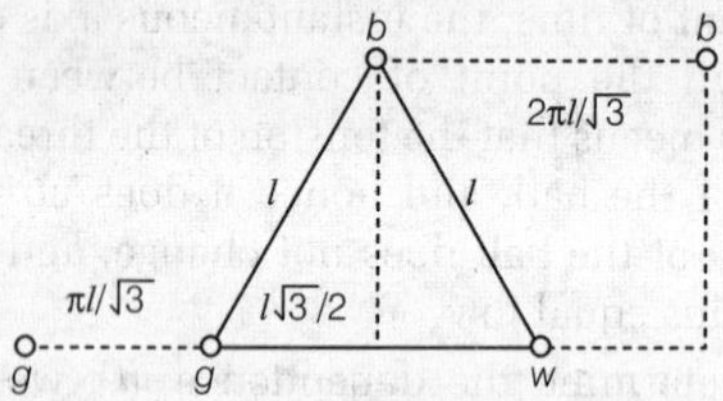

Fig. 174

and the white ball will be displaced by a distance $\omega(l/2\sqrt{3})T = \pi l/\sqrt{3}$. The rod connecting the green and the white ball will simultaneously turn through an angle 2π since the period of revolution of the balls around their centre of mass coincides with the period T. Therefore, the required distance is

$$L = l\sqrt{\frac{3}{4} + \left(\pi\sqrt{3} + \frac{1}{2}\right)^2},$$

or for another arrangement of the balls (the white and the green ball change places in the figure),

$$L = l\sqrt{\frac{3}{4} + \left(\pi\sqrt{3} - \frac{1}{2}\right)^2}.$$

1.73. The centre of mass of the system consisting of the blocks and the thread is acted upon in the horizontal direction only by the force exerted by the pulley.

Obviously, the horizontal component of this force, equal to $T(1 - \cos\phi)$, where T is the tension of the thread, is always directed to the right (Fig. 175).

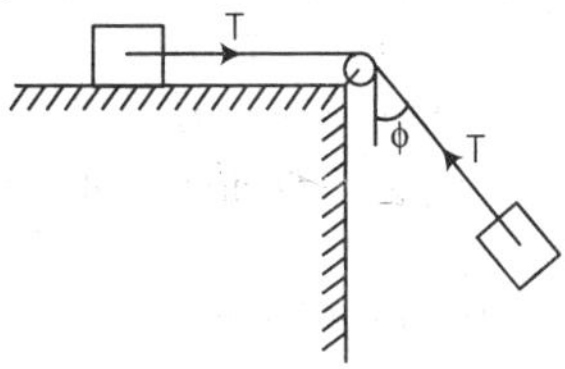

Fig. 175

Since at the initial moment the centre of mass is at rest above the pulley, during motion it will be displaced along the horizontal to the right. Hence it follows that the left block reaches the pulley before the right block strikes the table since otherwise the centre of mass would be to the left of the pulley at the moment of impact.

1.74. According to the initial conditions (the left load is at rest, and the right load acquires the velocity v), the left load will move in a straight line, while the right load will oscillate in addition to the motion in a straight line. At a certain instant, the left load is acted upon along the vertical by a force $mg - T$, and the right load by a force $mg - T\cos\phi$ (Fig. 176, the vertical axis is directed downwards). Here T is the tension of the thread.

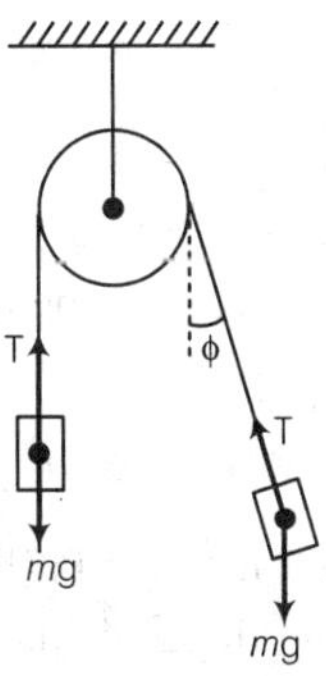

Fig. 176

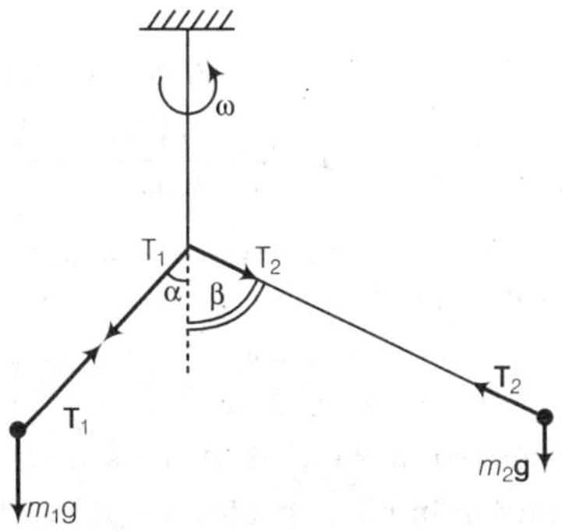

Fig. 177

Hence it follows that the difference in the vertical components of the accelerations of the right (a_1) and left (a_2) loads, given by

$$a_1 - a_2 = \left(g - \frac{T}{m}\cos\phi\right) - \left(g - \frac{T}{m}\right) = \frac{T}{m}(1 - \cos\phi),$$

is always nonnegative. Since at the initial moment the relative distance and the relative vertical velocity of the loads are equal to zero, the difference in the ordinates of the right and left loads will increase with time, i.e. at any instant the right load is lower than the left one.

1.75. Let the right and left threads be deflected respectively through angles β and α from the vertical (Fig. 177). For the rod to remain in the vertical position, the following condition must be satisfied:

$$T_1 \sin\alpha = T_2 \sin\beta, \tag{1}$$

where T_1 and T_2 are the tensions of the relevant threads.

Let us write the equations of motion for the two bodies in the vertical and horizontal directions:

$$T_1 \sin\alpha = m_1\omega^2 l_1 \sin\alpha, \qquad T_1 \cos\alpha = m_1 g,$$

$$T_2 \sin\beta = m_2\omega^2 l_2 \sin\beta, \qquad T_2 \cos\beta = m_2 g.$$

Solving this system of equations and taking into account Eq. (1), we obtain

$$\omega = g^{1/2}\left(\frac{m_1^2 - m_2^2}{m_1^2 l_1^2 - m_2^2 l_2^2}\right)^{1/4} \approx 14 \text{ rad/s}.$$

1.76. We denote by l_1 and l_2 the lengths of the springs connecting the axle to the first ball and the first and the second ball. Since the balls move in a circle, their equations of motion can be written in the form

$$m\omega^2 l_1 = k(l_1 - l_0) - k(l_2 - l_0),$$

$$m\omega^2 (l_1 + l_2) = k(l_2 - l_0)$$

whence

$$l_1 = \frac{l_0}{1 - 3m\omega^2/k + (m\omega^2/k)^2},$$

$$l_2 = \frac{(1 - m\omega^2/k)\, l_0}{1 - 3m\omega^2/k + (m\omega^2/k)^2}.$$

The solution has a physical meaning when the following inequalities are satisfied:

$$1 - \frac{3m\omega^2}{k} + \frac{m\omega^2}{k} > 0, \quad 1 - \frac{m\omega^2}{k} \geq 0.$$

Let us suppose that $m\omega^2/k = x$. Since $m\omega^2/k > 0$, the second condition implies that $0 < x < 1$. The first condition yields

$$x^2 - 3x + 1 > 0,$$

whence either $x > (3 + \sqrt{5})/2 \simeq 2.6$

or $x < (3 - \sqrt{5})/2 \simeq 0.4$.

Consequently, the region of admissible values of x lies between 0 and $(3 - \sqrt{5})/2$, whence

$$\omega < \sqrt{\frac{3 - \sqrt{5}}{2}\frac{k}{m}}.$$

1.77. The change in the kinetic energy W_k of the body as a result of a small displacement Δs can be written in the form

$$\Delta W_k = F\Delta s,$$

where F is the force acting on the body. Therefore, the force at a certain point of

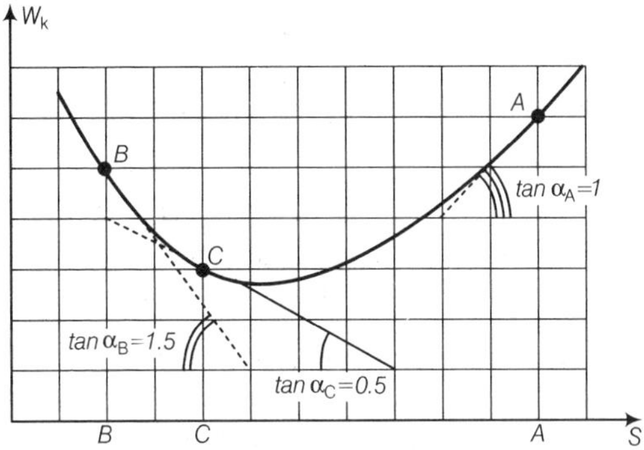

Fig. 178

the trajectory is defined as the slope of the tangent at the relevant point of the curve describing the kinetic energy as a function of displacement in a rectilinear motion. Using the curve given in the condition of the problem, we find that (Fig. 178) $F_C \simeq -1\text{N}$ and $F_B \simeq -3\text{N}$.

1.78. The amount of liberated heat will be maximum if the block traverses the maximum distance relative to the conveyer belt. For this purpose, it is required that the velocity of the block relative to the ground in the vicinity of the roller A must be zero (see Fig. 41). The initial velocity of the block relative to the ground is determined from the conditions

$$-v_0 + at = 0,\ l = v_0 t - \frac{at^2}{2},$$

where $a = \mu g$ is the acceleration imparted to the block by friction. Hence

$$v_0 = \sqrt{2\mu g l}.$$

The time of motion of the block along the conveyer belt to the roller A is

$$t = \sqrt{\frac{2l}{\mu g}}.$$

The distance covered by the block before it stops is

$$s_1 = l + vt = l + v\sqrt{\frac{2l}{\mu g}}.$$

Then the block starts moving with a constant acceleration to the right. The time interval in which the slippage ceases is $\tau = v/a = v/\mu g$. The distance by which the block is displaced relative to the ground during this time is

$$x = \frac{a\tau^2}{2} = \frac{v^2}{2\mu g}.$$

Since $v < \sqrt{2\mu g l}$ by hypothesis, the block does not slip from the conveyer belt during this time i.e. $s < l$.

'The distance covered by the block relative to the conveyer belt during this time is

$$s_2 = \left|\frac{v^2}{2a} - v\tau\right| = \frac{v^2}{2\mu g}.$$

The total distance traversed by the block relative to the conveyer belt is

$$s = s_1 + s_2 = l + v\sqrt{\frac{2l}{\mu g}} + \frac{v^2}{2\mu g}$$

$$= \frac{(v + \sqrt{2\mu g l})^2}{2\mu g}.$$

The amount of heat liberated at the expense of the work done by friction is

$$Q = \mu m g s = \frac{m(v + \sqrt{2\mu g l})^2}{2}.$$

1.79. In the former case (the motion of the pipe without slipping), the initial amount of potential energy stored in the gravitational field will be transformed into the kinetic energy of the pipe, which will be equally distributed between the energies of rotary and translatory motion.

In the latter case (the motion with slipping), not all the potential energy will be converted into the kinetic energy at the end of the path because of the work done against friction.

Since in this case the energy will also be equally distributed between the energies of translatory and rotary motions, the velocity of the pipe at the end of the path will be smaller in the latter case.

1.80. After the spring has been released, it is uniformly stretched. In the process, very fast vibrations of the spring emerge, which also attenuate very soon. During this time, the load cannot be noticeably displaced, i.e. if the middle of the spring has been displaced by a distance x in doing the work A, the entire spring is now stretched by x.

Therefore, the potential energy of the spring, which is equal to the maximum kinetic energy in the subsequent vibratory motion, is $W_K = kx^2/2$, where k is the rigidity of the entire spring.

When the spring is pulled downwards at the midpoint, only its upper half (whose rigidity is $2k$) is stretched, and the work equal to the potential energy of extension of the upper part of the spring is $A = 2kx^2/2 = kx^2$. Hence we may conclude that the maximum kinetic energy of the load in the subsequent motion is $W_k = A/2$.

1.81. Since the system is closed, the stars will rotate about their common centre of mass in concentric circles. The equations of motion for the stars have the form

$$m_1\omega_1^2 l_1 = F$$

$$m_2\omega_2^2 l_2 = F. \qquad (1)$$

Here ω_1 and ω_2 are the angular velocities of rotation of the stars, l_1 and l_2 are the radii of their orbits, F is the force of interaction between the stars, equal to Gm_1m_2 / l^2, where l is the separation between the stars, and G is the gravitational constant. By the definition of the centre of mass,

$$m_1 l_1 = m_2 l_2$$

$$l_1 + l_2 = l. \qquad (2)$$

Solving Eqs. (1) and (2) together, we obtain

$$\omega_1 = \omega_2 = \sqrt{\frac{G(m_1 + m_2)}{l^3}}$$

$$= l^{-1}\sqrt{\frac{G(m_1 + m_2)}{l}},$$

and the required period of revolution of these stars is

$$T = 2\pi l\sqrt{\frac{l}{G(m_1 + m_2)}}.$$

1.82. Let v_1 be the velocity of the station before the collision, v_2 the velocity of the station and the meteorite immediately after the collision, m the mass of the meteorite, and $10m$ the mass of the station.

Before the collision, the station moved around a planet in a circular orbit of radius R. Therefore, the velocity v_1 of the station can be found from the equation

$$\frac{10mv_1^2}{R} = G\frac{10mM}{R^2}.$$

Hence $v_1 = GM / R$. In accordance with the momentum conservation law, the velocities u, v_1 and v_2 are connected through the following relation:

$$mu + 10\,mv_1 = 11mv_2.$$

We shall write the momentum conservation law in projections on the x-and y-axes (Fig. 179):

$$10\,mv_1 = 11mv_{2x}, \qquad (1)$$

$$mu = 11\,mv_{2y}. \qquad (2)$$

After the collision, the station goes over to an elliptical orbit. The energy of the station with the meteorite stuck in it remains constant during the motion in the elliptical orbit.

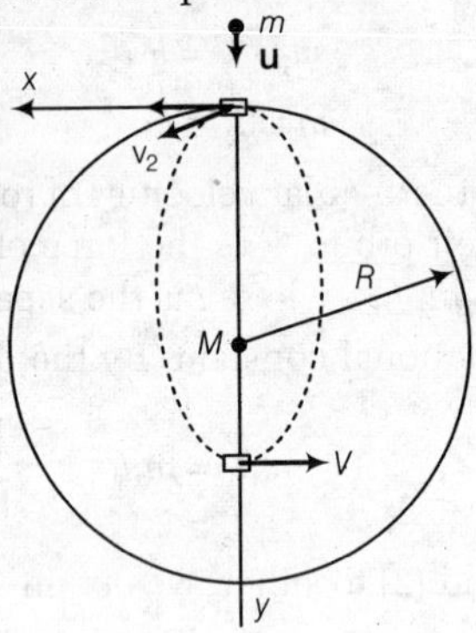

Fig. 179

$$\text{Consequently, } -G\frac{11mM}{R} + \frac{11m}{2}(v_{2x}^2 + v_{2y}^2) = -G\frac{11mM}{R/2} + \frac{11m}{2}V^2, \qquad (3)$$

where V is the velocity of the station at the moment of the closest proximity to the planet. Here we have used the formula for the potential energy of gravitational interaction of two bodies (of mass m_1 and m_2): $W_p = -Gm_1m_2/r$. According to Kepler's second law, the velocity V is connected to the velocity v_2 of the station immediately after the collision through the relation

$$\frac{VR}{2} = v_{2x}R. \qquad (4)$$

Solving Eqs. (1)-(4) together and considering that $v_1 = \sqrt{GM/R}$, we determine the velocity of the meteorite before the collision:

$$u = \sqrt{\frac{58GM}{R}}.$$

1.83. For a body of mass m resting on the equator of a planet of radius R, which rotates at an angular velocity ω, the equation of motion has the form

$$m\omega^2 R = mg' - N,$$

where N is the normal reaction of the planet surface, and $g' = 0.01\,g$ is the free-fall acceleration on the planet. By hypothesis, the bodies on the equator are weightless, i.e. $N = 0$. Considering that $\omega = 2\pi/T$, where T is the period of rotation of the planet about its axis (equal to the solar day), we obtain $R = \dfrac{T^2}{4\pi^2}g'$.

Substituting the values $T = 8.6 \times 10^4$ s and $g' \simeq 0.1$ m/s^2, we get

$$R \simeq 1.8 \times 10^7 \text{ m} = 18000 \text{ km}.$$

1.84. We shall write the equation of motion for Neptune and the Earth around the Sun (for the sake of simplicity, we assume that the orbits are circular):

$$m_N \omega_N^2 R_N = \frac{GMm_N}{R_N^2},$$

$$m_E \omega_E^2 R_E = \frac{GMm_E}{R_E^2}.$$

Here $m_N, m_E, \omega_N, \omega_E, R_N$, and R_E are the masses, angular velocities, and orbital radii of Neptune and the Earth respectively, and M is the mass of the Sun. We now take into account the relation between the angular velocity and the period of revolution around the Sun:

$$\omega_N = \frac{2\pi}{T_N}, \quad \omega_E = \frac{2\pi}{T_E}$$

Here T_N and T_E are the periods of revolution of Neptune and the Earth. As a result, we find that the period of revolution of Neptune around the Sun is

$$T_N = T_E\sqrt{\frac{R_N^3}{R_E^3}} \simeq 165 \text{ years}.$$

A similar result is obtained for elliptical orbits from Kepler's third law.

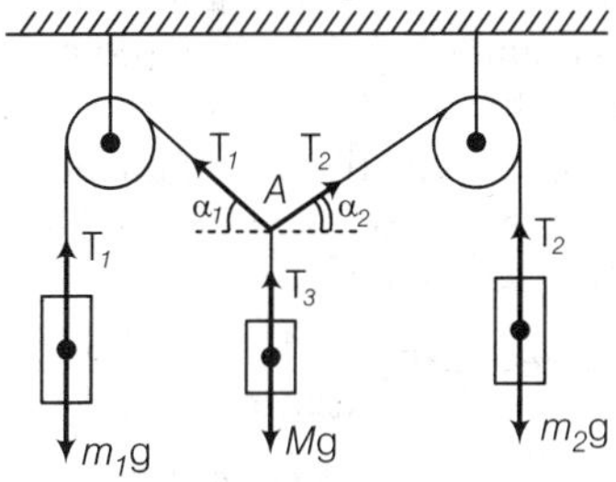

Fig. 180

1.85. Let us consider two methods of solving this problem.

1. The equilibrium conditions for the loads have the form (Fig. 180)

$$T_1 = m_1 g, T_2 = m_2 g,$$
$$Mg = T_1 \sin\alpha_1 + T_2 \sin\alpha_2,$$
$$T_1 \cos\alpha_1 = T_2 \cos\alpha_2.$$

From these relations, we can determine the angles corresponding to the equilibrium, position of the system:

$$\sin\alpha_1 = \frac{M^2 - m_2^2 + m_1^2}{2M\, m_1},$$

$$\sin\alpha_2 = \frac{M^2 - m_1^2 + m_2^2}{2M\, m_2}.$$

Obviously, equilibrium can be attained only under the conditions that $0 < \alpha_1 < \pi/2$ and $0 < \alpha_2 < \pi/2$, i.e.

$$0 < \frac{M^2 - m_2^2 + m_1^2}{2M\, m_1} < 1, 0 < \frac{M^2 - m_1^2 + m_2^2}{2M\, m_2} < 1.$$

These inequalities imply that the entire system will be in equilibrium only provided that

$$M < m_1 + m_2, \quad M^2 > |m_1^2 - m_2^2|.$$

2. Let us consider the equilibrium of point A. At this point, three forces are applied:

$$T_1 = m_1 g, T_2 = m_2 g, T_3 = Mg.$$

Point A is in equilibrium when T_1, T_2, and T_3 form a triangle. Since the sum of two sides of a triangle is larger than the third side, we obtain the relation between the masses m_1, m_2, and M required for the equilibrium of point A:

$$m_1 + m_2 > M, \; M + m_1 > m_2, \; M + m_2 > m_1.$$

1.86. Let us consider the equilibrium conditions for the rod at the instant when it forms an angle α with the horizontal. The forces acting on the rod are shown in Fig. 181. While solving this problem, it is convenient to make use of the equality to zero of the sum of the torques about the point of intersection of the force of gravity mg and the force F applied by the person perpendicular to the rod (point O) since the moments of these forces about this point are zero.

If the length of the rod is $2l$, the arm of the normal reaction N is $l\cos\alpha$, while the arm of the friction is $l/\sin\alpha + l\sin\alpha$, and the equilibrium condition will be written in the form

$$Nl\cos\alpha = F_{fr} l\left(\frac{1}{\sin\alpha} + \sin\alpha\right)$$

$$= F_{fr} l \frac{1 + \sin^2\alpha}{\sin\alpha},$$

whence

$$F_{fr} = N\frac{\cos\alpha \sin\alpha}{1 + \sin^2\alpha} = N\frac{\cos\alpha \sin\alpha}{2\sin^2\alpha + \cos^2\alpha}$$

$$= N\frac{1}{2\tan\alpha + \cot\alpha}.$$

On the other hand, the friction cannot exceed the sliding friction μN, and hence

$$\mu \geq \frac{1}{2\tan\alpha + \cot\alpha}.$$

This inequality must be fulfilled at all values of the angle α. Consequently, in order to find the

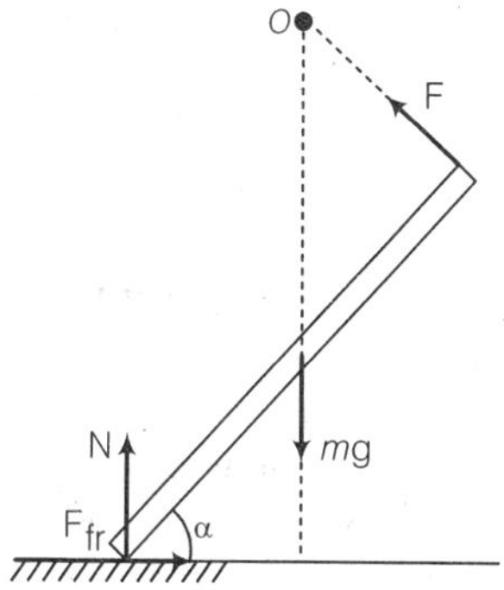

Fig. 181

minimum coefficient of friction $\mu_{\min}$, we must find the maximum of the function $(2x^2 + 1/x^2)^{-1}$, where $x^2 = \tan\alpha$. The identity $2x^2 + 1/x^2 = (\sqrt{2}x - 1/x)^2 + 2\sqrt{2}$ implies that the maximum value of $1/(2\tan\alpha + \cot\alpha)$ is $1/2\sqrt{2} = \sqrt{2}/4$ and is attained at $x^2 = \tan\alpha = \sqrt{2}/2$. Thus, the required minimum coefficient of friction is

$$\mu_{\min} = \frac{\sqrt{2}}{4}.$$

1.87. Since the hinge C is in equilibrium, the sum of the forces applied to it is zero.

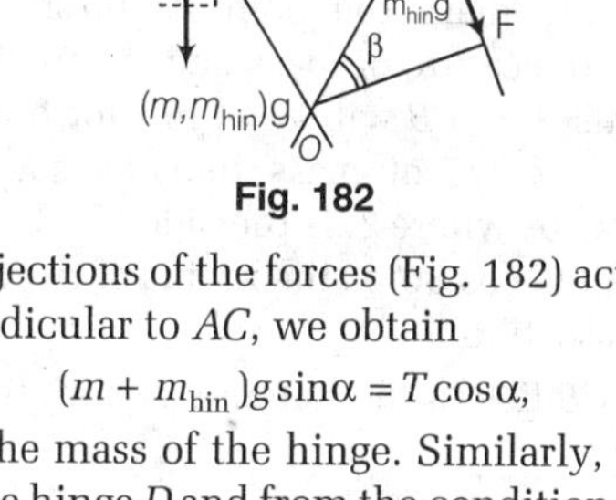

Fig. 182

Writing the projections of the forces (Fig. 182) acting on the hinge C on the axis perpendicular to AC, we obtain

$$(m + m_{\text{hin}})g\sin\alpha = T\cos\alpha, \tag{1}$$

where m_{hin} is the mass of the hinge. Similarly, from the equilibrium condition for the hinge D and from the condition that the middle rod is horizontal, we obtain

$$T\cos\alpha = F\cos\beta + m_{\text{hin}}g\sin\alpha. \tag{2}$$

Solving Eqs. (1) and (2) together, we find that

$$F = \frac{T\cos\alpha - m_{\text{hin}} g\sin\alpha}{\cos\beta} = \frac{mg\sin\alpha}{\cos\beta} \geq mg\sin\alpha.$$

Thus, the minimum force $F_{\min}$ for which the middle rod retains its horizontal position is

$$F_{\min} = mg\sin\alpha = \frac{mg}{2}$$

and directed at right angles to the rod BD.

1.88. By hypothesis, the coefficient of sliding friction between the pencil and the inclined plane satisfies the condition $\mu \geq \tan\alpha$. Indeed, the pencil put at right angles to the generatrix is in equilibrium, which means that $mg\sin\alpha = F_{\text{fr}}$, where mg is the force of gravity, and F_{fr} is the force of friction. But $F_{\text{fr}} \leq \mu mg\cos\alpha$. Consequently, $mg\sin\alpha \leq \mu mg\cos\alpha$, whence $\mu \geq \tan\alpha$.

Thus, the pencil will not slide down the inclined plane for any value of the angle ϕ.

The pencil may start rolling down at an angle ϕ_0 such that the vector of

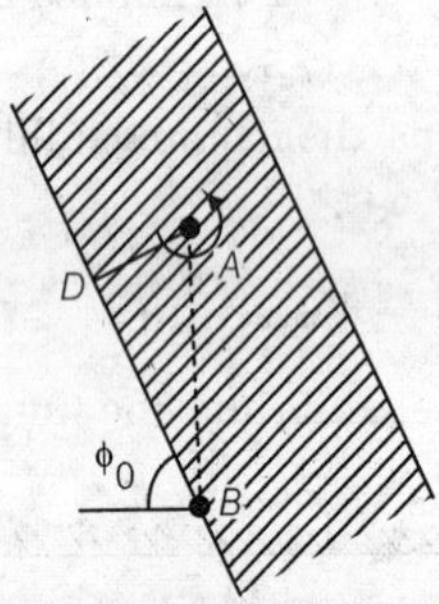

Fig. 183

the force of gravity "leaves" the region of contact between the pencil and the inclined plane (hatched region in Fig. 183). In order to find this angle, we project the centre of mass of the pencil (point A) on the inclined plane and mark the point of intersection of the vertical passing through the centre of mass and the inclined plane (points B). Obviously, points A and B will be at rest for different orientations of the pencil if its centre of mass remains stationary. In this case, $AB = 2l\cos 30° \tan\alpha$, where $2l$ is the side of a hexagonal cross section of the pencil, and $2l\cos 30°$ is the radius of the circle inscribed in the hexagonal cross section.

As long as point B lies in the hatched region, the pencil will not roll down the plane.

Let us write the condition for the beginning of rolling down

$$\frac{AD}{\cos\phi_0} = AB\text{ , or } \frac{l}{\cos\phi_0} = l\sqrt{3}\tan\alpha,$$

whence

$$\phi_0 = \arccos\left(\frac{1}{\sqrt{3}\tan\alpha}\right).$$

Thus, if the angle ϕ satisfies the condition

$$\arccos\left(\frac{1}{\sqrt{3}\tan\alpha}\right) \le \phi \le \frac{\pi}{2},$$

the pencil remains in equilibrium. The expression for the angle ϕ_0 is meaningful provided that $\tan\alpha > 1/\sqrt{3}$. The fact that the pencil put parallel to the generatrix rolls down indicates that $\tan\alpha > 1/\sqrt{3}$ (prove this!).

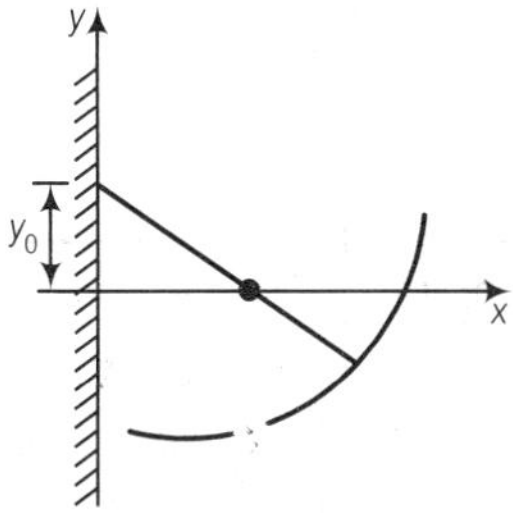

Fig. 184

1.89. Let the cross section of the surface be described by the function $y(x)$ shown in Fig. 184. Since the rod must be in equilibrium in any position, the equilibrium can be only neutral, i.e. the centre of mass of the rod must be on the same level for any position of the rod. If the end of the rod leaning against the surface has an abscissa (x) the ordinate (y_0) of its other end touching the vertical wall can be found from the condition

$$l^2 = [y(x) - y_0]^2 + x^2, \quad y_0 = y(x) \pm \sqrt{l^2 - x^2}.$$

Since the rod is homogeneous, its centre of mass is at the midpoint. Assuming for definiteness that the ordinate of the centre of mass is zero, we obtain

$$\frac{y_0 + y(x)}{2} = 0,$$

whence $$y(x) = \pm\frac{\sqrt{l^2 - x^2}}{2}.$$

Only the solution with the minus sign has the physical meaning. Therefore, in general, the cross section of the surface is described by the function

$$y(x) = a - \frac{\sqrt{l^2 - x^2}}{2},$$

where a is an arbitrary constant.

1.90. In the absence of the wall, the angle of deflection of the simple pendulum varies harmonically with a period T and an angular amplitude α. The projection of the point rotating in a circle of radius α at an angular velocity $\omega = 2\pi / T$ performs the same motion. The perfectly elastic collision of the rigid rod with the wall at an angle of deflection β corresponds to an instantaneous jump from point B to point C

(Fig. 185). The period is reduced by $\Delta t = 2\gamma + \omega$, where $\gamma = \arccos(\beta / \alpha)$. Consequently,

$$T_1 = \frac{2\pi}{\omega} - \frac{2\gamma}{\omega},$$

and the sought solution is $\frac{T_1}{T} = 1 - \frac{1}{\pi} \arccos \frac{\beta}{\alpha}$.

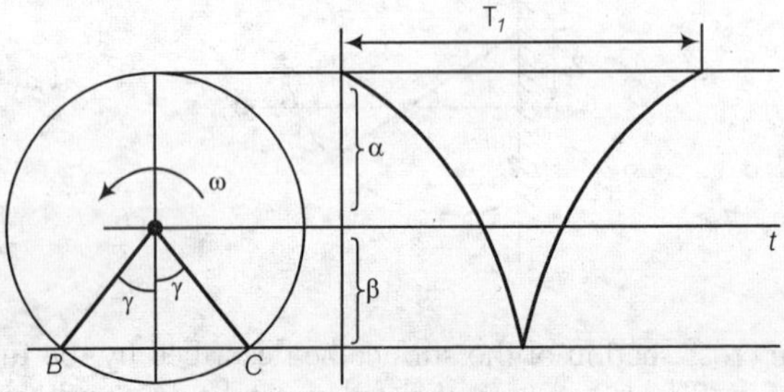

Fig. 185

1.91*. Let the ball of mass m falling from a height h elastically collide with a stationary horizontal surface. Assuming that the time of collision of the ball with the surface is small in comparison with the time interval Δt between two consecutive collisions, we obtain

$$\Delta t = 2\sqrt{\frac{2h}{g}}.$$

As a result of each collision, the momentum of the ball changes by $\Delta p = 2mv = 2m\sqrt{2gh}$. Therefore, the same momentum $\Delta p = 2m\sqrt{2gh}$ is transferred to the horizontal surface in one collision.

In order to determine the mean force exerted by the ball on the horizontal surface we consider the time interval $\tau >> \Delta t$. The momentum transferred to the horizontal surface during the time τ is

$$\Delta P = \Delta p \frac{\tau}{\Delta t} = 2m \frac{\sqrt{2gh}\tau}{2\sqrt{2h/g}} = mg\tau.$$

Consequently, the force exerted by the jumping ball on the horizontal surface and averaged during the time interval τ can be obtained from the relation

$$F_m = \frac{\Delta P}{\tau} = mg.$$

By hypothesis, the mass M of the pan of the balance is much larger than the mass m of the ball. Therefore, slow vibratory motion of the balance pan will be superimposed by nearly periodic impacts of the ball. The mean force exerted by the ball on the pan is $F_m = mg$. Consequently, the required displacement Δx of the equilibrium position of the balance is

$$\Delta x = \frac{mg}{k}.$$

1.92. The force acting on the bead at a certain point A in the direction tangential to the wire is $F = mg \cos \alpha$, where α is the angle between the tangent at point A and the ordinate axis (Fig. 186).

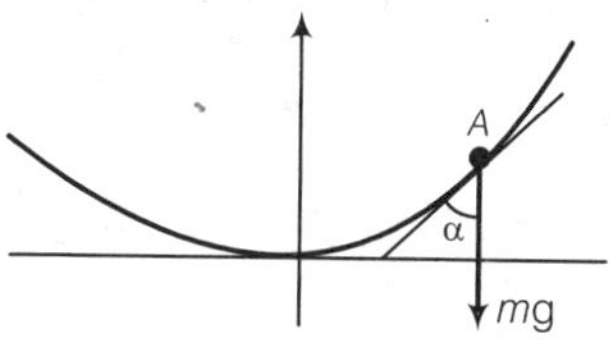

Fig. 186

For the length of the region of the wire from the origin to the bead to vary harmonically, the force F acting at point A must he proportional to the length l_A. But $F \leq mg$, and l_A increases indefinitely. Consequently, there must be a point B at which the proportionality condition is violated. This means that oscillations with the amplitude l_B cannot be harmonic.

1.93. It follows from the equations of motion for the blocks

$$ma_1 = F_{el}, 2ma_2 = -F_{el}$$

where F_{el} is the elastic force of the spring, that their accelerations at each instant of time are connected through the relation $a_2 = -a_1/2$. Hence the blocks vibrate in antiphase in the inertial reference frame fixed to the centre of mass of the blocks, and the relative displacements of the blocks with respect to their equilibrium positions are connected through the same relation as their accelerations:

$$\Delta x_2 = -\frac{\Delta x_1}{2}$$

Then

$$F_{el} = -\left(\frac{3}{2}\right)k\Delta x_1 = 3k\Delta x_2 .$$

Consequently, the period of small longitudinal oscillations of the system is

$$T = 2\pi\sqrt{\frac{2m}{3k}}.$$

1.94. Let us mark the horizontal diameter $AB = 2r$ of the log at the moment it passes through the equilibrium position.

Let us now consider the log at the instant when the ropes on which it is suspended are deflected from the vertical by a small angle α (Fig. 187). In the absence of slippage of the ropes, we can easily find from geometrical considerations that the diameter AB always remains horizontal in the process of oscillations. Indeed, if $EF \perp DK$, $FK = 2r \tan\alpha \approx 2r\alpha$. But $BD \approx FK/2 \approx r\alpha$ Consequently, $\angle BOD = \alpha$ as was indicated above.

Since the diameter AB remains horizontal all the time, the log performs translatory motion, i.e. the velocities of all its points are the same at each instant. Therefore, the motion of the log is synchronous to the oscillation of a simple pendulum of length l. Therefore, the period of small oscillations of the log is

$$T = 2\pi\sqrt{\frac{l}{g}}.$$

1.95. The period of oscillations of the pendulum in the direction perpendicular to the rails is $T_1 = 2\pi\sqrt{\frac{l}{g}}$ (l is the length of the weightless inextensible thread) since the load M is at rest in this case (Fig. 188).

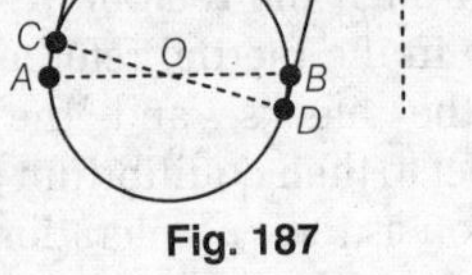

Fig. 187

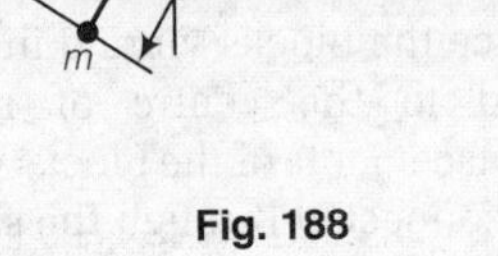

Fig. 188

The period of oscillations in the plane parallel to the rails ("parallel" oscillations) can be found from the condition that the centre of mass of the system remains stationary. The position of the centre of mass of the system is determined from the equation $ml_1 = M(l - l_1)$. Thus, the ball performs oscillations with point O remaining at rest and is at a distance $l_1 = ml/(M + m)$ from point O. Hence the period of "parallel" oscillations of the pendulum is

$$T_2 = 2\pi\sqrt{\frac{Ml}{(m + M)g}}.$$

Consequently, $$\frac{T_2}{T_1} = \sqrt{\frac{M}{m + M}}.$$

1.96. The force exerted by the rods on the load is $F_1 = 2F_{ten}\cos\alpha$, while the force exerted on the spring is $F_2 = 2F_{ten}\sin\alpha$ (see Fig. 48).

According to Hooke's law, $F_2 = (1.5l - 2l\sin\alpha)k$, where k is the rigidity of the spring. As a result, $F_1 = 1.5lk\cot\alpha - 2lk\cos\alpha$.

In order to determine the period of small oscillations, we must determine the force ΔF acting on the load for a small change Δh in the height of the load relative to the equilibrium position $h_0 = 2l\cos\alpha_0$. We obtain

$$\Delta F = 1.5\,lk\,\Delta(\cot\alpha) - 2lk\,\Delta(\cos\alpha),$$

where

$$\Delta(\cot\alpha) = \left(\frac{\Delta\cot\alpha}{d\alpha}\right)_{\alpha=\alpha_0}\Delta\alpha = -\frac{\Delta\alpha}{\sin^2\alpha_0},$$

$$\Delta(\cos\alpha) = -\sin\alpha_0\Delta\alpha.$$

Consequently, since $\Delta k = -2l\sin\alpha_0\,\Delta\alpha$, we find that

$$\Delta F = -1.5k\frac{l\Delta\alpha}{\sin^2\alpha_0} + 2kl\sin\alpha_0\Delta\alpha$$

$$= -5kl\,\Delta\alpha = -5k\Delta h$$

because $\sin\alpha_0 = 1/2$.

The period of small oscillations of the load can be found from the formula $T = 2\pi\sqrt{m/(5k)}$, where m is the mass of the load determined from the equilibrium condition:

$$1.5\,kl\cot\alpha_0 - 2kl\cos\alpha_0 = mg,$$

$$m = \frac{\sqrt{3}/2}{kl/g}.$$

Thus,
$$T = 2\pi\sqrt{\frac{\sqrt{3}l}{10g}}.$$

1.97. At each instant of time, the kinetic energy of the hoop is the sum of the kinetic energy of the centre of mass of the hoop and the kinetic energy of rotation of the hoop about its centre of mass.

Since the velocity of point A of the hoop is always equal to zero, the two kinetic energy components are equal (the velocity of the centre of mass is equal to the linear velocity of rotation about the centre of mass).

Therefore, the total kinetic energy of the hoop is mv^2 (m is its mass, and v is the velocity of the centre of mass).

According to the energy conservation law, $mv^2 = mg(r - h_A)$, where h_A is the height of the centre of mass of the hoop above point A at each instant of time. Consequently, the velocity of the centre of mass of the hoop is $v = \sqrt{g(r - h_A)}$.

On the other hand, the velocity of the pendulum B at the moment when it is at a height h_A above the rotational axis A is $v = \sqrt{2g(r - h_A)}$, i.e. is $\sqrt{2}$ times larger. Thus, the pendulum attains equilibrium $\sqrt{2}$ times sooner than the hoop, i.e. in $t = \frac{\tau}{\sqrt{2}} \simeq 0.35$ s.

1.98. It should be noted that small oscillations of the load occur relative to the stationary axis AB (Fig. 189).

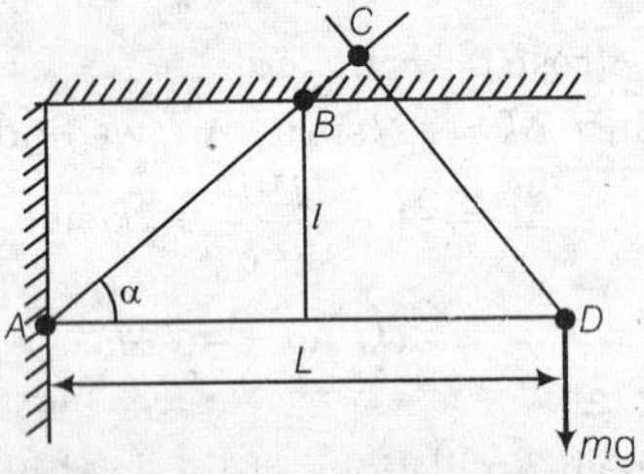

Fig. 189

Let $DC \perp AB$. Then small oscillations of the load are equivalent to the oscillations of a simple pendulum of the same mass, but with the length of the thread

$$l' = L \sin\alpha = L\frac{l}{\sqrt{l^2 + (L/2)^2}},$$

and the free-fall acceleration

$$g' = g\cos\alpha = g\frac{L/2}{\sqrt{l^2 + (L/2)^2}}$$

where $L = AD$.

Thus, the required period of small oscillations of the system is

$$T = 2\pi\sqrt{\frac{l'}{g'}} = 2\pi\sqrt{\frac{2l}{g}}.$$

1.99. In order to solve the problem, it is sufficient to note that the motion of the swing is a rotation about an axis passing through the points where

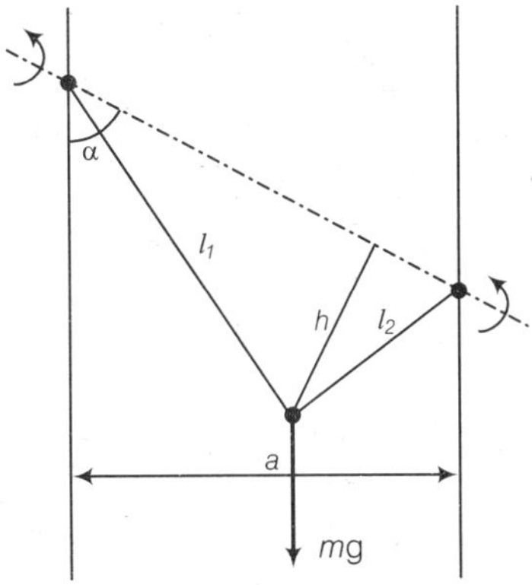

Fig. 190

the ropes are fixed, i.e. the system is a "tilted simple pendulum" (Fig. 190). The component of the force of gravity mg along the rotational axis does not influence the oscillations, while the normal component $mg \sin\alpha$ is in fact the restoring force.

Therefore, using the formula for the period of a simple pendulum, we can write

$$T = 2\pi\sqrt{\frac{h}{g\sin\alpha}},$$

where
$$h = \frac{l_1 l_2}{\sqrt{l_1^2 + l_2^2}} = \frac{l_1 l_2}{\sqrt{a^2 + b^2}},$$

$$\sin\alpha = \frac{a}{\sqrt{a^2 + b^2}}.$$

Consequently, the period of small oscillations of the swing is

$$T = 2\pi\sqrt{\frac{l_1 l_2}{ag}}.$$

1.100. The period of a simple pendulum is inversely proportional to the square root of the free-fall acceleration:

$$T \propto \frac{1}{\sqrt{g}}.$$

Let the magnitude of the acceleration of the lift be a. Then the period of the pendulum for the lift moving upwards with an acceleration a will be

$$T_{\text{up}} \propto \frac{1}{\sqrt{g + a}}$$

and for the lift moving downwards with the same acceleration

$$T_{\text{down}} \propto \frac{1}{\sqrt{g-a}}.$$

Obviously, the time measured by the pendulum clock moving upwards with the acceleration a is proportional to the ratio of the time t_{up} of the upward uniformly accelerated motion to the period T_{up}:

$$t'_{\text{up}} = \frac{t_{\text{up}}}{T_{\text{up}}} \propto t_{\text{up}}\sqrt{g+a}.$$

The time measured by the pendulum clock moving downwards with the acceleration a is

$$t'_{\text{down}} = \frac{t_{\text{down}}}{T_{\text{down}}} \propto t_{\text{down}}\sqrt{g-a}.$$

By hypothesis, the times of the uniformly accelerated downward and upward motions are equal: $t_{\text{down}} = t_{\text{up}} = t_1/2$, where t_1 is the total time of accelerated motion of the lift. Therefore, the time measured by the. pendulum clock during a working day is

$$t' \approx \frac{t_1}{2}\left(\sqrt{\frac{g+a}{g}} + \sqrt{\frac{g-a}{g}}\right) + t_0.$$

Here t_0 is the time of the uniform motion of the lift. The stationary pendulum clock would indicate

$$t \approx t_1 + t_0.$$

It can easily be seen that the inequality $\sqrt{g+a} + \sqrt{g-a} < 2\sqrt{g}$ is fulfilled. Indeed,

$$\left(\frac{\sqrt{g+a} + \sqrt{g-a}}{2\sqrt{g}}\right)^2 = \frac{g + \sqrt{g^2 - a^2}}{2g} < 1.$$

Hence it follows that on the average the pendulum clock in the lift lags behind: $t' < t$, and hence the operator works too much.

1.101. Pascal's law implies that the pressure of a gas in communicating vessels is the same at the same altitude. Since the tubes of the manometer communicate with the atmosphere, the pressure in them varies with altitude according to the same law as the atmospheric air pressure.

This means that the pressure exerted by the air on the liquid in different arms of the manometer is the same and equal to the atmospheric pressure at the altitude of manometer. Thus, the reading of the manometer corresponds to the zero level since there is no pressure difference.

1.102. We choose the zero level of potential energy at the bottom of the outer tube. Then the potential energy of mercury at the initial instant of time is $W_1 = 2Sl\rho_{mer}g\left(\frac{1}{2}\right) = \rho_{mer}gSl^2$.

The potential energy of mercury at the final instant

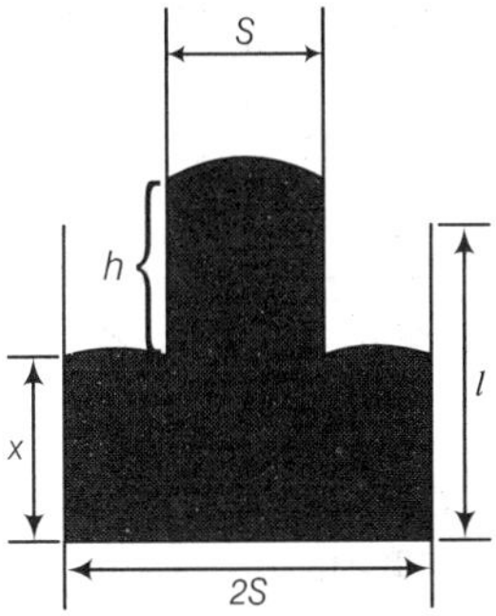

Fig. 191

(the moment of separation of the inner tube, Fig. 191) is
(by hypothesis, $l > h$)

$$W_f = 2S\,x\rho_{mer}g\left(\frac{x}{2}\right) + Sh\rho_{mer}g\left(x + \frac{h}{2}\right),$$

where x is the level of mercury in the outer tube at the moment of separation. This level can be found from the condition of the constancy of the mercury volume:

$$2Sx + Sh = 2Sl,$$

$$x = l - \frac{h}{2}$$

The difference in the potential energies is equal to the sum of the required work A done by external forces and the work done by the force of atmospheric pressure acting on the surface of mercury in the outer tube and on the upper (sealed) end of the inner tube. The displacement of mercury in the outer tbue is $l - x$, the corresponding work of the force of atmospheric pressure being $p_0S(l - x) = \rho_{mer}gSh\,(l - x)$.

The displacement of the sealed end of the inner tube is $l - (l + x)$, the corresponding work being $-p_0\,S\,x = -\rho_{mer}gShx$.

Therefore, the required work of external forces is

$$A = W_f - W_1 - \rho_{mer}gSh(l - 2x)$$

$$= \rho_{mer}gSh\left(l - \frac{3h}{4}\right).$$

1.103. The pressure at the bottom of the "vertical" cylinder is $p = p_0 + \rho_w gh$, where p_0 is the atmospheric pressure, ρ_w is the density of water, and g is the free-fall acceleration. According to Pascal's

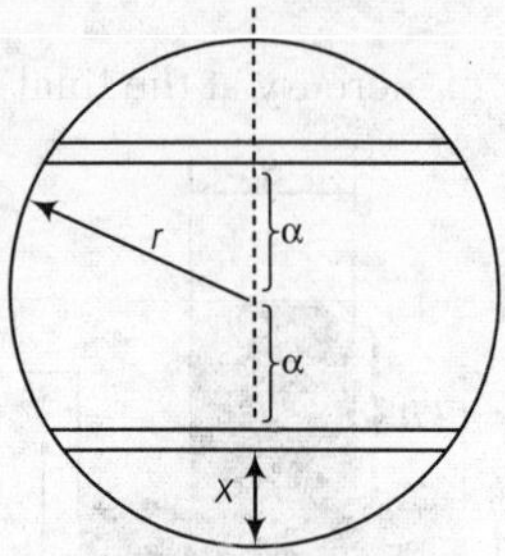

Fig. 192

law, the same pressure is exerted on the lower part of the piston in the "horizontal" cylinder. The total pressure of water on the part of the piston separated from the lower part by a distance x along the vertical is $p - \rho gx$ (Fig. 192).

Let us consider the parts of the piston in the form of narrow (of width Δx) horizontal strips separated by equal distances a from its centre. The force of pressure exerted by water on the upper strip is $[p - \rho_w g(r + a)]\,\Delta S$,

while the force of pressure on the lower strip is

$$[p - \rho_w g\,(r - a)]\,\Delta S,$$

where ΔS is the area of a strip, The sum of these forces is proportional to the area of the strip, the proportionality factor $2(p - \rho gr)$ being independent of a. Hence it follows that the total force of pressure of water on the piston is $(p - p_w gr)\pi r^2 = [p_0 + \rho_w g(h - r)]\pi r^2$.

The piston is in equilibrium when this force is equal to the force of atmospheric pressure acting on the piston from the left and equal to $p_0 \pi r^2$. Hence $h = r$, i.e. the piston is in equilibrium when the level of water in the vertical cylinder is equal to the radius of the horizontal cylinder. An analysis of the solution shows that this equilibrium is stable.

1.104. The condition of complete submergence of a body is $M \geq \rho_w V$, where M is the mass of the body, and V is its volume. In the case under consideration, we have

$$M = m_{cork} + m_{al},\ V = \frac{m_{cork}}{\rho_{cork}} + \frac{m_{al}}{\rho_{al}}.$$

Hence it follows that the minimum mass of the wire is

$$m_{al} = \frac{\rho_{al}(\rho_w - \rho_{cork})}{(\rho_{al} - \rho_w)\rho_{cork}} m_{cork} \approx 1.6 m_{cork}.$$

1.105. Obviously, in equilibrium, the sphere is at a certain height h above the bottom of the reservoir, and some part of the chain lies at the bottom, while the other part hangs vertically between the bottom and the sphere (Fig. 193). By hypothesis, we can state that the sphere is completely submerged in water (otherwise, nearly the whole chain would hang, which is impossible in view of the large density of iron).

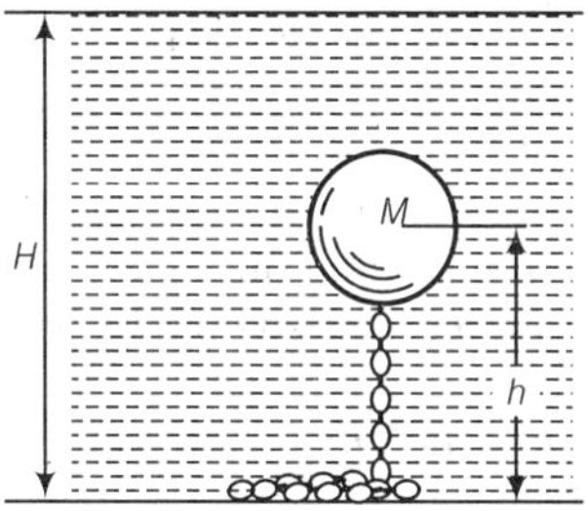

Fig. 193.

Then the height h can be obtained from the equality of the total force of gravity of the sphere and the hanging part of the chain and the buoyant force acting on them:

$$\left(M + m\frac{h - D/2}{l}\right)g = \rho_w\left(V + \frac{m}{\rho_{iron}}\frac{h - D/2}{l}\right)g.$$

Hence $h = \dfrac{D}{2} + \dfrac{P_w V - M}{m(1 - P_w / P_{iron})}l = 1.6\,\text{m}.$

The depth at which the sphere floats is $H - h = 1.4\,\text{m}$.

1.106. The equilibrium condition for the lever is the equality of the moments of forces (Fig. 194). In air, these forces are the forces of gravity $m_1 g$ and $m_2 g$ of thc bodies. Since they are different, their arms l_1 and l_2 are also different since

$$m_1 g l_1 = m_2 g l_2.$$

When the lever is immersed in water, the force of gravity is supplemented by the buoyan of water, which is proportional to the

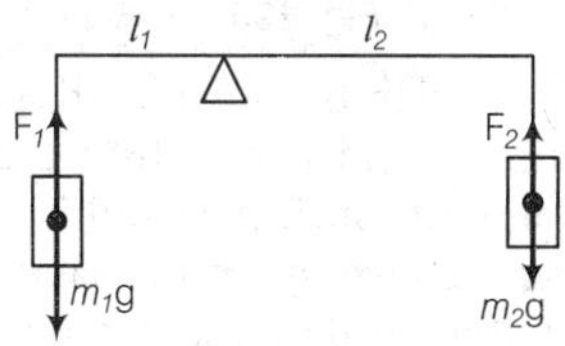

Fig. 194

volume of the body. By hypothesis, $F_1 = F_2$, and therefore

$$(m_1 g - F_1)l_1 \neq (m_2 g - F_2)l_2.$$

Thus, the equilibrium of the lever lever will be violated.

1.107. The volume of the submerged part of each box changes by the same amount $\Delta V = m/\rho_w$, where m is the mass of the body, and ρ_w is the density of water. Since the change in the level of water in each vessel is determined only by ΔV and the vessels are identical, the levels of water in them will change by the same amount.

1.108. Let the volume of the steel ball be V, and let the volume of its part immersed in mercury be V_0 before water is poured and V_1 after water covers the ball completely. The value of V_0 can be found from the condition $\rho_{st} V = \rho_{mer} V_0$,

where ρ_{st} and ρ_{mer} are the densities of steel and mercury. Since the pressure of water is transmitted through mercury to the lower part of the ball, the buoyant force exerted on it by water is $\rho_w (V - V_1) g$, where ρ_w is the density of water, while the buoyancy of mercury is $\rho_{mer} V_1 g$. The condition of floating for the ball now becomes $\rho_{st} V = \rho_{mer} V_1 + \rho_w (V - V_1)$,

whence
$$V_1 = \frac{\rho_{st} - \rho_w}{\rho_{mer} - \rho_w} V.$$

Thus, the ratio of the volumes of the parts of the ball submerged in mercury in the former and latter cases is
$$\frac{V_0}{V_1} = \frac{\rho_{st}}{\rho_{mer}} \frac{\rho_{mer} - \rho_w}{\rho_{st} - \rho_w} = \frac{1 - \rho_w / \rho_{mer}}{1 - \rho_w / \rho_{st}}.$$

Since $\rho_{mer} > \rho_{st}$, $V_0 > V_1$, i.e. the volume of the part of the ball immersed in mercury will become smaller when water is poured.

1.109. The level of water in the vessel in which the piece of ice floats is known to remain unchanged after melting of ice.

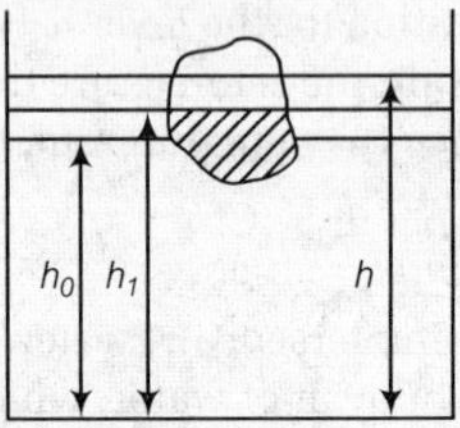

Fig. 195.

In the case under consideration, we shall assume that the level of water at the initial moment (measured from the bottom of the vessel) is h_0, and that the level of the surface of hill is h (Fig. 195). If the vessel contained only water, its level h_1 for the same position of the piece of ice relative to the bottom of the vessel would obey the condition
$$h_0 < h_1 < h.$$
Water formed as a result of melting ice has a volume corresponding to the hatched region in the figure. Since a part of this volume is above the surface of water ($h_1 > h_0$), the level of water rises after melting of ice. On the other hand, since $h_1 < h$, oil fills the formed "hole", i.e. the total level of liquid in the vessel falls.

1.110. Let x be the length of the part of the rod in the tumbler, and y be the length of its outer part. Then the length of the rod is $x + y$, and the centre of mass of the rod is at a distance $(x + y)/2$ from its ends and at a distance $(y - x)/2$ from the outer end. The condition of equilibrium is the equality to zero of the sum of the moments of force about the brim of the tumbler.

$$(F_b - F_A)x = \frac{Mg(y - x)}{2},$$

where $F_b = m_b g = \rho_{al} gV$ is the force of gravity of the ball, and $F_A = \rho_w gV/2$ is the buoyant force, where $V = (4/3)\pi r^3$ is the volume of the ball.

The required ratio is

$$\frac{y}{x} = \frac{1 + 2(F_b - F_A)}{Mg} \simeq 1.5.$$

1.111. When the barometer falls freely, the force of atmospheric pressure is no longer compensated by the weight of the mercury column irrespective of its height. As a result, mercury fills the barometer tube completely, i.e. to the division 1050 mm.

1.112. In a vessel with a liquid moving horizontally with an acceleration a, the surface of the liquid becomes an inclined plane. Its slope ϕ is determined from the condition that the sum of the force of pressure F and the force of gravity mg acting on an area element of the surface is equal to ma, and the force of pressure is normal to the surface. Hence $\tan\phi = \frac{a}{g}$.

According to the law of communicating vessels, the surfaces of the liquid in the arms of the manometer belong to the above-mentioned inclined plane (Fig. 196).

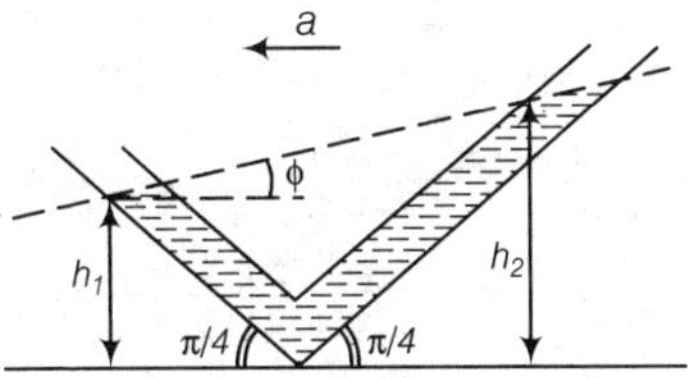

Fig. 196

It follows from geometrical considerations that

$$\tan\phi = \frac{h_2 - h_1}{h_2 + h_1},$$

whence

$$a = \frac{g(h_2 - h_1)}{h_2 + h_1}.$$

1.113. The air layer of thickness Δx at a distance x from the front of the cabin experiences the force of pressure

$$[p(x + \Delta x) - p(x)]\, S,$$

where S is the cross-sectional area of the cabin. Since air is at rest relative to the cabin, the equation of motion for the mass of air under consideration has the form

$$\rho S\ \Delta x a = [p(x + \Delta x) - p(x)]S.$$

Making Δx tend to zero, we obtain $\dfrac{dp}{dx} = \rho a,$

whence $p(x) = p_1 + \rho a x.$

Since the mean pressure in the cabin remains unchanged and equal to the atmospheric pressure ρ_0, the constant p_1 can be found from the condition

$$p_0 = p_1 + \frac{\rho a l}{2},$$

where l is the length of the cabin. Thus, in the middle of the cabin, the pressure is equal to the atmospheric pressure, while in the front and rear parts of the cabin, the pressure is lower and higher than the atmospheric pressure by

$$\Delta p = \frac{\rho a l}{2} \simeq 0.03\,\text{Pa respectively.}$$

1.114. Let us consider the conditions of equilibrium for the mass of water contained between cross sections separated by x and $x + \Delta x$ from the rotational axis relative to the tube. This part of the liquid, whose mass is $\rho_w S\ \Delta x$, uniformly rotates at an angular velocity ω under the action of the forces of pressure on its lateral surfaces. Denoting the pressure in the section x by $p(x)$, we obtain

$$[p(x + \Delta x) - p(x)]\, S = \rho S\ \Delta x \omega^2 \left(x + \frac{\Delta x}{2} \right).$$

Making Δx tend to zero, we obtain the following equation:

$$\frac{dp}{dx} = \rho_w\, \omega^2 x,$$

whence

$$p(x) = \rho_w\, \omega^2 \left(\frac{x^2}{2} \right) + p_0.$$

Using the conditions of the problem

$$p_1 = p(r_1) = \rho_w \omega^2 \left(\frac{r_1^2}{2} \right) + p_0,$$

$$p_2 = p(r_2) = \rho_w \omega^2 \left(\frac{r_2^2}{2} \right) + p_0,$$

we obtain the angular velocity of the tube: $\omega = \sqrt{\dfrac{2}{\rho_w} \dfrac{p_2 - p_1}{r_2^2 - r_1^2}}.$

1.115. Let the exponent α be such that the body having an initial velocity v traverses a finite distance $s(v)$ in the medium. Since the velocity of the body monotonically decreases during its motion in the medium, $s(v) > s(v_1)$ for $v > v_1$. It is also clear that $s(v)$ tends to zero as $v \to 0$. The condition under which the body comes to a halt is that the work A of the drag is equal to the initial kinetic energy of the body:

$$\frac{mv^2}{2} = A. \tag{1}$$

Since the drag monotonically decreases with the velocity of the body during its motion, we can write

$$A \le \mu v^{\alpha} s(v). \tag{2}$$

Substituting Eq. (2) into Eq. (1), we obtain

$$s(v) \ge \frac{m}{2\mu} v^{2-\alpha},$$

whence it follows that for $\alpha \ge 2$ the condition $\lim_{v \to 0} s(v) = 0$ is violated. Therefore, for $\alpha \ge 2$, the body cannot be decelerated on the final region of the path.

1.116. According to the law of universal gravitation, the force of attraction of the body of mass m to Mars on its surface is $\frac{M_M m}{R_M^2}$, where M_M is the mass of Mars, and R_M is its radius. This means that the free-fall acceleration on the surface of Mars is $g_M = GM_M / R_M^2$. If the mass of the Martian atmosphere is m_M, it is attracted to the surface of the planet with the force $m_M g_M$, which is equal to the force of pressure of the atmosphere, i.e. the pressure on the surface of Mars is $p_M = m_M g_M / (4\pi R_M^2)$. Similarly, for the corresponding parameters on the Earth, we obtain $p_E = m_E g_E / (4\pi R_E^2)$.

The ratio of the masses of the Martian and the Earth's atomospheres is

$$\frac{m_M}{m_E} = \frac{p_M \cdot 4\pi R_M^2 g_E}{p_E \cdot 4\pi R_E^2 g_M}.$$

Considering that $M_M = (4/3)\pi R_M^3 \rho_M$ (a similar expression can be obtained for the Earth) and substituting the given quantities, we get

$$\frac{m_M}{m_E} = \frac{p_M}{p_E} \frac{R_M}{R_E} \frac{\rho_E}{\rho_M} \simeq 3.4 \times 10^{-3}.$$

It should be noted that we assumed in fact that the atmosphere is near the surface of a planet. This is really so since the height of the atmosphere is much smaller than the radius of a planet (e.g. at an altitude of 10 km above the surface of the Earth it is impossible to breathe, and the radius of the Earth is $R_E \simeq 6400$ km!).

2. Heat and Molecular Physics

2.1. Since the vertical cylinders are communicating vessels, the equilibrium sets in after the increase in the mass of the first piston only when it "sinks" to the bottom of its cylinder, i.e. the whole of the gas flows to the second cylinder. Since the temperature and pressure of the gas remain unchanged, the total volume occupied by the gas must remain unchanged. Hence we conclude that $S_1h_0 + S_2h_0 = S_2h$, where S_1 and S_2 are the cross-sectional areas of the first and second cylinders, and h is the height at which the second piston will be located, i.e. just the required difference in heights (since the first piston lies at the bottom). The initial pressures produced by the pistons are equal. Therefore,

$$\frac{m_1g}{S_1} = \frac{m_2g}{S_2}, \quad \frac{S_1}{S_2} = \frac{m_1}{m_2}$$

and hence

$$h = h_0\left(\frac{m_1}{m_2} + 1\right) = 0.3\,\text{m}.$$

2.2. If the temperature T_{wall} of the vessel walls coincides with the gas temperature T, a molecule striking the wall changes the normal component p_x of its momentum by $-p_x$. Consequently, the total change in the momentum is $2p_x$. When $T_{\text{wall}} > T$, the gas is heated. This means that gas molecules bounce off the wall at a higher velocity than that at which they impinge on the wall, and hence have a higher momentum. As a result, the change in the momentum will be larger than $2p_x$ (Fig. 197). If, however, $T_{\text{wall}} < T$, the gas is cooled, i.e. gas molecules bounce off the wall with a smaller momentum than that with which they impinge on the wall. In this case, the change in the momentum will be obviously smaller than $2p_x$ (Fig. 198).

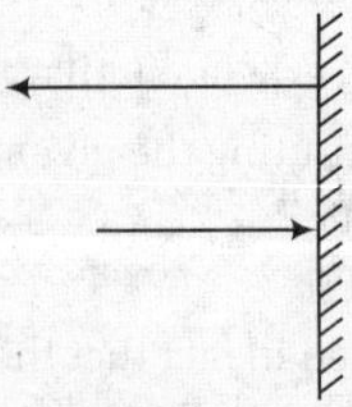

$T_{\text{wall}} > T$

Fig. 197

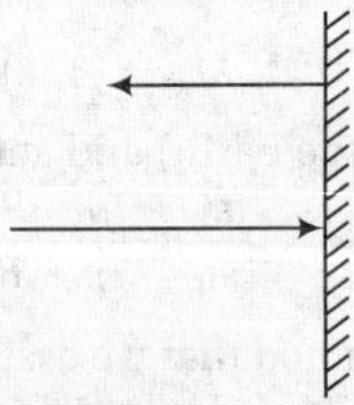

$T_{\text{wall}} < T$

Fig. 198

Since according to Newton's second law, the change in momentum is proportional to the mean force, the pressure exerted by the gas on the walls is higher when the walls are warmer than the gas.

2.3. The work A done by the gas during the cycle is determined by the area of the p-V diagram bounded by the cycle, i.e. by the area of the trapezoid (see Fig. 57) :

$$A = (p_2 - p_1)\left(\frac{V_3 - V_2 + V_4 - V_1}{2}\right).$$

All these quantities can easily be expressed in terms of pressure and volume p_1 and V_1 at point 1. Indeed, according to Charles' law, $V_3 = V_2T_3 / T_2 = V_1T_3 / T_2$ and $V_4 = V_1T_4 / T_1 = V_1T_2 / T_1$, while the Gay-Lussac law implies that $p_2 = p_1T_2 / T_1$. Substituting these values into the expression for work, we obtain

$$A = p_1V_1\left(\frac{T_2 - T_1}{T_1}\right)\left(\frac{T_2}{T_1} + \frac{T_3}{T_2} - 2\right).$$

The equation of state for n moles of an ideal gas is $p_1V_1 = nRT_1$, and we can finally write

$$A = nR\,(T_2 - T_1)\left(\frac{T_2}{T_1} + \frac{T_3}{T_2} - 2\right).$$

2.4. Figure 58 shows that on segments 1-2 and 3-4, pressure is directly proportional to temperature. It follows from the equation of state for an ideal gas that the gas volume remains unchanged in this case, and the gas does no work. Therefore, we must find the work done only in isobaric processes 2-3 and 4-1. The work $A_{23} = p_2(V_3 - V_2)$ is done on segment 2-3 and $A_{41} = p_1(V_1 - V_4)$ on segment 4-1. The total work A done by the gas during a cycle is

$$A = p_2(V_3 - V_2) + p_1(V_1 - V_4).$$

The equation of state for three moles of the ideal gas can be written as $pV = 3RT$,and hence

$$p_1V_1 = 3RT_1, \qquad p_1V_4 = 3RT_4,$$
$$p_2V_2 = 3RT_2, \qquad p_2V_3 = p_3V_3 = 3RT_3.$$

Substituting these values into the expression for work, we finally obtain

$$A = 3R\,(T_1 + T_3 - T_2 - T_4)$$
$$= 2 \times 10^4\,\text{J} = 20\ \text{kJ}.$$

2.5. The cycle $1 \to 4 \to 3 \to 2 \to 1$ is in fact equivalent to two simple cycles $1 \to 0 \to 2 \to 1$ and $0 \to 4 \to 3 \to 0$ (see Fig. 59). The work done by the gas is determined by the area of the corresponding cycle on the p-V diagram. In the first cycle the work is positive, while in the second cycle it is negative (the work is done on the gas). The work done in the first cycle can easily be calculated:

$$A_1 = \frac{(p_0 - p_1)(V_2 - V_1)}{2}.$$

As regards the cycle $0 \to 4 \to 3 \to 0$, the triangle on the p-V diagram corresponding to it is similar to the triangle corresponding to the first cycle. Therefore, the work A_2 done in the second cycle will be

$$A_2 = -A_1 \frac{(p_2 - p_0)^2}{(p_0 - p_1)^2}.$$

(The areas of similar triangles are to each other as the squares of the lengths of the corresponding elements, in our case, altitudes.) The total work A done during the cycle $1 \to 4 \to 3 \to 2 \to 1$ will therefore be

$$A = A_1 \left[\frac{1 - (p_2 - p_0)^2}{(p_0 - p_1)^2} \right] \simeq 750 \text{ J}.$$

2.6. According to the first law of thermodynamics, the amount of heat ΔQ_1 received by a gas going

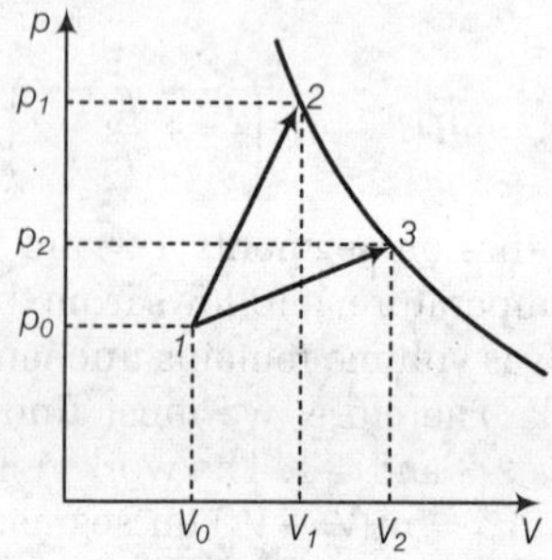

Fig. 199

over from state $1\,(p_0, V_0)$ to state $2\,(p_1, V_1)$ (Fig. 199) is $\Delta Q_1 = \Delta U_1 + A_1$, where ΔU_1 is the change in its internal energy, and A_1 is the work done by the gas,

$$A_1 = \frac{(p_0 + p_1)(V_1 - V_0)}{2}.$$

As the gas goes over from state 1 to state 3 (p_2, V_2) (points 2 and 3 lie on the same isotherm), the following relations are fulfilled:

$$\Delta Q_2 = \Delta U_2 + A_2,\ A_2 = \frac{(p_0 + p_2)(V_2 - V_0)}{2}.$$

Since the final temperature of the gas in states 2 and 3 is the same, $\Delta U_1 = \Delta U_2$. In order to find out in which process the gas receives a larger amount of heat, we must compare the works A_1 and A_2 :

$$A_1 - A_2 = \frac{(p_0 + p_1)(V_1 - V_0)}{2} - \frac{(p_0 + p_2)(V_2 - V_0)}{2}$$

$$= \frac{(p_0 V_1 - p_0 V_2) + (p_2 V_0 - p_1 V_0)}{2} < 0$$

since $p_0 V_1 < p_0 V_2$ and $p_2 V_0 < p_1 V_0$. Consequently, $A_2 > A_1$ and $\Delta Q_2 > \Delta Q_1$, i.e. the amount of heat received by the gas in the process $1 \to 3$ is larger.

2.7. Since hydrogen diffuses through all the partitions, it uniformly spreads over the entire vessel, and in all the three parts of the vessel, the pressure of hydrogen is

$$p_{H_2} = \frac{m_{H_2}}{\mu_{H_2}} \frac{RT}{V}$$

(if a gas penetrates through a partition, its pressure on both sides of the partition must be the same in equilibrium).

Nitrogen can diffuse only through the right partition, and hence will fill the middle and right parts of the vessel (see Fig. 61) having the volume $(2/3)V$. The pressure of nitrogen is

$$p_{N_2} = \frac{m_{N_2}}{\mu_{N_2}} \frac{3RT}{2V}.$$

Oxygen does not diffuse through the partitions, and its pressure in the middle part of the vessel is

$$p_{O_2} = \frac{m_{O_2}}{\mu_{O_2}} \frac{3RT}{V}.$$

According to Dalton's law, the pressure in a part of a vessel is equal to the sum of the partial pressures of the gases it contains:

$$p_1 = p_{H_2} \simeq 1.3 \times 10^9 \text{ Pa} = 1.3 \text{ GPa},$$

$$p_2 = p_{H_2} + p_{O_2} + p_{N_2} \simeq 4.5 \times 10^9 \text{ Pa} = 4.5 \text{ GPa},$$

$$p_3 = p_{H_2} + p_{N_2} \simeq 2.0 \times 10^9 \text{ Pa} = 2.0 \text{ GPa}.$$

2.8*. Let us first determine the velocity of the descent module. We note that the change in pressure Δp is connected with the change in altitude Δh through the following relation:

$$\Delta p = -\rho g \Delta h, \tag{1}$$

where ρ is the gas density. The equation of state for an ideal gas implies that $p = (\rho/\mu)RT$ (here T is the gas temperature at the point where the change in pressure is considered). Taking into account that $\Delta h = -v\,\Delta t$, where v is the velocity of the descent, and Δt is the time of the descent, we can write expression (1) in the form

$$\frac{\Delta p}{p} = g\frac{\mu v \Delta t}{RT}. \tag{2}$$

Knowing the ratio $\Delta p/\Delta t$, i.e. the slope of the tangent at the final point A of the graph, we can determine the velocity v from Eq. (2). (It should be noted that since the left-hand side of (2) contains the ratio $\Delta p/p$, the scale on the ordinate axis is immaterial.) Having determined $(\Delta p/\Delta t)p^{-1}$ from the graph and substituting $\mu = 44$ g/mol for CO_2, we find that the velocity of the descent module of the spacecraft is

$$v = \frac{RT}{g\mu}\frac{\Delta p}{p\Delta t} = \frac{8.3 \text{ J}/(\text{K}\cdot\text{mol}) \times 7 \times 10^2 \text{ K}}{10 \text{ m/s}^2 \times 44 \times 10^{-3} \text{ kg/mol} \times 1150 \text{ s}} \simeq 11.5 \text{ m/s}.$$

Let us now solve the second part of the problem. Considering that the module has a velocity of 11.5 m/s, it was at an altitude $h = 15$ km above the surface of the planet 1300 s before landing, i.e. this moment corresponds to $t = 2350$ s. Using the relation $(\Delta p / \Delta t)\, p^{-1}$, we can find the required temperature T_h at this point of the graph from Eq. (2):

$$T_h = \frac{g\mu v}{R}\left(\frac{p\Delta t}{\Delta p}\right)_t \simeq 430\,\text{K}.$$

2.9. Since the piston has been displaced by h under the action of the load, the volume of the gas has decreased by hS and has become $V - hS$. The gas pressure under the piston is equal to the atmospheric pressure p_0 plus the pressure Mg/S produced by the load, i.e. $p_0 + Mg/S$. Therefore, we can write the equation of state for the gas before and after loading:

$$p_0 V = nRT_i, \quad (1)$$

$$\frac{p_0 + Mg/S}{V - hS} = nRT_f. \quad (2)$$

Here T_i and T_f are the initial and final temperatures of the gas.

Since the gas is thermally insulated by hypothesis, it follows from the first law of thermodynamics that the entire work A done on the gas is spent to change its internal energy, i.e. $A = (3/2)nR\,(T_f - T_i)$ (the internal energy of a mole of an ideal gas is $U = (3/2)RT$). It can easily be seen that the work is $A = Mgh$, and hence

$$Mgh = \frac{3}{2}nR(T_f - T_i). \quad (3)$$

Subtracting Eq. (1) from Eq. (2) termwise and using expression (3) for $T_f - T_i$, we obtain the following equation in h:

$$\frac{MgV}{S} - Mgh - p_0 hS = \frac{2}{3}Mgh.$$

Hence we find that $h = \dfrac{MgV}{S\,(p_0 S + Mg/3)}$.

Substituting h into Eq. (2), we determine the final temperature of the gas:

$$T_f = \frac{(p_0 S + Mg)(3p_0 S - 2Mg)V}{(3p_0 S + Mg)SnR}$$

2.10. According to the first law of thermodynamics, the amount of heat Q supplied to the gas is spent on the change ΔU in its internal energy and on the work A done by the gas:

$$Q = \Delta U + A.$$

The internal energy U of a mole of an ideal gas can be written in the form $U = c_V T = (3/2)\,RT$, i.e. $\Delta U = (3/2)\,R\Delta T$. The work done by the gas at constant pressure p is $A = p\Delta V = pS\Delta x$, where Δx is the displacement of the piston.

The gas pressure is $p = p_0 + \frac{Mg}{S}$,

i.e. is the sum of the atmospheric pressure and the pressure produced by the piston. Finally, the equation of state $pV = RT$ leads to the relation between the change ΔV in volume and the change ΔT in temperature at a constant pressure:

$$p\Delta V = R\Delta T.$$

Substituting the expressions for ΔU and A into the first law of thermodynamics and taking into account the relation between ΔV and ΔT, we obtain

$$Q = p\Delta V + \frac{3}{2}p\Delta V = \frac{5}{2}pS\Delta x. \quad (1)$$

Since the amount of heat liberated by the heater per unit time is q, $Q = q\Delta t$, where Δt is the corresponding time interval. The velocity of the piston is $v = \Delta x / \Delta t$. Using Eq. (1), we obtain

$$v = \frac{2}{5}\frac{q}{p_0 S + Mg}.$$

2.11*. For a very strong compression of the gas, the repulsion among gas molecules becomes significant, and finiteness of their size should be taken into account. This means that other conditions being equal, the pressure of a real gas exceeds the pressure of an ideal gas the stronger, the larger the extent to which the gas is compressed. Therefore, while at a constant temperature the product pV is constant for an ideal gas, it increases with decreasing volume for a real gas.

2.12*. Let us consider an intermediate position of the piston which has been displaced by a distance y from its initial position. Suppose that the gas pressure is p_2 in the right part of the vessel and p_1 in the left part. Since the piston is in equilibrium, the sum of the forces acting on it is zero:

$$(p_2 - p_1)S - 2ky = 0, \quad (1)$$

where S is the area of the piston.

The total work done by the gas over the next small displacement Δy of the piston is $\Delta A = \Delta A_1 + \Delta A_2$, where ΔA_2 is the work done by the gas contained in the right part, and ΔA_1 is the work done by the gas in the left part, and

$$\Delta A_1 + \Delta A_2 = p_2\Delta yS - p_1\Delta yS$$
$$= (p_2 - p_1)\Delta yS = 2ky\Delta y. \quad (2)$$

Thus, by the moment of displacement of the piston by $x = l/2$, the total work done by the gas will be equal to the sum of the potential energies stored in the springs:

$$A = 2\frac{k}{2}\left(\frac{l}{2}\right)^2. \quad (3)$$

If an amount of heat Q is supplied to the gas in the right part of the vessel, and the gas in the left part transfers an amount of heat Q' to the thermostat, the total amount of heat supplied to the system is $Q - Q'$, and we can write (the first law of thermodynamics)

$$Q - Q' = 2\frac{k}{2}\left(\frac{l}{2}\right)^2 + \Delta U, \qquad (4)$$

where ΔU is the change in the internal energy of the gas. Since the piston does not conduct heat, the temperature of the gas in the left part does not change, and the change ΔU in the internal energy of the gas is due to the heating of the gas in the right part by ΔT. For n moles of the ideal gas, we have $\Delta U = n(3/2)R\Delta T$. The temperature increment ΔT can be found from the condition of equilibrium at the end of the process.

In accordance with the equation of state, the pressure of the gas in the right part of the vessel is $p = nR(T + \Delta T)/[S(l + l/2)]$. On the other hand, it must be equal to the sum of the gas pressure $p' = nRT/[S(l - l/2)]$ in the left part and the pressure $p'' = 2kl/(2S)$ created by the springs, i.e.

$$\frac{2nR(T + \Delta T)}{3\,Sl} = \frac{2nRT}{Sl} + \frac{kl}{S}.$$

Hence we can find that $\Delta T = 2T + 3kl^2/(2nR)$.

Using Eq. (4), we finally obtain

$$Q' = Q - 3nRT - \frac{5}{2}kl^2.$$

2.13. Let T_1 be the initial temperature of the gas under the piston, and T_2 the gas temperature after the amount of heat ΔQ has been supplied to the system. Since there is no friction and the vessel is thermally insulated, the entire amount of heat ΔQ is spent on the change ΔW in the internal energy of the system:

$$\Delta Q = \Delta W.$$

The change in the internal energy of the system is the sum of the changes in the internal energy of the gas and in the potential energy of the compressed spring (since we neglect the heat capacity of the vessel, piston, and spring).

The internal energy of a mole of an ideal monatomic gas increases as a result of heating from T_1 to T_2 by

$$\Delta W_1 = \frac{3}{2}R(T_2 - T_1). \qquad (1)$$

The potential energy of the compressed spring changes by

$$\Delta W_2 = \frac{k}{2}(x_2^2 - x_1^2), \qquad (2)$$

where k is the rigidity of the spring, and x_1 and x_2 are the values of the absolute displacement (deformation) of the left end of the spring at temperatures T_1 and T_2 respectively. Let us find the relation between the parameters of the gas under the piston and the deformation of the spring.

The equilibrium condition for the piston implies that

$$p = \frac{F}{S} = \frac{kx}{S}, \qquad x = \frac{pS}{k}, \tag{3}$$

where p is the gas pressure, and S is the area of the piston. According to the equation of state for an ideal gas, for one mole we have $pV = RT$. For the deformation x of the spring, the volume of the gas under the piston is $V = xS$ and the pressure $p = RT/(xS)$. Substituting this expression for p into Eq. (3), we obtain

$$x^2 = \frac{RT}{k}. \tag{4}$$

Thus, the change in the potential energy of the compressed spring as a result of heating of the system is

$$\Delta W_2 = \frac{R}{2}(T_2 - T_1).$$

The total change in the internal energy of the system as a result of heating from T_1 to T_2 is

$$\Delta W = \Delta W_1 + \Delta W_2 = 2R(T_2 - T_1),$$

and the heat capacity of the system is

$$C = \frac{\Delta Q}{\Delta T} = \frac{\Delta U}{T_2 - T_1} = 2R.$$

2.14. Let us analyze the operation of the heat engine based on the cycle formed by two isotherms and two isochores (Fig. 200).

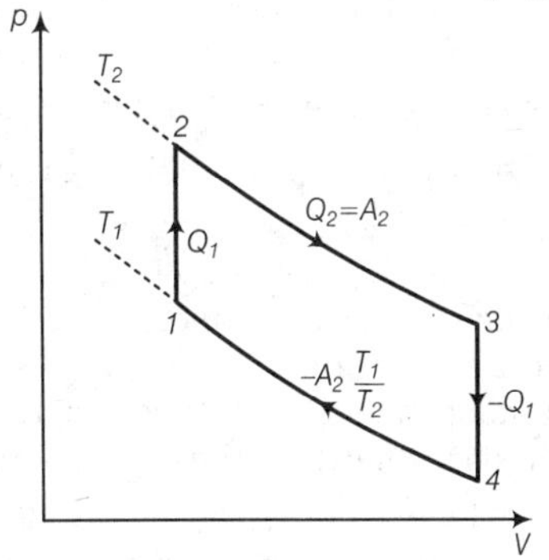

Fig. 200

Suppose that the temperature of the cooler (corresponding to the lower isotherm) is T_1, and the temperature of the heater (corresponding to the upper isotherm) is T_2. On the isochoric segment 1-2, the gas volume does not change, i.e. no work is done, but the temperature increases from T_1 to T_2. It means that a certain amount of heat Q_1 is supplied to the gas. On the isothermal segment 2-3, the internal energy of the gas remains constant, and the entire amount of heat Q_2 supplied to the gas is spent on doing work: $Q_2 = A_2$.

On the isochoric segment *3-4*, the gas temperature returns to its initial value T_1, i.e. the amount of heat Q_1 is removed from the gas. On the isothermal segment 4-1, the work done by the gas is negative, which means that some amount of heat is taken away from the gas. Thus, the total amount of heat supplied to the gas per cycle is $Q_1 + A_2$.

Figure 200 shows that the work done by the gas per cycle is the sum of the positive work A_2, on the segment *2-3* and the negative work A_4 on the segment 4-1.

Let us compare the pressures at the points corresponding to equal volumes on the segments 4-1 and 2-3. The Gay-Lussac law indicates that the ratio of these pressures is T_1 / T_2, and hence the work done by the gas is $A_4 = -(T_1 / T_2)A_2$. The total work per cycle is given by

$$A = A_2 + A_4 = \left(1 - \frac{T_1}{T_2}\right)A_2,$$

and the efficiency is $\eta = \dfrac{A}{Q_1 + A_2} = \dfrac{1 - T_1 / T_2}{1 + Q_1 / A_2} < 1 - \dfrac{T_1}{T_2}$.

Therefore, the efficiency of the heat engine based on the cycle consisting of two isotherms and two isochores is lower than the efficiency $1 - T_1 / T_2$ of Carnot's heat engine.

2.15*. Let us first determine the free-fall acceleration g_{pl} on the surface of the planet. On the one hand, we know that the force of attraction of a body of mass m to the planet is mg_{pl}. On the other hand, it follows from the law of universal gravitation that this force is GmM / r^2, where G is the gravitational constant. Hence we obtain $g_{pl} = GM / r^2$. The pressure p exerted by the atmospheric column of height h on the surface of the planet is

$$p = \rho g_{pl} h, \qquad (1)$$

where ρ is the density of the atmosphere. While determining the pressure of the atmospheric column, we assume that the free-fall acceleration is independent of altitude. This assumption is justified since by hypothesis the height of the atmosphere is much smaller than the radius r of the planet ($h \ll r$).

Using the equation of state for an ideal gas of mass M occupying a volume V in the form $pV = (M / \mu)RT$ and considering that $\rho = M / V$, we find that

$$\rho = \frac{p\mu}{RT}.$$

Substituting this expression for ρ into Eq. (1) and cancelling out p, we determine the temperature T of the atmosphere on the surface of the planet:

$$T = \frac{\mu g_{pl} h}{R} = \frac{\mu GMh}{Rr^2}.$$

2.16. We must take into account here that the heat transferred per unit time is proportional to the temperature difference. Let us introduce the following notation: T_{out1}, T_{out2} and T_{r_1}, T_{r_2} are the temperatures outdoors and in the room in the first and second cases respectively. The thermal power dissipated by the radiator in the room is $k_1(T - T_r)$, where k_1 is a certain coefficient. The thermal power dissipated from the room is $k_2(T_r - T_{out})$, where k_2 is another coefficient. In thermal equilibrium, the power dissipated by the radiator is equal to the power dissipated from the room. Therefore, we can write

$$k_1(T - T_{r_1}) = k_2(T_{r_1} - T_{out1}).$$

Similarly, in the second case,

$$k_1(T - T_{r_2}) = k_2(T_{r_2} - T_{out2}).$$

Dividing the first equation by the second, we obtain

$$\frac{T - T_{r_1}}{T - T_{r_2}} = \frac{T_{r_1} - T_{out1}}{T_{r_2} - T_{out2}}.$$

Hence we can determine T:

$$T = \frac{T_{r_2} T_{out1} - T_{r_1} T_{out2}}{T_{r_2} + T_{out1} - T_{out2} - T_{r_1}} = 60\,\text{C}.$$

2.17. The total amount of heat q liberated by the space object per unit time is proportional to its volume: $q = \alpha R^3$, where α is a coefficient. Since the amount of heat given away per unit surface area is proportional to T^4, and in equilibrium, the entire amount of the liberated heat is dissipated into space, we can write $q = \beta R^2 T^4$ (the area of the surface is proportional to R^2, and β is a coefficient). Equating these two expressions for q, we obtain

$$T^4 = \frac{\alpha}{\beta} R.$$

Consequently, the fourth power of the temperature of the object is proportional to its radius, and hence a decrease in radius by half leads to a decrease in temperature only by a factor of $\sqrt[4]{2} \simeq 1.19$.

2.18*. For definiteness, we shall assume that the liquid flowing in the inner tube 2 is cooled, i.e. $T_{i_2} > T_{f_2}$ and hence $T_{i1} < T_{f1}$.

Since the cross-sectional area $2S - S = S$ of the liquid flow in the outer tube 1 is equal to the cross-sectional area S of the liquid flow in the inner tube 2, and their velocities coincide, the decrease in temperature of the liquid flowing in tube 2 from the entrance to the exit is equal to the decrease in temperature of the liquid flowing in tube 1. In other words, the temperature difference in the liquids remains constant along the heat exchanger, and hence

$$T_{i2} - T_{f1} = T_{f2} - T_{i1}. \quad (1)$$

In view of the constancy of the temperature difference, the rate of heat transfer is constant along the heat exchanger. The amount of heat Q transferred from the liquid flowing in tube *2* to the liquid flowing in tube *1* during a time t is

$$Q = S_{lat} kt(T_{i2} - T_{f1}). \quad (2)$$

Here S_{lat} is the lateral surface of the inner tube, $S_{lat} = 2\pi rl$, where r is the radius of the inner tube, i.e. $\pi r^2 = S$, and $r = \sqrt{S/\pi}$. The amount of heat Q is spent for heating the liquid flowing in tube 1. During the time t, the mass of the liquid flowing in the outer tube 1 is $m = \rho vtS$, and its temperature increases from T_{i1} to T_{f1}. Consequently,

$$Q = \rho vt Sc\,(T_{f1} - T_{i1}). \quad (3)$$

Equating expressions (2) and (3), we obtain

$$2\pi\sqrt{\frac{S}{\pi}} lk\,(T_{i2} - T_{f1}) = \rho vSc(T_{f1} - T_{i1}).$$

Hence we can find T_{f_1}, and using Eq. (1), T_{f_2} as well. Therefore, we can write

$$T_{f1} = T_{i2} + (T_{i1} - T_{i2})\left(\frac{1 + 2\sqrt{\pi/S}lk}{\rho vc}\right)^{-1}$$

$$T_{f2} = T_{i1} + (T_{i2} - T_{i1})\left(\frac{1 + 2\sqrt{\pi/S}lk}{\rho vc}\right)^{-1}$$

2.19*. As a result of redistribution, the gas pressure obviously has the maximum value at the rear (relative to the direction of motion) wall of the vessel since the acceleration a is imparted to the gas just by the force of pressure exerted by this wall. We denote this pressure by p_{max}. On the other hand, $p_{max} \le p_{sat}$. Considering that $p_{sat} >> p$ and hence neglecting the force of pressure exerted by the front wall, on the basis of Newton's second law, we can write

$$p_{max} = \frac{m_{gas}a}{S} \le p_{sat},$$

where m_{gas} is the mass of the substance in the gaseous state contained in the vessel. Consequently, for $a \le p_{sat}S/M$, no condensation will take place, while for $a > p_{sat}S/M$, the mass of the gas will become $m = p_{sat}S/a$, and the vessel will contain a liquid having the mass

$$m_{liq} = M - m = \frac{M - p_{sat}S}{a}.$$

2.20. Boiling of water is the process of intense formation of steam bubbles. The bubbles contain saturated water vapour and can be formed when the pressure of saturated water vapour becomes equal to the atmospheric pressure (760 mmHg, or 10^5 Pa).

It is known that this condition is fulfilled at a temperature equal to the boiling point of water: $T_{boil} = 100°C$ (or 373 K). By hypothesis, the pressure of saturated water vapour on the planet is $p_0 = 760$ mm Hg, and hence the temperature on the planet is $T = T_{boil} = 373$ K. Using the equation of state for an ideal gas $\rho = \dfrac{p_0\mu}{RT_{boil}}$,

where μ is the molar mass of water, and p_0 is the atmospheric pressure, and substituting the numerical values, we obtain $\rho = 0.58$ kg/m^3.

2.21. When we exhale air in cold weather, it is abruptly cooled. It is well known that the saturated vapour pressure drops upon cooling. Water vapour contained in the exhaled air becomes saturated as a result of cooling and condenses into tiny water drops ("fog").

If we open the door of a warm hut on a chilly day, cold air penetrating into the hut cools water vapour contained in the air of the hut. It also becomes saturated, and we see "fog", viz. the drops of condensed water.

2.22*. It is easier to solve the problem graphically. The total pressure p in the vessel is the sum of the saturated water vapour pressure p_{sat} and the pressure of hydrogen p_{H_2}. According to the equation of state for an ideal gas, the pressure of hydrogen is

$$p_{H_2} = \frac{m_{H_2}}{\mu_{H_2} V} RT$$

$$= \frac{2 \times 10^{-3} \text{ kg} \times 8.3 \text{ J/(mol} \cdot \text{K)}}{2 \times 10^{-3} \text{kg/mol} \times 2 \times 10^{-3} \text{m}^3} T$$

$$= 4.15 \times 10^3 T,$$

where p_{H_2} is measured in pascals. The $p_{H_2}(T)$ dependence is linear. Therefore, having calculated $p_{H_2}(T)$ for two values of temperature, say, for

$$T_1 = 373 \text{ K},$$

$$p_{H_2} = 15.5 \times 10^5 \text{ Pa},$$

$$T_2 = 453 \text{ K},$$

$$p_{H_2} = 18.8 \times 10^5 \text{ Pa},$$

we plot the graph of $p_{H_2}(T)$.

Using the hint in the conditions of the problem, we plot the graph of the function $p_{sat}(T)$.

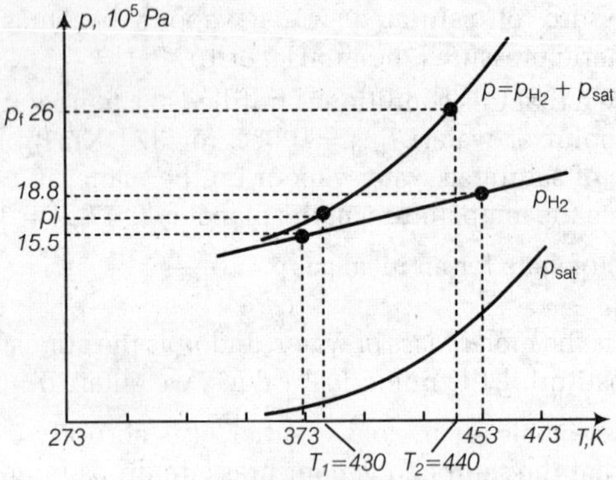

Fig. 201

"Composing" the graphs of $p_{H_2}(T)$ and $p_{sat}(T)$, we obtain the graph of the temperature dependence of the total pressure in the vessel, $p(T)$ (Fig. 201).

Using the $p(T)$ curve, from the initial and final values of pressure specified in the conditions of the problem, we obtain the initial and final temperatures in the vessel:

$$p_i = 17 \times 10^5 \text{ Pa}, \qquad T_1 = T_i \simeq 380 \text{ K},$$

$$p_f = 26 \times 10^5 \text{ Pa}, \qquad T_2 = T_f \simeq 440 \text{ K}.$$

Let us now determine the mass of evaporated water. Assuming that water vapour is an ideal gas, we calculate the initial p_{v_1} and final p_{v_2} pressures of water vapour in the vessel. For this purpose, we make use of the obtained graphs. For $T_1 = 380$ K, the pressure of hydrogen is $p'_{H_2} \simeq 15.5 \times 10^5$ Pa, and $p_{v1} = p_i - p'_{H_2} \simeq 1.5 \times 10^5$ Pa.

$$\text{For } T_2 = 440 \text{ K}, \; p''_{H_2} \simeq 18 \times 10^5 \text{ Pa, and}$$

$$p_{v_2} = p_f - p''_{H_2} \simeq 8 \times 10^5 \text{ Pa}.$$

Let us write the equations of state for water vapour at p_{v1}, T_1 and p_{v2}, T_2:

$$p_{v_1} V = \frac{m_{v_1}}{\mu_v} RT_1, \qquad p_{v_2} V = \frac{m_{v_2}}{\mu_v} RT_2,$$

where m_{v_1} and m_{v_2} are the initial and final masses of vapour in the vessel. Hence we can determine the mass of evaporated water:

$$\Delta m = m_{v_2} - m_{v_1} = \frac{\mu_v V}{R}\left(\frac{p_{v_2}}{T_2} - \frac{p_{v_1}}{T_1}\right)$$

$$= \frac{18 \times 10^{-3} \text{ kg/mol} \times 2 \times 10^{-3} \text{ m}^3}{8.3 \text{ J/(K} \cdot \text{mol)}}$$

$$\times \left(\frac{8 \text{ Pa}}{440 \text{ K}} - \frac{1.5 \text{ Pa}}{380 \text{ K}}\right) \times 10^5 = 6 \times 10^{-3} \text{ kg} = 6 \text{ g}.$$

2.23. If h is the height of water column in the capillary, the temperature of the capillary, and hence of water at this height, is

$$T_h = \frac{T_{up}h}{l}.$$

Water is kept in the capillary by surface tension. If σ_h is the surface tension at the temperature T_h, we can write

$$h = \frac{2\sigma_h}{\rho_w gr},$$

where ρ_w is the density of water. Hence we obtain

$$\sigma_h = \frac{\rho grh}{2} = \left(\frac{\rho grl}{2}\right)\left(\frac{T_h}{T_{up}}\right).$$

Using the hint in the conditions of the problem, we plot the graph of the function $\sigma(T)$.

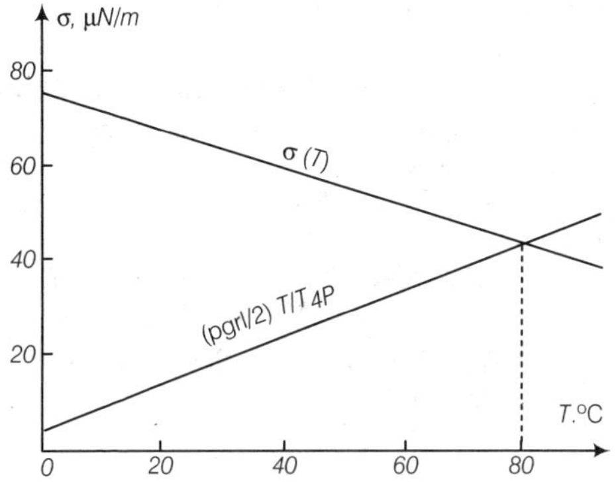

Fig. 202

The temperature T_h on the level of the maximum ascent of water is determined by the point of intersection of the curves describing the $(\rho grl/2)T/T_{up}$ and σ (T) dependences. Figure 202 shows that $T_h \simeq 80$ °C. Consequently, $h = \dfrac{lT_h}{T_{up}} \simeq 6.4$ cm.

The problem can also be solved analytically if we note that the $\sigma(T)$ dependence is practically linear.

2.24. The condition of equilibrium for the soap bubble film consists in that the air pressure p_{bub1} is the sum of the external pressure p_1 and the excess pressure $4\sigma/r$ due to surface tension. It should be noted that there are two air-soap film interfaces in the soap bubble, each of which produces a pressure $2\sigma/r$. For this reason, the excess pressure is $2\times 2\sigma/r = 4\sigma/r$. Therefore, we can first write the equilibrium condition in the form

$$p_{bub1} = p_1 + \frac{4\sigma}{r}.$$

After the radius of the bubble has been reduced by half, the pressure produced by surface tension becomes $8\sigma / r$. By hypothesis, the temperature is maintained constant, and hence (according to Boyle's law) a decrease in the volume of the bubble by a factor of eight (its radius has decreased by half) leads to an eight-fold increase in the air pressure in the bubble (it becomes $8\ p_{\text{bub1}}$),

so that we can write $8 p_{\text{bub1}} = p_2 + \dfrac{8\sigma}{r}$.

Substituting p_{bub1} into this formula from the first equation, we can finally write

$$p_2 = 8p_1 + \frac{24\sigma}{r}.$$

2.25. In the fireplace, large temperature gradients may take place. If the bricks and the mortar are made of different materials, i.e. materials with different temperature expansion coefficients, the fireplace can crack.

2.26. Let us suppose that the temperature of the mixture of the liquids having the initial temperatures T_1 and T_2 has become T. Since the vessel containing the mixture is thermally insulated ($\Delta Q = 0$), we can write

$$c_1 m_1 (T - T_1) + c_2 m_2 (T - T_2) = 0,$$

whence

$$\frac{m_1}{m_2} = \left(\frac{c_2}{c_1}\right)(T - T_2)(T_1 - T)^{-1}.$$

By hypothesis, $2(T_1 - T) = T_1 - T_2$, and hence $T - T_2 = T_1 - T$, and the ratio $(T - T_2)/(T_1 - T) = 1$. Therefore,

$$\frac{m_1}{m_2} = \frac{c_2}{c_1},$$

i.e. the ratio of the masses of these liquids is inverse to the ratio of their specific heats.

2.27. In the former case, the water in the test tube is mainly heated due to convection since warm water is lighter than cold water. In the latter case, water is cooled only as a result of heat exchange between water layers in the test tube. Since the conditions of heat exchange between the test tube and outer water remain the same, $t_1 < t_2$.

It should be noted that if we change the parameters of the problem ($20°\text{C} \to 0°\text{C}$ and $80°\text{C} \to 4,°\text{C}$), we shall obtain a reverse answer. The reason lies in the anomaly of water. In the temperature interval from 0 to 4°C, cold water is lighter than warm water.

2.28. For the system under consideration (vessel-water, vessel-water-ball), the heat flux per unit time $q = \Delta Q / \Delta t$ through the surface of contact with the ambient depends on the temperature difference:

$$\frac{\Delta Q}{\Delta t} = \alpha F (T_{\text{ves}} - T),$$

where t is the time, T_{ves} is the temperature of the vessel, T is the temperature of the ambient, and F is a certain function of temperature. The coefficient α is determined by the conditions at the contact of the system under consideration with the ambient. In our case, the conditions at the contact are identical for the two vessels, and hence the coefficient α is the same in both cases. The amount of heat ΔQ lost by the vessel leads to a decrease in the temperature of the vessel by ΔT_{ves}.

For the * vessel with water, we obtain

$$\Delta Q_1 = (M_w c_w + m_{ves} c_{ves})\,\Delta T_{ves},$$

where M_w and c_w are the mass and specific heat of water, m_{ves} and c_{ves} are the relevant quantities for the vessel.

For the vessel with water and the ball, we obtain

$$\Delta Q_2 = (M_w c_w + m_w c_w + m_b c_b)\,\Delta T_{ves},$$

where m_b and c_b are the mass and specific heat of the ball. By hypothesis, $m_{ves} << M_w$ and $m_b = M_w$. Besides, $c_{ves} << c_w$, and hence we can write

$$\Delta Q_1 = M_w c_w\,\Delta T_{ves}, \qquad \Delta Q_2 = M_w\,(c_w + c_b)\,\Delta T_{ves}.$$

It can easily be seen that the change ΔT_{ves} of temperature in the two vessels occurs during different time intervals Δt_1 and Δt_2 so that

$$\frac{\Delta T_{ves}}{F(T_{ves} - T)} = \frac{\alpha}{M_w c_w}\Delta t_1,$$

$$\frac{\Delta T_{ves}}{F(T_{ves} - T)} = \frac{\alpha}{M_w (c_w + c_b)}\Delta t_2.$$

Hence we obtain $$\frac{\Delta t_1}{\Delta t_2} = \frac{c_w}{c_w + c_b}.$$

Therefore, the following relation will be fulfilled for the total times t_1 and t_2 of cooling of the vessels:

$$\frac{t_2}{t_1} = \frac{c_w + c_b}{c_w} = k,$$

whence $$c_b / c_w = k - 1.$$

2.29. If the level of water in a calorimeter has become higher, it means that a part of water has been frozen (the volume of water increases during freezing). On the other hand, we can state that some amount of water has not been frozen since otherwise its volume would have increased by a factor of $\rho_w / \rho_{ice} \simeq 1.1$, and the level of water in the calorimeter would have increased by $(h/3)(1.1 - 1) \simeq 2.5$ cm, while by hypothesis $\Delta h = 0.5$ cm. Thus, the temperature established in the calorimeter is 0 °C.

Using this condition, we can write

$$c_w m_w (T_w - 0\,°C) = -\lambda\,\Delta m + c_{ice} m_{ice}\,(0\,°C - T_{ice}), \qquad (1)$$

where Δm is the mass of frozen water, and T_{ice} is the initial temperature of ice. As was mentioned above, the volume of water increases as a result of freezing by a factor of ρ_w / ρ_{ice}, and hence

$$\Delta h S = \left(\frac{\rho_w}{\rho_{ice}} - 1 \right) \frac{\Delta m}{\rho_w}, \quad (2)$$

where S is the cross-sectional area of the calorimeter. Substituting Δm from Eq. (2) into Eq. (1) and using the relations $m_w = (h/3)\rho_w S$ and $m_{ice} = (h/3)\rho_{ice} S$, we obtain

$$c_w S \frac{h}{3} \rho_w T_w = -\lambda S\, \Delta h \frac{\rho_{ice}\rho_w}{\rho_w - \rho_{ice}} - c_{ice}\, \rho_{ice} S T_{ice} \frac{h}{3}.$$

Hence
$$T_{ice} = -\frac{\lambda}{c_{ice}} \frac{3\Delta h}{h} \frac{\rho_w}{\rho_w - \rho_{ice}} - \frac{c_w}{c_{ice}} \frac{\rho_w}{\rho_{ice}} T_w \simeq -54\ °C.$$

2.30*. (1) Assuming that water and ice are incompressible, we can find the decrease in the temperature of the mixture as a result of the increase in the external pressure:

$$\Delta T = \left(\frac{p_1}{p} \right) \times 1\,K \simeq 0.18\,K.$$

Such a small change in temperature indicates that only a small mass of ice will melt, i.e. $\Delta m \ll m_{ice}$.

We write the energy conservation law:

$$4 = \lambda \Delta m - (c_{ice} + c_w)\, m\, \Delta T.$$

Let us estimate the work A done by the external force. The change in the volume of the mixture as a result of melting ice of mass Δm is

$$\Delta V = \frac{\Delta m}{\rho_{ice}} - \frac{\Delta m}{\rho_w} = \Delta m \frac{\rho_w - \rho_{ice}}{\rho_w \rho_{ice}} \ll 0.1 \frac{m}{\rho_{ice}} \simeq 10^{-4}\,m^3.$$

We have taken into account the fact that the density of water decreases as a result of freezing by about 10%, i.e. $(\rho_w - \rho_{ice})/\rho_w \simeq 0.1$.

Therefore, we obtain an estimate

$$A \le p_1\, \Delta V = 0.25\,kJ.$$

The amount of heat ΔQ required for heating the mass m of ice and the same mass of water by ΔT is

$$\Delta Q = (c_{ice} + c_w)\, m\, \Delta T \simeq 1.1\ kJ.$$

Since $A << \Delta Q$, we can assume that $\lambda\, \Delta m = \Delta Q$, whence

$$\Delta m = \frac{\Delta Q}{\lambda} = 3.2\,g.$$

The change in volume as a result of melting ice of this mass is

$$\Delta V_1 = \Delta m \frac{\rho_w - \rho_{ice}}{\rho_w \rho_{ice}} \simeq 3.5 \times 10^{-7} \text{ m}^3.$$

Considering that for a slow increase in pressure the change in the volume ΔV_1 is proportional to that in the pressure Δp, we can find the work done by the external force:

$$A = \frac{p_1 \Delta V_1}{2} \simeq 0.44 \text{ J}.$$

(2) We now take into account the compressibility of water and ice. The change in the volume of water and ice will be

$$\Delta V' = \frac{p_1}{p'} 10^{-2} V_{0w} + \frac{p_1}{2p'} 10^{-2} V_{0ice} \simeq 2 \times 10^{-6} \text{m}^3,$$

where $V_{0w} = 10^{-3}$ m^3 and $V_{0\,ice} = 1.1 \times 10^{-3}$ m^3

are the initial volumes of water and ice.

The work A' done by the external force to compress the mixture is

$$A' = \frac{p_1 \Delta V'}{2} \simeq 2.5 \text{ J}.$$

The total work of the external force is

$$A_{tot} = A + A' \simeq 3 \text{ J}.$$

Obviously, since we again have $A_{tot} \ll \Delta Q$, the mass of the ice that has melted will be the same as in case (1).

2.31. Considering that the gas density is $\rho = M / V$, we can write the equation of state for water vapour in the form $p = (\rho / \mu) RT$, where ρ and μ are the density and molar mass of water vapour. Boiling takes place when the saturated vapour pressure becomes equal to the atmospheric pressure.

If the boiling point of the salted water has been raised at a constant atmospheric pressure, it means that the density of saturated water vapour must have decreased.

2.32. Let us consider a cycle embracing the triple point: $A \to B \to C \to A$ (Fig. 203). The following phase transitions occur in turn: melting $\to$ vaporization $\to$ condensation of gas directly into the solid. Provided that the cycle infinitely converges to the triple point, we obtain from the first law of thermodynamics for the mass m of a substance

$$m\lambda + mq - mv = 0$$

since the work of the system during a cycle is zero, there is no inflow of heat from outside, and hence the total change in the internal energy is also equal to zero (the right-hand side of the equation).

Hence we can find the latent heat of sublimation of water at the triple point: $v = \lambda + q = 2.82 \times 10^6$ J/kg.

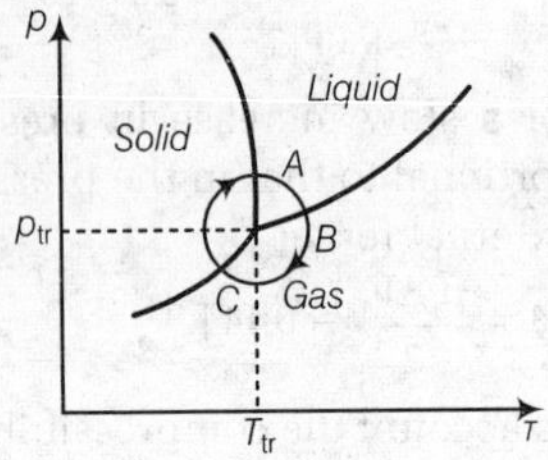

Fig. 203

2.33. The concentration of the solution of sugar poured above a horizontal surface practically remains unchanged.

After the equilibrium sets in, the concentration of the solution in the vessel will be $c = \dfrac{c_1 h_1}{h}$.

The concentration changes as a result of evaporation of water molecules from the surface (concentration increases) or as a result of condensation of vapour molecules into the vessel (concentration decreases). The saturated vapour pressure above the solution in the cylindrical vessel is lower than that above the solution at the bottom by $\Delta p = 0.05_{p_{sat}}\ (c - c_2)$. This difference in pressure is balanced by the pressure of the vapour column of height h:

$$\rho_v gh = 0.05 p_{sat}\ (c - c_2).$$

Hence we obtain $h = \dfrac{0.05\, p_{sat}\ (c - c_2)}{\rho vg}$.

The density ρ_v of vapour at a temperature $T = 293$ K can be found from the equation of state for an ideal gas:

$$\rho_v = -\frac{p_{sat}\ \mu}{RT}.$$

Thus, the height h of vapour column satisfies the quadratic equation

$$h = \frac{0.05 c_2 RT}{\mu g} \frac{2h_1}{h-1}.$$

Substituting the numerical values and solving the quadratic equation, we obtain $h \simeq 16.4$ cm.

It is interesting to note that, as follows from the problem considered above, if two identical vessels containing solutions of different concentrations are placed under the bell, the liquid will evaporate from the solution of a lower concentration. Conversely, water vapour will condense to the solution of a higher concentration.

Thus, the concentrations tend to level out. This phenomenon explains the wetting of sugar and salt in an atmosphere with a high moisture content.

2.34. Since the lower end of the duct is maintained at a temperature T_1 which is higher than the melting point of cast iron, the cast iron at the bottom will be molten. The temperature at the interface between the molten and solid cast iron is naturally equal to the melting point T_{melt}. Since the temperatures of the upper and lower ends of the duct are maintained constant, the amount of heat transferred per unit time through the duct cross-section must be the same in any region. In other words, the heat flux through the molten and solid cast iron must be the same (the brick duct is a poor heat conductor so that heat transfer through its walls can be neglected).

The heat flux is proportional to the thermal conductivity, the cross-sectional area, and the temperature difference per unit length. Let l_1 be the length of the lower part of the duct where the cast iron is molten, and l_2 be the length of the upper part where the cast iron is in the solid phase. Then we can write the condition of the constancy of heat flux in the form (the cross-sectional area of the duct is constant)

$$\frac{x_{liq}(T_1 - T_{melt})}{l_1} = \frac{x_{sol}(T_{melt} - T_2)}{l_2},$$

where x_{liq} and x_{sol} are the thermal conductivities of the liquid and solid cast iron. Considering that $x_{liq} = kx_{sol}$, we obtain

$$l_1 = \frac{l_2 k(T_1 - T_{melt})}{T_{melt} - T_2}.$$

The total length of the duct is $l_1 + l_2$. Therefore, the part of the duct occupied by the molten metal is determined from the relation

$$\frac{l_1}{l_1 + l_2} = \frac{k(T_1 - T_{melt})}{k(T_1 - T_{melt}) + (T_{melt} - T_2)}.$$

2.35*. The total amount of heat Q emitted in space per unit time remains unchanged since it is determined by the energy liberated during the operation of the appliances of the station. Since only the outer surface of the screen emits into space (this radiation depends only on its temperature), the temperature of the screen must be equal to the initial temperature $T = 500$ K of the station. However, the screen emits the same amount of heat Q inwards. This radiation reaches the envelope of the station and is absorbed by it. Therefore, the total amount of heat supplied to the station per unit time is the sum of the heat Q liberated during the operation of the appliances and the amount of heat Q absorbed by the inner surface of the screen, i.e. is equal to $2Q$. According to the heat balance condition, the same amount of heat must be emitted, and hence

$$\frac{Q}{2Q} = \frac{T^4}{T_x^4},$$

where T_x is the required temperature of the envelope of the station. Finally, we obtain $T_x = \sqrt[4]{2}T \simeq 600$ K.

2.36. It follows from the graph (see Fig. 67) that during the first 50 minutes the temperature of the mixture does not change and is equal to 0°C. The amount of heat received by the mixture from the room during this time is spent to melt ice. In 50 minutes, the whole ice melts and the temperature of water begins to rise.

In 10 minutes (from $\tau_1 = 50$ min to $\tau_2 = 60$ min), the temperature increases by $\Delta T = 2$ °C. The heat supplied to the water from the room during this time is $q = c_w m_w \Delta T = 84$ kJ. Therefore, the amount of heat received by the mixture from the room during the first 50 minutes is $Q = 5q = 420$ kJ. This amount of heat was spent for melting ice of mass m_{ice}: $Q = \lambda m_{ice}$. Thus, the mass of the ice contained in the bucket brought in the room is

$$m_{ice} = \frac{Q}{\lambda} \simeq 1.2 \text{ kg}.$$

2.37*. We denote by α the proportionality factor between the power dissipated in the resistor and the temperature difference between the resistor and the ambient. Since the resistance of the resistor is R_1 at $T_3 = 80$°C, and the voltage across it is U_1, the dissipated power is U_1^2 / R_1, and we can write

$$\frac{U_1^2}{R_1} = \alpha (T_3 - T_0). \quad (1)$$

The temperature of the resistor rises with the applied voltage since the heat liberated by the current increases. As the temperature becomes equal to $T_1 = 100$°C, the resistance of the resistor abruptly increases twofold. The heat liberated in it will decrease, and if the voltage is not very high, the heat removal turns out to be more rapid than the liberation of heat.

This leads to a temperature drop to $T_2 = 99$°C, which will cause an abrupt change in the resistance to its previous value, and the process will be repeated. Therefore, current oscillations caused by the jumpwise dependence of the resistance on temperature will emerge in the circuit.

During these oscillations, the temperature of the resistor is nearly constant (it varies between $T_2 = 99$ °C and $T_1 = 100$ °C) so that we can assume that the heat removal is constant, and the removed power is $\alpha (T_1 - T_0)$. Then, by introducing the time t_1 of heating (from 99 °C to 100 °C), the time t_2 of cooling, and the oscillation period $T = t_1 + t_2$, we can write the heat balance equations:

$$\frac{U_2^2 t_1}{R_1} = \alpha (T_1 - T_0) t_1 + C(T_1 - T_2),$$

$$\frac{U_2^2 t_2}{R_2} = \alpha (T_1 - T_0) t_2 - C(T_1 - T_2). \quad (2)$$

Using the value of α obtained from Eq. (1), we find that

$$t_1 = \frac{C(T_1 - T_2)}{U_2^2 / R_1 - U_1^2(T_1 - T_0)/[R_1(T_3 - T_0)]},$$

$$t_2 = \frac{C(T_1 - T_2)}{U_1^2(T_1 - T_0)/[R_1(T_3 - T_0)] - U_2^2 / R_2}.$$

Substituting the numerical values of the quantities, we obtain $t_1 = t_2 = 3/32$ s $\simeq 0.1$ s and $T \simeq 0.2$ s.

The maximum and minimum values of the current can easily be determined since the resistance abruptly changes from $R_1 = 50\ \Omega$ to $R_2 = 100\ \Omega$ in the process of oscillations. Consequently,

$$I_{max} = \frac{U_2}{R_1} = 1.6\ \text{A}\ ,\ I_{min} = \frac{U_2}{R_2} = 0.8\ \text{A}.$$

It should be noted that the situation described in the problem corresponds to a first-order phase transition in the material of the resistor. As a result of heating, the material goes over to a new phase at $T_1 = 100°C$ (this transition can be associated, for example, with the rearrangement of the crystal lattice of the resistor material). The reverse transition occurs at a lower temperature $T_2 = 99°C$. This phenomenon is known as hysteresis and is typical of first-order phase transitions.

2.38. Raindrops falling on the brick at first form a film on its surface (Fig. 204).

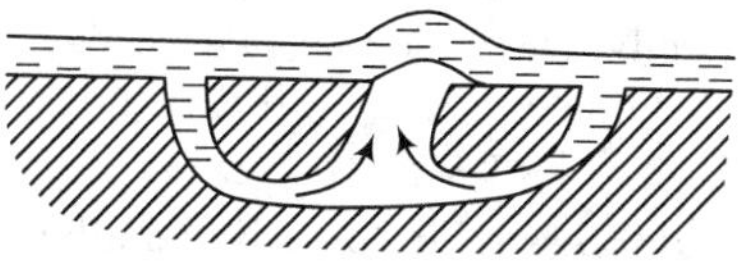

Fig. 204

The brick has a porous structure, and the pores behave like capillaries. Due to surface tension, water is sucked into pores-capillaries. The capillaries are interconnected and have various sizes, the number of narrow capillaries being larger. The force of surface tension sucking water in wide capillaries is weaker than the force acting in narrow capillaries.

For this reason, the water film in wide capillaries will bulge and break. This phenomenon is responsible for the hissing sounds.

2.39. The work A done by the gas is the sum of two components, viz. the work A_1 done against the force of atmospheric pressure and the work A_2 done against the force of gravity. The mercury-gas interface is shifted upon the complete displacement of mercury by $2l + l/2 = (5/2)l$, and hence $A_1 = \frac{5}{2} p_0 Sl$.

The work A_2 done against the force of gravity is equal to the change in the potential energy of mercury as a result of its displacement. The whole of mercury rises as a result of displacement by l relative to the horizontal part of the tube. This quantity should be regarded as the final height of the centre of mass of mercury. The initial position of the centre of mass of mercury is obviously $h_0 = l/8$. Hence we can conclude that

$$A_2 = Mg\left(l - \frac{l}{8}\right) = \frac{7}{8}Mgl,$$

where $M = 2lS\rho_{mer}$ is the mass of mercury.

Finally, we obtain

$$A = A_1 + A_2 = \frac{5}{2}p_0Sl + \frac{7}{4}\rho_{mer}gSl^2 \simeq 7.7\text{ J}.$$

2.40. The work A done by the external force as a result of the application and subsequent removal of the load is determined by the area $ABCD$ of the figure (see Fig. 69). According to the first law of thermodynamics, the change in the internal energy of the rod is equal to this work (the rod is thermally insulated), i.e.

$$\Delta W = A = kx_0(x - x_0).$$

On the other hand, $\Delta W = C\,\Delta T$, where ΔT is the change in the temperature of the rod, from which we obtain

$$\Delta T = \frac{\Delta W}{C} = \frac{kx_0(x - x_0)}{C}.$$

2.41. Let the cylinder be filled with water to a level x from the base. The c ınge in buoyancy is equal to the increase in the force of gravity acting on the cylinder with water. Hence we may conclude that $\Delta h = x$. From the equilibrium condition for the cylinder, we can write

$$p_2S = p_0S + mg,$$

where p_2 is the gas pressure in the cylinder after its filling with water, i.e. $p_2 = p_0 + mg/S$. Using Boyle's law, we can write $p_2(h - \Delta h) = p_1h$, where p_1 is the initial pressure of the gas. Finally, we obtain

$$p_1 = \frac{p_0 + mg/S}{1 - \Delta h/h}.$$

2.42. Let us choose the origin as shown in Fig. 205. Then the force acting on the wedge depends only on the x-coordinate of the shock front.

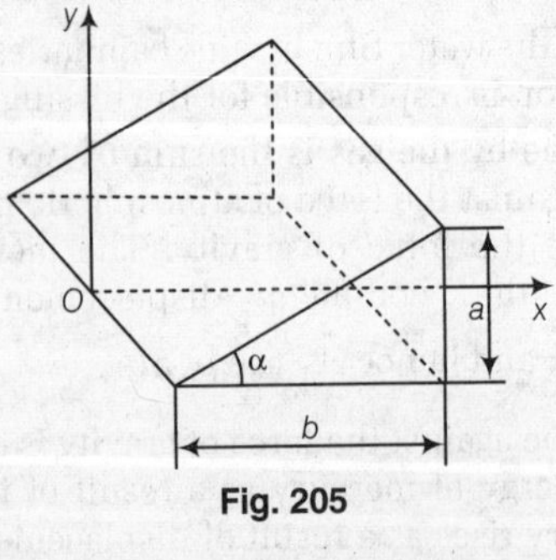

Fig. 205

The horizontal component of this force is

$$F_x = p_0 cx \tan\alpha = \frac{p_0 cxa}{b} = \frac{p_0 cavt}{b},$$

where $x = vt$ is the wavefront coordinate by the moment of time t from the beginning of propagation of the wave through the wedge. The acceleration imparted to the wedge at this moment of time is

$$a_t = \frac{F_x}{m} = \frac{p_0 cavt}{bm}.$$

At the moment of time t_0 when the wavefront reaches the rear face of the wedge, i.e. when the wavefront coordinate is $b = vt_0$, the acceleration of the wedge becomes

$$a_{t_0} = \frac{p_0 ca}{m}.$$

Since the acceleration of the wedge linearly depends on time, for calculating the velocity u of the wedge by the moment of time t_0 we can use the mean value of acceleration $a_m = p_0 ca/(2m)$:

$$u = a_m t_0 = \frac{p_0 abc}{2mv}.$$

When the entire wedge is in the region of an elevated pressure, the resultant force acting on the wedge is zero. The answer to the problem implies that the condition $u \ll v$ means that $p_0 \ll 2mv^2/(abc)$.

3. Electricity and Magnetism

3.1. Due to polarization of the insulator rod AB, the point charge $+q_1$ will be acted upon, in addition to the point charge $-q_2$, by the polarization charges formed at the ends of the rod (Fig. 206).

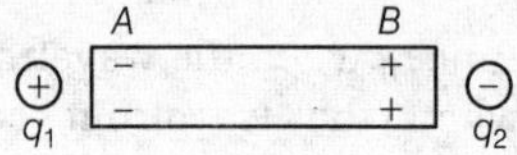

Fig. 206

The attractive force exerted by the negative charge induced at the end A will be stronger than the repulsive force exerted by the positive charge induced at the end B. Thus, the total force acting on the charge $+q_1$ will increase.

3.2. In the immediate proximity of each of point charges, the contribution from the other charge to the total field strength is negligibly small, and hence the electric field lines emerge from (enter) the charge in a spatially homogeneous bundle, their total number being proportional to the magnitude of the charge. Only a fraction of these lines gets into a cone with an angle 2α at the vertex near the charge $+q_1$. The ratio of the number of these lines to the total number of the lines emerging from the charge $+q_1$ is equal to the ratio of the areas of the corresponding spherical segments: $\dfrac{2\pi RR(1-\cos\alpha)}{4\pi R^2}=\dfrac{1}{2}(1-\cos\alpha)$.

Since the electric field lines connect the two charges of equal magnitude, the number of lines emerging from the charge $+q_1$ within the angle 2α is equal to the number of lines entering the charge $-q_2$ at an angle 2β. Consequently,

$$|q_1|(1-\cos\alpha)=|q_2|(1-\cos\beta),$$

whence
$$\sin\frac{\beta}{2}=\sin\frac{\alpha}{2}\sqrt{\frac{|q_1|}{q_2}}.$$

If $\sqrt{|q_1|/|q_2|}\,\sin(\alpha/2)>1$, an electric field line will not enter the charge $-q_2$.

3.3. Before solving this problem, let us formulate the theorem which will be useful for solving this and more complicated problems. Below we shall give the proof of this theorem applicable to the specific case considered in Problem 3.3.

If a charge is distributed with a constant density σ over a part of the spherical surface of radius R, the projection of the electric field strength due to this charge at the centre of the spherical surface on an arbitrary direction a is $E_a=\dfrac{1}{4\pi\varepsilon_0}\dfrac{\sigma}{R^2}S_{\perp a}$, where $S_{\perp a}$ is the area of the projection of the part of the surface on the plane perpendicular to the direction a.

Let us consider a certain region of the spherical surface ("lobule") and orient it as shown in Fig. 207, i.e. make the symmetry plane of the lobule coincide with the z- and x-axes. From the symmetry of charge distribution it follows that the total field strength at the origin of the coordinate system (point O) will be directed against the z-axis (if $\sigma > 0$), and the field strength components along the x-and y-axes will be zero.

Let us consider a small region of the surface ΔS of the lobule. The vertical component of the electric field strength at point O produced by the surface element ΔS is given by $\Delta E = \frac{1}{4\pi\varepsilon_0} \frac{\sigma}{R^2} \Delta S \cos\phi$,

where ϕ is the angle between the normal to the area element and the vertical.

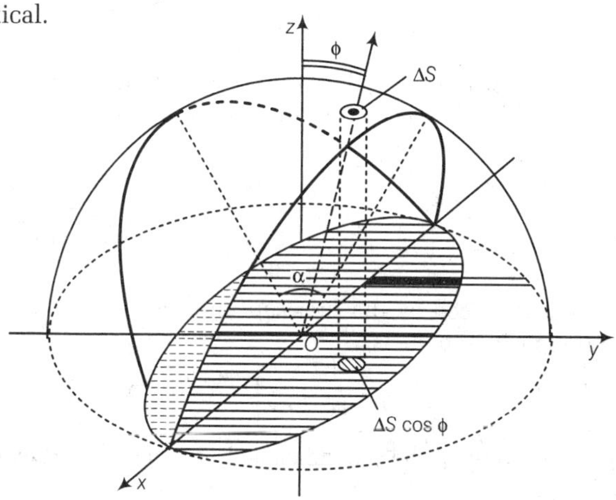

Fig. 207

But $\Delta S \cos\phi$ is the area of the projection of the element ΔS on the horizontal plane. Hence the total field strength at point O can be determined from the formula $E' = \frac{1}{4\pi\varepsilon_0} \frac{\sigma S}{R^2}$,

where S is the area of the hatched figure in Fig. 207, which is the projection of the lobule on the horizontal plane xOy. Since the area of any narrow strip of this region (black region in Fig. 207) is smaller than the area of the corresponding strip of the large circle by a factor of $\sin(\alpha/2)$, the entire area of the hatched region is smaller than the area of the large circle by a factor of $\sin(\alpha/2)$. Hence

$$E' = \frac{\sigma S}{4\pi\varepsilon_0 R^2} = \frac{\sigma}{4\pi\varepsilon_0 R^2} \pi R^2 \sin\frac{\alpha}{2} = \frac{\sigma \sin(\alpha/2)}{4\varepsilon_0}.$$

In the case of a hemisphere, $\alpha = \pi$ and $E = \frac{\sigma}{4\varepsilon_0}$.

3.4. It can easily be seen from symmetry considerations that the vector of the electric field strength produced by the "lobule" with an angle α lies in the planes of longitudinal and transverse symmetry of the lobule. Let the magnitude of this vector be E. Let us use the superposition principle and complement the lobule to a hemisphere charged with the same charge density. For this purpose, we append to the initial lobule another lobule with an angle $\pi - \alpha$. Let the magnitude of the electric field strength vector produced by this additional lobule at the centre of the sphere be E′. It can easily be seen that vectors **E** and **E′** are mutually perpendicular, and their vector sum is equal to the electric field vector of the hemisphere at its centre. By hypothesis, this sum is equal to E_0. Since the angle between vectors **E** and $\mathbf{E_0}$ is $\pi/2 - \alpha/2$, we obtain

$$E = E_0 \sin\frac{\alpha}{2}.$$

3.5*. Let us consider the case when the capacitors are oriented so that the plates with like charges face each other (Fig. 208).

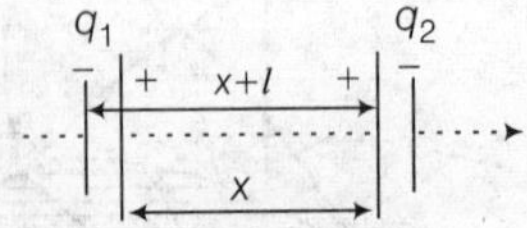

Fig. 208

The field produced by the first capacitor on the axis at a distance x from the positive plate is

$$E(x) = \frac{q_1}{4\pi\varepsilon_0}\left[\frac{1}{x^2} - \frac{1}{(x+l)^2}\right] \approx \frac{2q_1 l}{4\pi\varepsilon_0 x^3} \ (x \gg l).$$

The force acting on the second capacitor situated at a distance d from the first is

$$F = q_2[E(d) - E(d+l)] = \frac{q_1 q_2 l}{4\pi\varepsilon_0}\left[\frac{1}{d^3} - \frac{1}{(d+l)^3}\right] \approx \frac{3q_1 q_2 l^2}{2\pi\varepsilon_0 d^4}$$

Therefore, the capacitors will repel each other in this case.

A similar analysis can be carried out for the case when the capacitors are oriented so that the plates with unlike charges face each other. Then the capacitors will attract each other with the same force

$$F = \frac{3}{2}\frac{q_1 q_2 l^2}{\pi\varepsilon_0 d^4}.$$

3.6. We choose two small arbitrary elements belonging to the surfaces of the first and second hemispheres and having the areas ΔS_1 and ΔS_2. Let the separation between the two elements be r_{12}. The force of interaction between the two elements can be determined from Coulomb's law:

$$\Delta F_{12} = \frac{1}{4\pi\varepsilon_0}\frac{1}{r_{12}^2}\sigma_1 \Delta S_1 \sigma_2 \Delta S_2 = \frac{\Delta S_1 \Delta S_2}{4\pi\varepsilon_0 r_{12}^2}\sigma_1\sigma_2.$$

In order to determine the total force of interaction between the hemispheres, we must, proceeding from the superposition principle, sum up the forces ΔF_{12} for all the interacting pairs of elements so that the resultant force of interaction between the hemispheres is $F = k\sigma_1\sigma_2$,

where the coefficient k is determined only by the geometry of the charge distribution and by the choice of the system of units. If the hemispheres were charged with the same surface density σ, the corresponding force of interaction between the hemispheres would be

$$\widetilde{F} = k\sigma^2,$$

where the coefficient k is the same as in the previous formula.

Let us determine the force $\widetilde{F}$. For this purpose, we consider the "upper" hemisphere. Its small surface element of area ΔS carries a charge $\Delta q = \sigma\Delta S$ and experiences the action of the electric field whose strength E' is equal to half the electric field strength produced by the sphere having a radius R and uniformly charged with the surface density σ. (We must exclude the part produced by the charge Δq itself from the electric field strength.) The force acting on the charge Δq is end is directed along the normal to the surface element.

$$\Delta F = \Delta qE' = \sigma\Delta S\frac{1}{4\pi\varepsilon_0}\sigma\frac{4\pi R^2}{R^2 \cdot 2} = \frac{\sigma^2}{2\varepsilon_0}\Delta S$$

In order to find the force acting on the upper hemisphere, it should be noted that according to the expression for the force ΔF the hemisphere as if experiences the action of an effective pressure $p = \sigma^2/(2\varepsilon_0)$. Hence the resultant force acting on the upper hemisphere is

$$\widetilde{F} = p\pi R^2 = \frac{\sigma^2}{2\varepsilon_0}\pi R^2$$

(although not only the "lower" hemisphere, but all the elements of the "upper" hemisphere make a contribution to the expression ΔF for the force acting on the surface element ΔS, the forces of interaction between the elements of the upper hemisphere will be cancelled out in the general expression for the force of interaction between the hemispheres obtained above).

Since $\widetilde{F} = k\sigma^2$, we obtain the following expression for the force of interaction between the hemispheres for the case when they have different surface charge densities: $F = k\sigma_1\sigma_2 = \dfrac{\pi R^2}{2\varepsilon_0}\sigma_1\sigma_2$.

3.7. The density of charges induced on the sphere is proportional to the electric field strength: $\sigma \propto E$. The force acting on the hemispheres is proportional to the field strength: $F \propto \sigma SE \propto R^2E^2$,

where S is the area of the hemisphere, and R is its radius. As the radius of the sphere changes by a factor of n, and the field strength by a factor of k, the force will change by a factor of k^2n^2. Since the thickness of the sphere walls remains unchanged, the force tearing the sphere per unit length must remain unchanged, i.e. $k^2n^2 / n = 1$ and $k = 1/\sqrt{n} = 1/\sqrt{2}$. Consequently, the minimum electric field strength capable of tearing the conducting shell of twice as large radius is $E_1 = \dfrac{E_0}{\sqrt{2}}$.

3.8. Let l be the distance from the large conducting sphere to each of the small balls, d the separation between the balls, and r the radius of each ball. If we connect the large sphere to the first ball, their potentials become equal:
$$\frac{1}{4\pi\varepsilon_0}\left(\frac{Q}{l}+\frac{q_1}{r}\right)=\phi. \qquad (1)$$
Here Q is the charge of the large sphere, and ϕ is its potential. If the large sphere is connected to the second ball, we obtain a similar equation corresponding to the equality of the potentials of the large sphere and the second ball:
$$\frac{1}{4\pi\varepsilon_0}\left(\frac{Q}{l}+\frac{q_1}{d}+\frac{q_2}{r}\right)=\phi. \qquad (2)$$
(We assume that the charge and the potential of the large sphere change insignificantly in each charging of the balls.) When the large sphere is connected to the third ball, the first and second balls being charged, the equation describing the equality of potentials has the form
$$\frac{1}{4\pi\varepsilon_0}\left(\frac{Q}{l}+\frac{q_1}{d}+\frac{q_2}{d}+\frac{q_3}{r}\right)=\phi. \qquad (3)$$
The charge q_3 can be found by solving the system of equations (1)-(3):
$$q_3=\frac{q_2^2}{q_1}.$$

3.9. The charge q_1 of the sphere can be determined from the formula $q_1 = 4\pi\varepsilon_0\phi_1 r_1$.
After the connection of the sphere to the envelope, the entire charge q_1 will flow from the sphere to the envelope and will be distributed uniformly over its surface. Its potential ϕ_2 (coinciding with the new value of the potential of the sphere) will be
$$\phi_2=\frac{q_1}{4\pi\varepsilon_0 r_2}=\phi_1\frac{r_1}{r_2}.$$

3.10. We shall write the condition of the equality to zero of the potential of the sphere, and hence of any point inside it (in particular, its centre), by the moment of time t. We shall single out three time intervals:
(1) $t<\dfrac{a}{v}$, (2) $\dfrac{a}{v}\le t<\dfrac{b}{v}$, (3) $t\ge\dfrac{b}{v}$.
Denoting the charge of the sphere by $q(t)$, we obtain the following expression for an instant t from the first time interval:
$$\frac{q_1}{a}+\frac{q_2}{b}+\frac{q(t)}{vt}=0,$$

whence $q(t) = -v\left(\frac{q_1}{a} + \frac{q_2}{b}\right)t, \qquad I_1(t) = -v\left(\frac{q_1}{a} + \frac{q_2}{b}\right).$

For an instant t from the second time interval, we find that the fields inside and outside the sphere are independent, and hence

$$\frac{q(t) + q_1}{vt} = -\frac{q_2}{b}, \qquad I_2(t) = -v\frac{q_2}{b}.$$

Finally, as soon as the sphere absorbs the two point charges q_1 and q_2, the current will stop flowing through the "earthing" conductor, and we can write $I_3(t) = 0$.

Thus,
$$I(t) = \begin{cases} -v\left(\frac{q_1}{a} + \frac{q_2}{b}\right), & t < \frac{a}{v}, \\ -v\frac{q_2}{b}, & \frac{a}{v} \le t < \frac{b}{v}, \\ 0, & t \ge \frac{b}{v}. \end{cases}$$

3.11. Taking into account the relation between the capacitance, voltage, and charge of a capacitor, we can write the following equations for the three capacitors:

$$\phi_A - \phi_0 = \frac{q_1}{C_1}, \qquad \phi_B - \phi_0 = \frac{q_2}{C_2}, \qquad \phi_D - \phi_0 = \frac{q_3}{C_3},$$

where C_1, C_2, and C_3 are the capacitances of the corresponding capacitors, and q_1, q_2 and q_3 are the charges on their plates. According to the charge conservation law, $q_1 + q_2 + q_3 = 0$, and hence the potential of the common point O is

$$\phi_0 = \frac{\phi_A C_1 + \phi_B C_2 + \phi_D C_3}{C_1 + C_2 + C_3}.$$

3.12*. Since the sheet is metallic, the charges must be redistributed over its surface so that the field in the bulk of the sheet is zero. In the first approximation, we can assume that this distribution is uniform and has density $-\sigma$ and σ over the upper and the lower surface respectively of the sheet. According to the superposition principle, we obtain the condition for the absence of the field in the bulk of the sheet:

$$\frac{q}{4\pi\varepsilon_0 l^2} - \frac{\sigma}{\varepsilon_0} = 0.$$

Let us now take into consideration the nonuniformity of the field produced by the point charge since it is the single cause of the force F of interaction. The upper surface of the sheet must be attracted with a force $\sigma Sq / (4\pi\varepsilon_0 l^2)$, while the lower surface must be repelled with a force $\sigma Sq / [4\pi\varepsilon_0 (l + d)^2]$. Consequently, the force of attraction of the sheet to the charge is

$$F = \frac{\sigma Sq}{4\pi\varepsilon_0 l^2}\left[1 - \frac{1}{(1 + d/l)^2}\right] \approx \frac{q^2 Sd}{8\pi^2\varepsilon_0 l^5}.$$

3.13. It can easily be seen that the circuit diagram proposed in the problem is a "regular" tetrahedron whose edges contain six identical capacitors.

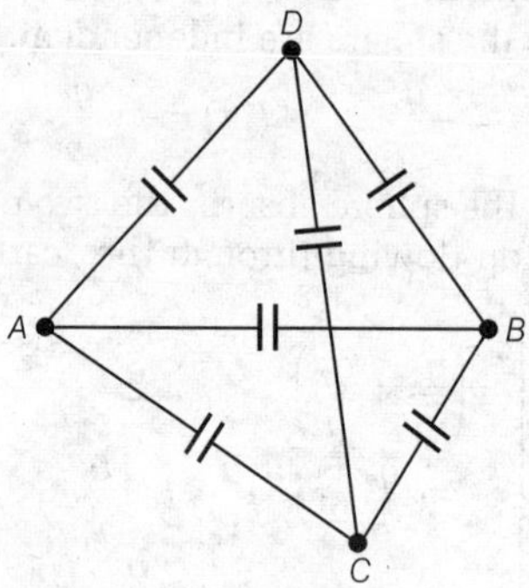

Fig. 209

Therefore, we conclude from the symmetry considerations that irrespective of the pair of points between which the current source is connected, there always exists an uncharged capacitor in the circuit (the capacitor in the edge crossed with the edge containing the source). For example, if the current source is connected between points A and B in Fig. 209, the capacitor between points C and D will be uncharged since the potentials of points C and D are equal.

3.14. The capacitance of the nonlinear capacitor is

$$C = \varepsilon C_0 = \alpha U C_0,$$

where C_0 is the capacitance of the capacitor without a dielectric. The charge on the nonlinear capacitor is $q_n = CU = \alpha C_0 U^2$, while the charge on the normal capacitor is $q_0 = C_0 U$. It follows from the charge conservation law $q_n + q_0 = C_0 U_0$

that the required voltage is $U = \dfrac{\sqrt{4\alpha U_0 + 1} - 1}{2\alpha} = 12\text{ V}.$

3.15. Let us go over to the inertial reference frame fixed to the moving centre of the thread. Then the balls have the same velocity v at the initial instant. The energy stored initially in the system is

$$W_1 = \frac{q^2}{4\pi\varepsilon_0 \cdot 2l} + \frac{2mv^2}{2}.$$

At the moment of the closest approach, the energy of the system is

$$W_2 = \frac{q^2}{4\pi\varepsilon_0 d}.$$

Using the energy conservation law, we find that

$$d = \frac{2lq^2}{q^2 + 8\pi\varepsilon_0 mv^2 l}.$$

3.16. Let v_1 and v_2 be the velocities of the first and second balls after the removal of the uniform electric field. By hypothesis, the angle between the velocity v_1 and the initial velocity v is 60°. Therefore, the change in the momentum of the first ball is $\Delta p_1 = q_1 E\,\Delta t = m_1 v \sin 60°$.

Here we use the condition that $v_1 = v/2$, which implies that the change in the momentum Δp_1 of the first ball occurs in a direction perpendicular to the direction of its velocity v_1.

Since $E \,||\, \Delta p_1$ and the direction of variation of the second ball momentum is parallel to the direction of Δp_1, we obtain for the velocity of the second ball (it can easily be seen that the charges on the balls have the same sign) $v_2 = v \tan 30° = \dfrac{v}{\sqrt{3}}$.

The corresponding change in the momentum of the second ball is

$$\Delta p_2 = q_2 E \Delta t = \frac{m_2 v}{\cos 30°}.$$

Hence we obtain $\dfrac{q_1}{q_2} = \dfrac{m_1 \sin 60°}{m_2 / \cos 30°}$, $\dfrac{q_2}{m_2} = \dfrac{4}{3}\dfrac{q_1}{m_1} = \dfrac{4}{3} k_1$.

3.17. The kinetic energy of the first ball released at infinity (after a long time) can be determined from the energy conservation law:

$$\frac{mv_1^2}{2} = \frac{q^2}{4\pi\varepsilon_0}\left(\frac{1}{a_1} + \frac{1}{a_2} + \ldots + \frac{1}{a_{N-1}}\right),$$

where $a_1, a_2, \ldots, a_{N-1}$ are the distances from the first ball (before it was released) to the remaining balls in the circle, a_1 and a_{N-1} being the distances to the nearest neighbours, i.e. $a_1 = a_{N-1} = a$ $(N = 1977)$.

Analyzing the motion of the second ball, we neglect the influence of the first released ball. Then

$$\frac{mv_2^2}{2} = \frac{q^2}{4\pi\varepsilon_0}\left(\frac{1}{a_1} + \frac{1}{a_2} + \ldots + \frac{1}{a_{N-2}}\right),$$

i.e. one of the nearest neighbours is missing in the parentheses. Therefore,

$$K = \frac{mv_1^2}{2} - \frac{mv_2^2}{2} = \frac{q^2}{4\pi\varepsilon_0 a}, \quad \text{or} \quad q = \sqrt{4\pi\varepsilon_0 K a}.$$

3.18. According to the momentum conservation law, $mv = (m + M)u$,

where m is the mass of the accelerated particle, M is the mass of the atom, and u is their velocity immediately after the collision.

We denote by W_{ion} the ionization energy and write the energy conservation law in the form,

$$\frac{mv^2}{2} = W_{\text{ion}} + \frac{(m + M)u^2}{2}.$$

Eliminating the velocity u from these equations, we obtain

$$\frac{mv^2}{2} = W_{\text{ion}}\left(1 + \frac{m}{M}\right).$$

If m is the electron mass, then $m/M << 1$, and the kinetic energy required for the ionization is $\frac{mv^2}{2} \approx W_{\text{ion}}$.

When an atom collides with an ion of mass $m \approx M$, $mv^2/2 \approx 2W_{\text{ion}}$, i.e. the energy of the ion required for the ionization must be twice as high as the energy of the electron.

3.19. From the equality of the electric and elastic forces acting on the free ball,

$$\frac{q^2}{4\pi\varepsilon_0 \cdot 4l^2} = kl$$

we obtain the following expression for the length l of the unstretched spring: $l^3 = \frac{q^2}{16\pi\varepsilon_0 k}$,

where k is the rigidity of the spring, and q are the charges of the balls. Let us suppose that the free ball is deflected from the equilibrium position by a distance x which is small in comparison with l. The potential energy of the system depends on x as follows:

$$W(x) = \frac{1}{2}k(l - x)^2 + \frac{q^2}{4\pi\varepsilon_0(2l - x)} \approx \frac{5}{2}kl^2 + kx^2.$$

Here we have taken into account the relation between q_1, k, and l obtained above and retain the terms of the order of $[x/(2l)]^2$ in the expression $\frac{1}{2l - x} = \frac{1}{2l(1 - x/2l)} = \frac{1}{2l}\left[1 + \left(\frac{x}{2l}\right) + \left(\frac{x}{2l}\right)^2 + \ldots\right]$.

Thus, it is as if the stretched spring has double the rigidity, and the ratio of the frequencies of harmonic vibrations of the system is $\frac{\nu_2}{\nu_1} = \frac{\sqrt{2k}}{\sqrt{k}} = \sqrt{2}$.

3.20. Let us consider the two charged balls to be a single mechanical system. The Coulomb interaction between the balls is internal, and hence it does not affect the motion of the centre of mass. The only external force acting on the system is the force of gravity. It is only this force that will determine the motion of the centre of mass of the system. Since the masses of the balls are equal, the initial position of the centre of mass is at a height $(h_1 + h_2)/2$, and its initial velocity v is horizontal. Then the centre of mass will move along a parabola characterized by the following equation:

$$h = \frac{h_1 + h_2}{2} - \left(\frac{g}{2}\right)\left(\frac{x}{v}\right)^2, \quad (1)$$

where x is the horizontal coordinate of the centre of mass, and h is its vertical coordinate. At the moment the first ball touches the ground at a distance $x = l$, the height H of the centre of mass, according to expression (1), is

$$H = \frac{h_1 + h_2}{2} - \left(\frac{g}{2}\right)\left(\frac{l}{v}\right)^2.$$

Since the masses of the balls are equal, the second ball must be at a height $H_2 = 2H$ at this instant. Therefore,

$$H_2 = h_1 + h_2 - g\left(\frac{l}{v}\right)^2.$$

3.21. Let the resistance of half the turn be R. Then in the former case, we have fifteen resistors of resistance R connected in parallel, the total resistance being $R/15$.

In the latter case, we have the same fifteen resistors connected in series, the total resistance being $15R$. Therefore, as a result of unwinding, the resistance of the wire will increase by a factor of 225.

3.22. It can easily be noted from symmetry considerations that the potentials of points A and C (Fig. 210) at any instant of time will be the same. Therefore, the closure of the key K will not lead to any change in the operation of the circuit, and the coil AC will not be heated.

3.23. After adding two conductors, the circuit will acquire the form shown in Fig. 211. From symmetry considerations, we conclude that the central conductor will not participate in electric charge transfer.

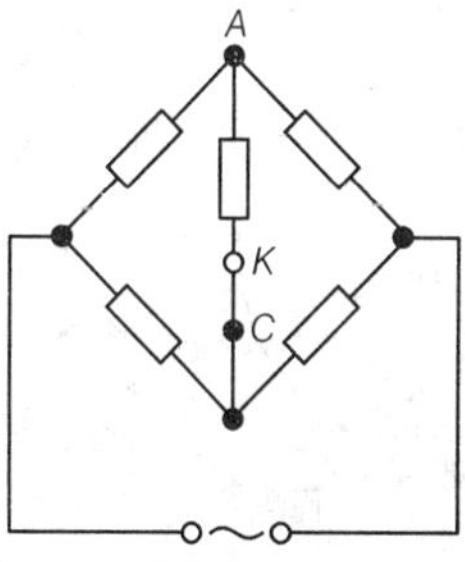

Fig. 210

Therefore, if the initial resistance R_1 of the circuit was $5r$, where r is the resistance of a conductor,

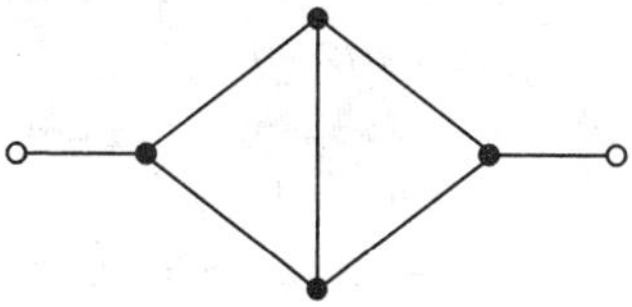

Fig. 211

the new resistance of the circuit will become

$$R_2 = 2r + \frac{2r}{2} = 3r.$$

Therefore, $$\frac{R_2}{R_1} = \frac{3}{5}.$$

3.24. The total resistance R_{AB} of the frame can easily be calculated by noting from symmetry considerations that there is no current in the edge $CD: R_{AB} = R/2$, where R is the resistance of an edge. Therefore, $I = \frac{2U}{R}$, where U is the applied voltage.

The total current can be changed in two ways:

(1) if we remove one of the edges *AD*, *AC*, *BC* or *BD*, the change in the current will be the same;

(2) if we remove the edge *AB*, the change will be different. In the first case, the change in the current will be $\Delta I = -(2/5)\,U/R = -I/5$, and in the second case, the total resistance will be R, and hence $\Delta I = -U/R = -I/2 = \Delta I_{max}$.

3.25. It follows from symmetry considerations that the potentials of points C and D are equal. Therefore, this circuit can be replaced by an equivalent one (we combine the junctions C and D, Fig. 212).

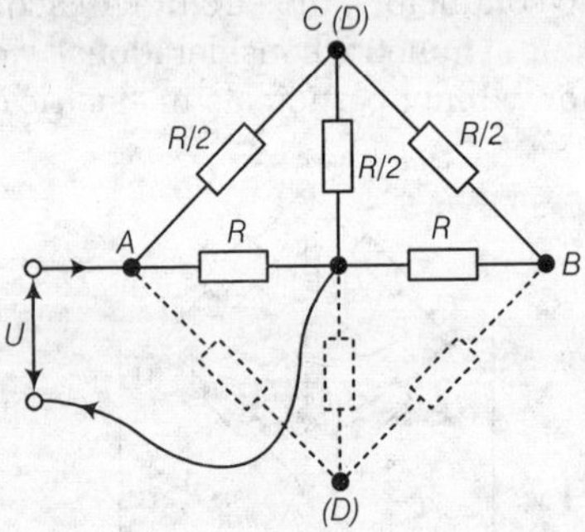

Fig. 212

The resistance between points A and B of the circuit can be determined from the formulas for parallel and series connection of conductors:

$$R_{C(D)B} = \frac{R/2(R/2 + R)}{R/2 + R/2 + R} = \frac{3}{4}\frac{R}{2} = \frac{3}{8}R,$$

$$R_{AC(D)B} = \frac{R}{2} + \frac{3}{8}R = \frac{7}{8}R,\; R_{AB} = \frac{R(7/8)\,R}{R + (7/8)\,R} = \frac{7}{15}R.$$

Thus, the current I in the leads can be determined from the formula

$$I = \frac{U}{(7/15)R} = \frac{15}{7}\frac{U}{R}.$$

3.26*. In order to simplify the solution, we present the circuit in a more symmetric form (Fig. 213). The obtained circuit cannot be simplified by connecting or disconnecting junctions (or by removing some conductors) so as to obtain parallel- or series-connected subcircuits. However, any problem involving a direct current has a single solution, which we shall try to "guess" by using the symmetry of the circuit and the similarity of the currents in the circuit.

Let us apply a voltage U to the circuit and mark currents through each element of the circuit.

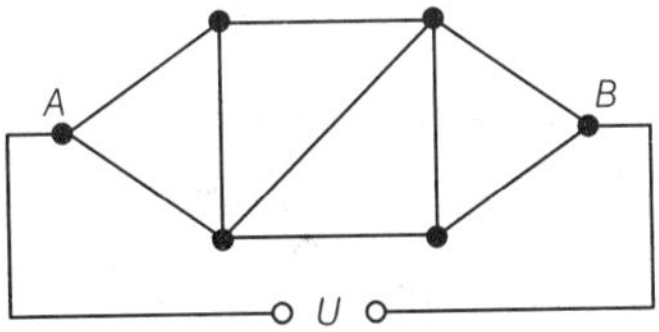

Fig. 213

We shall require not nine values of current (as in the case of arbitrary resistances of circuit elements) but only five values I_1, I_2, I_3, I_4, and I_5 (Fig. 214). For such currents, Kirchhoff's first rule for the junction C

$$I_1 = I_3 + I_5$$

and for the junction D

$$I_2 + I_3 = I_4 + I_5$$

will automatically be observed for the junctions E and F (this is due to the equality of the resistances of all resistors of the circuit).

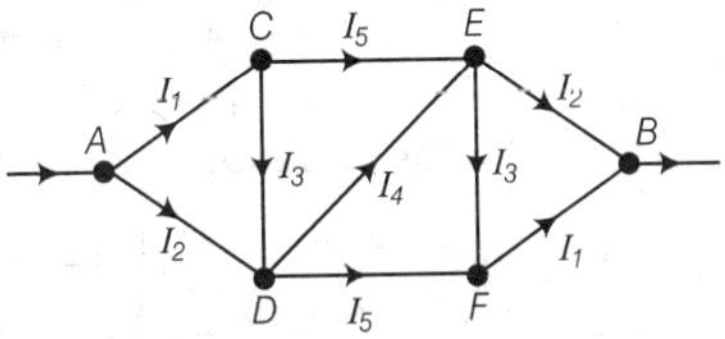

Fig. 214

Let us now write Kirchhoff's second rule in order to obtain a system of five independent equations:

$$(I_2 + I_5 + I_1)R = U,$$
$$(I_3 + I_4)R = I_5R,$$
$$(I_1 + I_3)R = I_2R,$$

where R is the resistance of each resistor. Solving this system of five equations, we shall express all the currents in terms of I_1:

$$I_2 = \frac{6}{5}I_1, \quad I_3 = \frac{I_1}{5}, \quad I_4 = \frac{3}{5}I_1, \quad I_5 = \frac{4}{5}I_1.$$

Besides, $U = \left(I_1 + \frac{4}{5}I_1 + \frac{6}{5}I_1\right)R.$

Consequently, $U / I_1 = R$.

Considering that the resistance R_{AB} of the circuit satisfies the equation $R_{AB} = U/(I_1 + I_2)$, we obtain

$$R_{AB} = \frac{U}{I_1 + I_2} = \frac{U}{I_1 + (6/5)I_1} = \frac{5}{11}\frac{U}{I_1}.$$

Taking into account the relation obtained above, we get the following expression for the required resistance: $R_{AB} = \frac{15}{11}R.$

3.27 It follows from symmetry considerations that the initial circuit can be replaced by an equivalent one (Fig. 215).

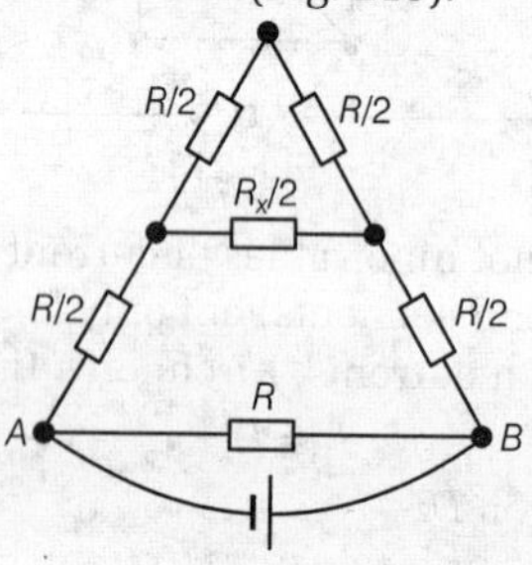

Fig. 215

We replace the "inner" triangle consisting of an infinite number of elements by a resistor of resistance $R_{AB} / 2$, where the resistance R_{AB} is such that $R_{AB} = R_x$ and $R_{AB} = a\rho$. After simplification, the circuit becomes a system of series- and parallel-connected conductors. In order to find R_x, we write the equation

$$R_x = R\left(R + \frac{RR_x/2}{R + R_x/2}\right)\left(R + R + \frac{RR_x/2}{R + R_x/2}\right)^{-1}$$

Solving this equation, we obtain $R_{AB} = R_x = \frac{R(\sqrt{7}-1)}{3} = \frac{a\rho(\sqrt{7}-1)}{3}.$

3.28. It follows from symmetry considerations that if we remove the first element from the circuit, the resistance of the remaining circuit between points C and D will be $R_{CD} = kR_{AB}$. Therefore, the equivalent circuit of the infinite chain will have the form shown in Fig. 216.

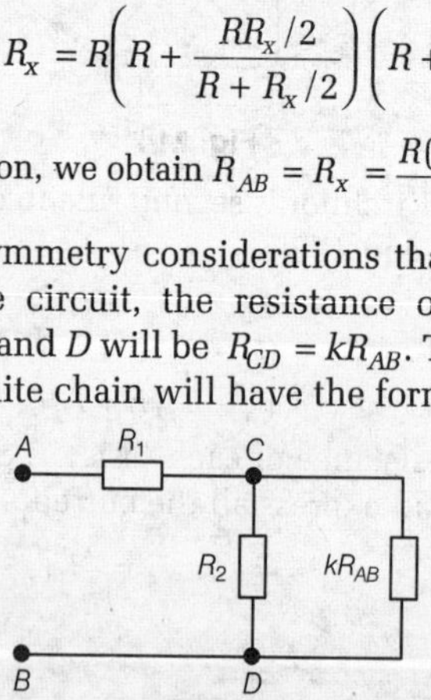

Fig. 216

Applying to this circuit the formulas for the resistance of series- and parallel-connected resistors, we obtain

$$R_{AB} = \frac{R_1 + R_2 kR_{AB}}{R_2 + kR_{AB}}.$$

Solving the quadratic equation for R_{AB}, we obtain (in particular, for $k = 1/2$)

$$R_{AB} = \frac{R_1 - R_2 + \sqrt{R_1^2 + R_2^2 + 6R_1 R}}{2}.$$

3.29. The potentiometer with the load is equivalent to a resistor of resistance

$$R_1 = \frac{R}{2} + \frac{RR/2}{R + R/2} = \frac{5}{6}R.$$

Hence the total current in the circuit will be $I_1 = \dfrac{U}{(5/6)R} = \dfrac{6}{5}\dfrac{U}{R}.$

The voltage across the load will be

$$U_{1l} = U - I_1 \frac{R}{2} = \frac{2}{5}U.$$

If the resistance of the load becomes equal to $2R$, the total current will be

$$I_2 = \frac{U}{\dfrac{R}{2} + \dfrac{(R/2)(2R)}{R/2 + 2R}} = \frac{10}{9}\frac{U}{R}.$$

The voltage across the load will become

$$U_{21} = U - I_2 \frac{R}{2} = \frac{4}{9}U.$$

Thus, the voltage across the load will change by a factor of $k = U_{21} / U_{11}$:

$$k = \frac{U_{21}}{U_{11}} = \frac{10}{9}.$$

3.30. In the former case, the condition $I_1 = I_2$ is fulfilled, where $I_1 = \alpha_1 n_1$ and $I_2 = \alpha_2 n_2$. Consequently, $\alpha_1 n_1 = \alpha_2 n_2$. In the latter case, $I'_1 R_1 = I'_2 R_x$, where R_x is the resistance of the second resistor. Besides, $I'_1 = \alpha_1 n'_1$ and $I'_2 = \alpha_2 n'_2$, and hence

$$R_1 \alpha_1 n'_1 = R_x \alpha_2 n'_2.$$

Finally, we obtain

$$\frac{R_1 n'_1}{n_1} = \frac{R_x n'_2}{n_2}.$$

Therefore, $$R_x = \frac{R_1 n_2 n'_1}{n_1 n'_2}.$$

3.31. The condition required for heating and melting the wire is that the amount of Joule heat liberated in the process must be larger than the amount of heat dissipated to the ambient:

$$I^2R > kS(T - T_{am}).$$

By hypothesis, the current required for melting the first wire must exceed 10 A. Therefore, $k.4d_1l(T_{melt} - T_{am}) = I_1^2R_1$,

where l is the length of the wires, T_{melt} is the melting point of the wire material, and I_1 and R_1 are the current and resistance of the first wire. The resistance of the second wire is $R_2 = R_1/16$. Therefore, the current I_2 required for melting the second wire must satisfy the relation

$$I_2^2R_2 > k \cdot 4d_2l(T_{melt} - T_{am}).$$

Finally, we obtain

$$I_2 > 8I_1 = 80 \text{ A}.$$

3.32. Let the emf of the second source be ξ_2 .Then, by hypothesis,

$$I = \frac{\xi_1 + \xi_2}{R + R_x} = \frac{\xi_2}{R},$$

where R is the resistance of the varying resistor for a constant current. Hence we obtainthe answer:

$$R_x = \frac{\xi_1}{I}.$$

3.33. The current through the circuit before the source of emf ξ_2 is short-circuited satisfies the condition $I_1 = \dfrac{\xi_1 + \xi_2}{R + r_1 + r_2}$,

where r_1 and r_2 are the internal resistances of the current sources. After the short-circuiting of the second source of emf ξ_2, the current through the resistor of resistance R can be determined from the formula

$$I_2 = \frac{\xi_1}{R + r_1}.$$

Obviously, if

$$\frac{\xi_1}{R + r_1} > \frac{\xi_2 + \xi_1}{R + r_1 + r_2},$$

the answer will be affirmative.

Thus, if the inequality $\xi_1(R + r_1 + r_2) > (\xi_1 + \xi_2)(R + r_1)$ is satisfied, and hence $\xi_1r_2 > \xi_2(R + r_1)$, the current in the circuit increases. If, on the contrary, $\xi_1r_2 < \xi_2(R + r_1)$, the short-circuiting of the current source leads to a decrease in the current in the circuit.

3.34*. Let us make use of the fact that any "black box" circuit consisting of resistors can be reduced to a form (Fig. 217),

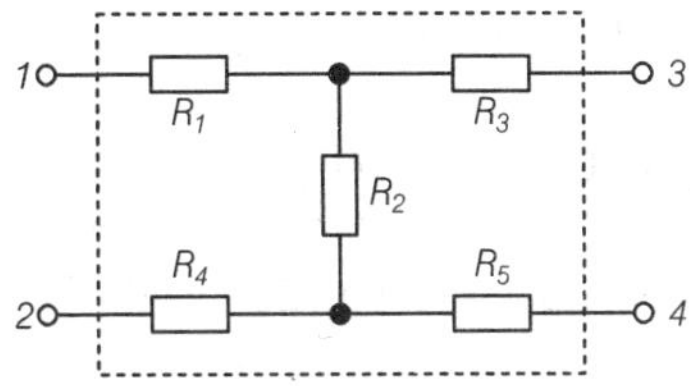

Fig. 217

where the quantities $R_1, R_2, \ldots, R_5$ are expressed in terms of the resistances of the initial resistors of the "black box" circuit (this can be verified by using in the initial circuit the transformations of the star-delta type and reverse transformations).

By hypothesis, equal currents pass each time through resistors of resistance R_1 and R_4 and also through R_3 and R_5 (or there is no current through them when the clamps are disconnected). Using this circumstance, we can simplify the circuit as shown in Fig. 218. Then, by hypothesis,

$$N_1 = \frac{U^2}{R'_1 + R'_2}, \quad N_2 = \frac{U^2}{R'_1 + R'_2 R'_3/(R'_2 + R'_3)},$$

$$N_3 = \frac{U^2}{R'_2 + R_3}, \quad N_4 = \frac{U^2}{R'_3 + R'_1 R'_2/(R'_1 + R'_2)}.$$

It can easily be verified that

$$N_1 N_4 = N_2 N_3 .$$

Consequently,
$$N_4 = \frac{N_2 N_3}{N_1} = 40 \text{ W}.$$

3.35. At the first moment after the connection of the key K, the capacitors are not charged, and hence the voltage between points A and B is zero (see Fig. 93).

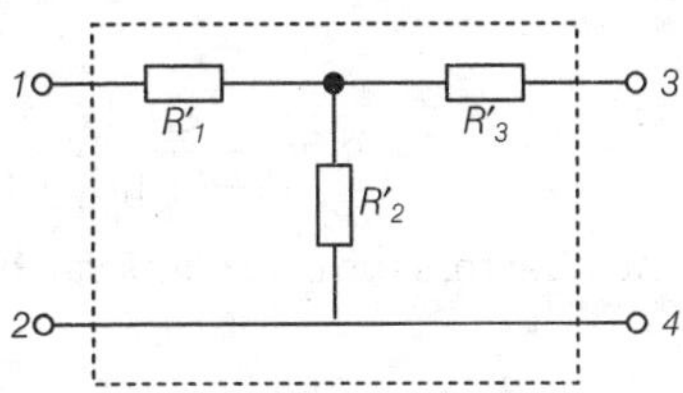

Fig. 218

The current in the circuit at this instant can be determined from the condition

$$I_1 = \frac{\xi}{R_1}.$$

Under steady-state conditions, the current between points A and B will pass through the resistors R_1 and R_3. Therefore, the current passing through these conductors after a long time is $I_2 = \frac{\xi}{R_1 + R_3}$.

3.36. Let us consider the steady-state conditions when the voltage across the capacitor practically does not change and is equal on the average to U_{st}. When the key is switched to position *1*, the charge on the capacitor will change during a short time interval Δt by

$$\frac{\Delta t\,(\xi_1 - U_{st})}{R_1}.$$

When the key is switched to position *2*, the charge will change by

$$\frac{\Delta t\,(\xi_2 - U_{st})}{R_2}.$$

During cycle, the total change in charge must be zero:

$$\frac{(\xi_1 - U_{st})}{R_1} + \frac{(\xi_2 - U_{st})}{R_2} = 0.$$

Hence the voltage U_{st} and the capacitor charge q_{st} in the steady state can be found from the formulas

$$U_{st} = \frac{\xi_2 R_1 + \xi_1 R_2}{R_1 + R_2},\quad q_{st} = CU_{st} = \frac{C\,(\xi_2 R_1 + \xi_1 R_2)}{R_1 + R_2}.$$

3.37. A direct current cannot pass through the capacitors of capacitance C_1 and C_2. Therefore, in the steady state, the current through the current source is

$$I = \frac{\xi}{r + R_2}.$$

Since the capacitors are connected in series, their charges q will be equal, and

$$\frac{q}{C_1} + \frac{q}{C_2} = IR_2.$$

Consequently,

$$q = \frac{\xi R_2 C_1 C_2}{(r + R_2)(C_1 + C_2)}.$$

The voltages U_1 and U_2 across the capacitors can be calculated from the formulas

$$U_1 = \frac{q}{C_1} = \frac{\xi R_2 C_2}{(r + R_2)(C_1 + C_2)},$$

$$U_2 = \frac{q}{C_2} = \frac{\xi R_2 C_1}{(r + R_2)(C_1 + C_2)}$$

respectively.

3.38*. We shall mentally connect in series two perfect (having zero internal resistance) current sources of emf's equal to $-U_0$ and U_0 between points A and F. Obviously, this will not introduce any change in the circuit. The dependence of the current through the resistor of resistance R on the emf's of the sources will have the form

$$I = \alpha\xi - \beta U_0 + \beta U_0,$$

where ξ is the emf of the source contained in the circuit, and the coefficients α and β depend on the resistance of the circuit.

If we connect only one perfect source of emf equal to $-U_0$ between A and F, the potential difference between A and B will become zero. Therefore, the first two terms in the equation for I will be compensated: $I = \beta U_0$. The coefficient β is obviously equal to $1/(R + R_{\text{eff}})$, where R_{eff} is the resistance between A and B when the resistor R is disconnected. This formula is also valid for the case $R = 0$, which corresponds to the connection of the ammeter. In this case,

$$I_0 = \frac{U_0}{R_{\text{eff}}}.$$

Consequently, the required current is

$$I = \frac{U_0 I_0}{RI_0 + U_0}.$$

3.39. When the key K is closed, the voltage across the capacitor is maintained constant and equal to the emf ξ of the battery. Let the displacement of the plate B upon the attainment of the new equilibrium position be $-x_1$. In this case, the charge on the capacitor is $q_1 = C_1\,\xi = \varepsilon_0\, S\xi\,/(d - x_1)$, where S is the area of the capacitor plates.

The field strength in the capacitor is $E_1 = \xi\,/\,(d - x_1)$, but it is produced by two plates. Therefore, the field strength produced by one plate is $E_1/2$, and for the force acting on the plate B we can write

$$\frac{E_1 q_1}{2} = \frac{\varepsilon_0 S\xi^2}{2\,(d - x_1)^2} = kx_1, \qquad (1)$$

where k is the rigidity of the spring.

Let us now consider the case when the key K is closed for a short time. The capacitor acquires a charge $q_2, = \varepsilon_0 S\ \xi\,/\,d$ (the plates have no time to shift), which remains unchanged. Let the displacement of the plate B in the new equilibrium position be x_2. Then the field strength the capacitor becomes $E_2 = q_2\,/\,[C_2\ (d - x_2)]$ and $C_2 = \varepsilon_0 S\,/\,(d - x_2)$. In this case, the equilibrium condition for the plate B can be written in the form

$$\frac{E_2 q_2}{2} = \frac{q_2^2}{2\varepsilon_0 S} = \frac{\varepsilon_0 S\xi^2}{2d^2} = kx_2. \qquad (2)$$

Dividing Eqs. (1) and (2) termwise, we obtain $x_2 = x_1[(d - x_1)/d]^2$. Considering that $x_1 = 0.1\,d$ by hypothesis, we get $x_2 = 0.08\,d$.

3.40. Let us represent the central junction of wires in the form of two junctions connected by the wire 5-6 as shown in Fig. 219.

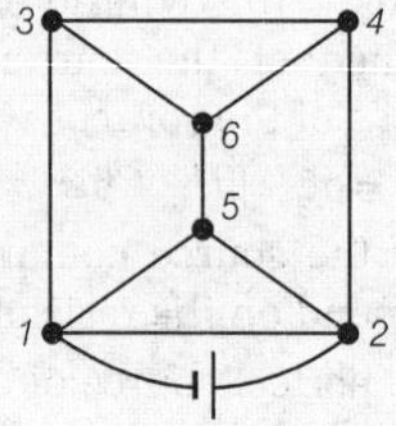

Fig. 219

Then it follows from symmetry considerations that there is no current through this wire. Therefore, the central junction can be removed from the initial circuit, and we arrive at the circuit shown in Fig. 220. By hypothesis,

$$R_{12} = R_{13} = R_{34} = R_{24} = r,$$

$$R_{15} = R_{25} = R_{36} = R_{46} = \frac{r}{\sqrt{2}}.$$

Let U be the voltage between points 1 and 2. Then the amount of heat liberated in the conductor 1-2 per unit time is $Q_{12} = \dfrac{U^2}{r}$.

From Ohm's law, we obtain the current through

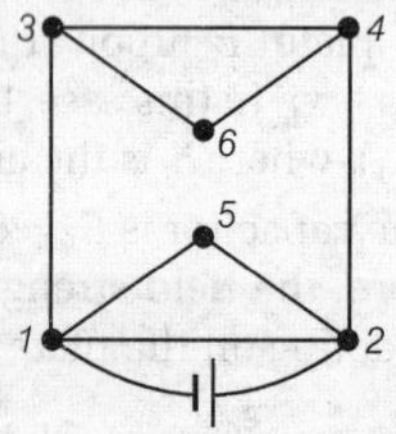

Fig. 220

the conductor 3-4:

$$I_{34} = \frac{U}{r(\sqrt{2} + 3)}.$$

The amount of heat liberated in the conductor 3-4 per unit time is

$$Q_{34} = I_{34}^2 r = \frac{U^2}{r(\sqrt{2} + 3)^2}.$$

Therefore, the required ratio is

$$\frac{Q_{12}}{Q_{34}} = (\sqrt{2} + 3)^2 = 11 + 6\sqrt{2}.$$

3.41. Since the anode current is I, the number of charge carriers (electrons) n arriving at the anode per unit time can be found from the formula

$$n = \frac{I}{|e|},$$

where e is the charge of a carrier. The momentum Δp transferred by the charge carriers to the anode per unit time is

$$\Delta p = nmv,$$

where m is the mass of a carrier, and v is its velocity. This momentum is equal to the mean force exerted on the anode by the charge carriers precipitating on it. Since $mv^2/2 = |e|U$, where U is the potential difference between the cathode and the anode, the mean pressure p_m exerted by electrons on the anode can be determined from the formula

$$p_m = \frac{nmv}{S} = \frac{I}{S}\frac{m}{|e|}\sqrt{\frac{2|e|U}{m}} = \frac{I}{S}\sqrt{\frac{2mU}{|e|}}.$$

3.42. It can be seen that during the time interval from 0 to t_0, the voltage across the capacitor is zero, the charge on it is also zero, there is no current through it, and hence U_{CD} is zero during this time interval (Fig. 221). During the time interval from t_0 to $2t_0$, the voltage across the capacitor, and hence the charge on its plates, grows linearly, and hence a direct current passes through the circuit.

This means that the voltage U_{CD} is constant. During the time interval from $2t_0$ to $3t_0$, the voltage across the capacitor does not change. Hence current does not flow, and U_{CD} is zero. Finally, during the time interval from $3t_0$ to $5t_0$, the capacitor is discharged, the current through the resistor is negative and constant, and its magnitude is half the value of the current during the time interval from t_0 to $2t_0$.

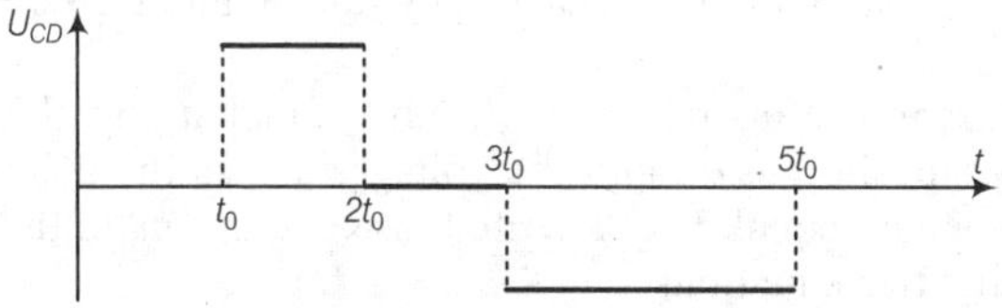

Fig. 221

3.43. Before switching the key K, the charge on the capacitor is $q_1 = \xi_1 C$, the positive charge being on the lower plate, and the negative charge, on the upper plate.

After switching the key K, as a result of recharging, the upper plate will acquire a positive charge, and the lower plate a negative charge equal to

$$q_2 = \xi_2 C.$$

Thus, the current source of emf ξ_2 will do the work $\xi_2 (q_1 + q_2)$. The required amount of heat liberated thereby in the resistor is

$$Q = \xi_2 (q_1 + q_2) - \left(\frac{q_2^2}{2C} - \frac{q_1^2}{2C} \right) = \frac{C(\xi_1 + \xi_2)^2}{2}.$$

3.44. Let us determine the current passing through the current source in the circuit:

$$I = \frac{\xi}{r + R_1 R_2 / (R_1 + R_2)} = \frac{\xi (R_1 + R_2)}{r(R_1 + R_2) + R_1 R_2}.$$

The voltage across each of the resistors R_1 and R_2 can be determined from the formula

$$U_{R_2} = \xi - Ir = \frac{\xi R_1 R_2}{rR_1 + R_2 (r + R_1)}.$$

The power liberated in the resistor R_2 can be calculated from the formula

$$N_{R_2} = \frac{U^2{}_{R_2}}{R_2} = \left[\frac{\xi R_1 R_2}{rR_1 + R_2 (R_1 + r)} \right]^2 \frac{1}{R_2}$$

$$= \frac{\xi^2 R_1^2}{(rR_1)^2 / R_2 + 2rR_1 (r + R_1) + (r + R_1)^2 R_2}.$$

The maximum power will correspond to the minimum value of the denominator. Using the classical inequality $a^2 + b^2 \geq 2ab$, we find that for $R_2 = rR_1 / (r + R_1)$ the denominator of the fraction has the minimum value, and the power liberated in the resistor R_2 attains the maximum value.

3.45. At the moment when the current through the resistor attains the value I_0, the charge on the capacitor of capacitance C_1 is $q_1 = C_1 I_0 R$.

The energy stored in the capacitor by this moment is $W_1 = \dfrac{q_1^2}{2C_1}$.

After disconnecting the key, at the end of recharging, the total charge on the capacitors is q_1, and the voltages across the plates of the two capacitors are equal. Let us write these conditions in the form of the following two equations:

$$q'_1 + q'_2 = q_1, \quad \frac{q'_1}{C_1} = \frac{q'_2}{C_2},$$

where q'_1 and q'_2 are the charges on the capacitors after recharging. This gives

$$q'_1 = \frac{q_1 C_1}{C_1 + C_2}, \quad q'_2 = \frac{q_1 C_2}{C_1 + C_2}.$$

The total energy of the system after recharging is

$$W_2 = \frac{q'^2_1}{2C_1} + \frac{q'^2_2}{2C_2} = \frac{q_1^2}{2(C_1 + C_2)}.$$

The amount of heat liberated in the resistor during this time is

$$Q = W_1 - W_2 = \frac{(I_0 R)^2 C_2}{2(C_1 + C_2)}.$$

3.46. Before switching the key K, no current flows through the resistor of resistance R, and the charge on the capacitor of capacitance C_2 can be determined from the formula

$$q = \xi C_2.$$

The energy stored in this capacitor is found from the formula

$$W_{C_2} = \frac{\xi^2 C_2}{2}.$$

After switching the key K, the charge q is redistributed between two capacitors so that the charge q_1 on the capacitor of capacitance C_1 and the charge q_2 on the capacitor of capacitance C_2 can be calculated from the formulas $q_1 + q_2 = q$, $\dfrac{q_1}{C_1} = \dfrac{q_2}{C_2}$.

The total energy of the two capacitors will be

$$W_{C_1 + C_2} = \frac{q^2}{2(C_1 + C_2)} = \frac{\xi^2 C_2^2}{2(C_1 + C_2)}.$$

Therefore, the amount of heat Q liberated in the resistor can be obtained from the relation

$$Q = \frac{\xi^2 C_2}{2} - \frac{\xi^2 C_2}{2}\frac{C_2}{C_1 + C_2} = \frac{\xi^2 C_1 C_2}{2(C_1 + C_2)}.$$

3.47. By the moment when the voltage across the capacitor has become U, the charge q has passed through the current source. Obviously, $q/U = C$. From the energy conservation law, we obtain $\xi_q = \dfrac{Q + q^2}{2C}$,

where Q is the amount of heat liberated in both resistors. Since they are connected in parallel, $Q_1/Q_2 = R_2/R_1$, whence

$$Q_2 = C\left(\xi U - \frac{U^2}{2}\right)\frac{R_1}{R_1 + R_2}$$

$$= \frac{CUR_1}{2(R_1 + R_2)}(2\xi - U).$$

3.48. During the motion of the jumper, the magnetic flux through the circuit formed by the jumper, rails, and the resistor changes. An emf is induced in the circuit, and a current is generated. As a result of the action of the magnetic field on the current in the jumper, the latter will be decelerated.

Let us determine the decelerating force F. Let the velocity of the jumper at a certain instant be v. During a short time interval Δt, the jumper is shifted along the rails by a small distance $\Delta x = v\,\Delta t$. The change in the area embraced by the circuit is $vd\,\Delta t$, and the magnetic flux varies by $\Delta\Phi = Bvd\,\Delta t$ during this time. The emf induced in the circuit is

$$\xi = -\frac{\Delta\Phi}{\Delta t} = -Bvd.$$

According to Ohm's law, the current through the jumper is $I = \xi / R$. The force exerted by the magnetic field on the jumper is

$$F = IBd = -\frac{B^2d^2v}{R}$$

According to Lenz's law, the force F is directed against the velocity v of the jumper.

Let us now write the equation of motion for the jumper (over a small distance Δx):

$$ma = F = -\frac{B^2d^2v}{R}.$$

Considering that $a = \Delta v/\Delta t$ and $v = \Delta x/\Delta t$,

we obtain $$m\,\Delta v = -\frac{B^2d^2\Delta x}{R}.$$

It can be seen that the change in the velocity of the jumper is proportional to the change in its x-coordinate (at the initial instant, $x_0 = 0$). Therefore, the total change in velocity $v_f = v_0 = 0 - v_0 = -v_0$ is connected with the change in the coordinate (with the total displacement s) through the relation $m(-v_0) = -\dfrac{B^2d^2s}{R}$.

Hence we can determine the length of the path covered by the jumper before it comes to rest: $s = \dfrac{mRv_0}{B^2d^2}$.

When the direction of the magnetic induction **B** forms an angle α with the normal to the plane of the rails, we obtain

$$s = \frac{mRv_0}{B^2d^2\cos^2\alpha}.$$

Indeed, the induced emf, and hence the current through the jumper, is determined by the magnetic flux through the circuit, and in this case, the flux is determined by the projection of the magnetic induction **B** on the normal to the plane of the circuit.

3.49. The lines of the magnetic flux produced by the falling charged ball lie in the horizontal plane. Therefore, the magnetic flux Φ_B through the surface area bounded by the loop is zero at any instant of time. Therefore, the galvanometer will indicate zero.

3.50. Let us choose the coordinate system xOy with the origin coinciding with the instantaneous position of the ball (Fig. 222).

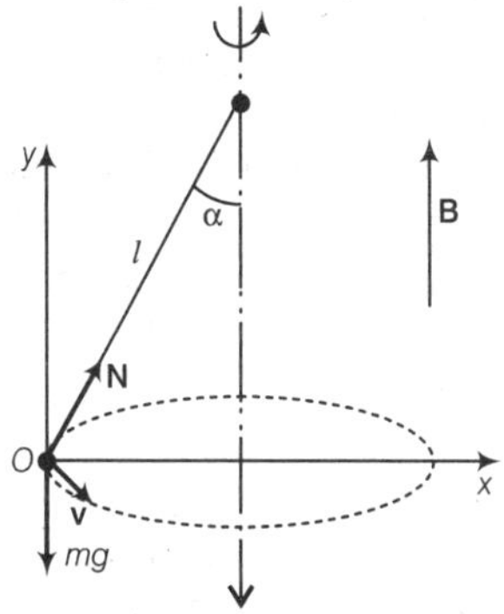

Fig. 222

The x-axis is "centripetal", while the y-axis is vertical just as the magnetic induction **B**.

The system of equations describing the motion of the ball (we assume that the ball moves in a circle counterclockwise) will be written in the form $N \sin \alpha - qvB = \dfrac{mv^2}{l \sin \alpha}$, $N \cos \alpha = mg$.

Besides, $\dfrac{2\pi r}{v} = T$, $r = l \sin \alpha$.

Solving this system of equations, we obtain

$$r = \sqrt{\frac{l^2 - (T/2\pi)^2}{[2\pi/(gT) \pm qB/(mg)]^2}}.$$

The plus sign corresponds to the counterclockwise rotation of the ball, and the minus sign to the clockwise rotation (if we view from the top).

3.51. When the metal ball moves in the magnetic field, the free electrons are distributed over the surface of the ball due to the action of the Lorentz force so that the resultant electric field in the bulk of the ball is uniform and compensates the action of the magnetic field. After the equilibrium has been attained, the motion of electrons in the bulk of the metal ceases. Therefore, the electric field strength is

$$E_{res} q + q\,[\mathbf{v} \times \mathbf{B}] = 0,$$

whence $$E_{res} = [\mathbf{B} \times \mathbf{v}].$$

We arrive at the conclusion that the uniform electric field emerging in the bulk of the ball has the magnitude

$$|E_{res}| = |\mathbf{B}|\,|\mathbf{v}|\sin\alpha.$$

The maximum potential difference $\Delta\phi_{max}$ emerging between the points on the ball diameter parallel to the vector $\mathbf{E}_{res}$ is

$$\Delta\phi_{max} = |E_{res}| \cdot 2r = |\mathbf{B}|\,|\mathbf{v}|\sin\alpha \cdot 2r.$$

3.52. The magnetic induction of the solenoid is directed along its axis. Therefore, the Lorentz force acting on the electron at any instant of time will lie in the plane perpendicular to the solenoid axis. Since the electron velocity at the initial moment is directed at right angles to the solenoid axis, the electron trajectory will lie in the plane perpendicular to the solenoid axis. The Lorentz force can be found from the formula $F = evB$.

The trajectory of the electron in the solenoid is an arc of the circle whose radius can be determined from the relation $evB = mv^2/r$, whence $r = \dfrac{mv}{eB}$.

The trajectory of the electron is shown in Fig. 223 (top view), where O_1 is the centre of the arc AC described by the electron, v' is the velocity at which the electron leaves the solenoid. The segments OA and OC are tangents to the electron trajectory at points A and C.

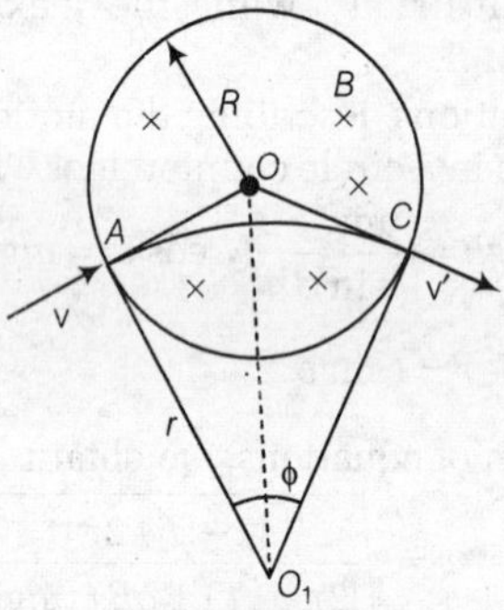

Fig. 223

The angle between v and v' is obviously $\phi = \angle AO_1C$ since $\angle OAO_1 = \angle OCO_1$.

In order to find ϕ, let us consider the right triangle OAO_1: side $OA = R$ and side $AO_1 = r$. Therefore, $\tan(\phi/2) = R/r = eBR/(mv)$.

Therefore, $\phi = 2 \text{ arc tan}\left(\dfrac{eBR}{mv}\right)$.

Obviously, the magnitude of the velocity remains unchanged over the entire trajectory since the Lorentz force is perpendicular to the velocity at any instant. Therefore, the transit time of electron in the solenoid can be determined from the relation

$$t = \frac{r\phi}{v} = \frac{m\phi}{eB} = \frac{2m}{eB}\arctan\left(\frac{eBR}{mv}\right).$$

3.53. During the motion of the jumper, the magnetic flux across the contour "closed" by the jumper varies. As a result, an emf is induced in the contour.

During a short time interval over which the velocity v of the jumper can be treated as constant, the instantaneous value of the induced emf is
$$\xi = -\frac{\Delta\Phi}{\Delta t} = -vbB\cos\alpha.$$

The current through the jumper at this instant is $I = \dfrac{\Delta q}{\Delta t}$,

where Δq is the charge stored in the capacitor during the time Δt, i.e.
$$\Delta q = C\,\Delta\xi = CbB\,\Delta v\cos\alpha$$
(since the resistance of the guides and the jumper is zero, the instantaneous value of the voltage across the capacitor is ξ). Therefore,
$$I = CbB\left(\frac{\Delta v}{\Delta t}\right)\cos\alpha = CbBa\cos\alpha,$$
where a is the acceleration of the jumper.

The jumper is acted upon by the force of gravity and Ampere's force. Let us write the equation of motion for the jumper:
$$ma = mg\sin\alpha - IbB\cos\alpha = mg\sin\alpha - Cb^2B^2\,a\cos^2\alpha.$$

Hence we obtain $a = \dfrac{mg\sin\alpha}{m + Cb^2B^2\cos^2\alpha}$.

The time during which the jumper reaches the foot of the "hump" can be determined from the condition $l = at^2/2$:
$$t = \sqrt{\frac{2l}{a}} = \sqrt{\frac{2l}{mg\sin\alpha}(m + Cb^2B^2\cos^2\alpha)}.$$

The velocity of the jumper at the foot will be
$$v_f = at = \sqrt{\frac{2lmg\sin\alpha}{m + Cb^2B^2\cos^2\alpha}}.$$

3.54*. The magnetic flux across the surface bounded by the superconducting loop is constant. Indeed, $\Delta\Phi/\Delta t = \xi$, but $\xi = IR = 0$ (since $R = 0$), and hence $\Phi = \text{const}$.

The magnetic flux through the surface bounded by the loop is the sum of the external magnetic flux and the flux of the magnetic field produced by the current I passing through the loop. Therefore, the magnetic flux across the loop at any instant is
$$\Phi = a^2B_0 + a^2\alpha z + LI.$$

Since $\Phi = B_0a^2$ at the initial moment ($z = 0$ and $I = 0$), the current I at any other instant will be determined by the relation
$$LI = -\alpha z a^2, \quad I = -\frac{\alpha z a^2}{L}.$$

The resultant force exerted by the magnetic field on the current loop is the sum of the forces acting on the sides of the loop which are parallel to the y-axis, i.e.

$$F = 2a|\alpha x|I = a^2\alpha I$$

and is directed along the z-axis.

Therefore, the equation of motion for the loop has the form

$$mz = -mg + a^2\alpha I = -\frac{mg - a^4\alpha^2 z}{L}.$$

This equation is similar to the equation of vibrations of a body of mass m suspended on a spring of rigidity $k = a^4\alpha^2/L$:

$$mz = -mg - kz.$$

This analogy shows that the loop will perform harmonic oscillations along the z-axis near the equilibrium position determined by the condition

$$\frac{a^4\alpha^2}{L} z_0 = -mg, \qquad z_0 = -\frac{mgL}{a^4\alpha^2}.$$

The frequency of these oscillations will be $\omega = \dfrac{a^2\alpha}{\sqrt{Lm}}$.

The coordinate of the loop in a certain time t after the beginning of motion will be

$$z = -\frac{mgL}{a^4\alpha^2}\left[-1 + \cos\left(\frac{a^2\alpha}{\sqrt{Lm}} t\right)\right].$$

3.55. The cross-sectional areas of the coils are $S_1 = \pi D_1^2/4$ and $S_2 = \pi D_2^2/4$. We shall use the well-known formula for the magnetic flux $\Phi = LI = BSN$, which gives $B = LI/(SN)$. Therefore, $\dfrac{B_2}{B_1} = \dfrac{L_2}{L_1}\dfrac{S_1 N_1}{S_2 N_2}\dfrac{I_2}{I_1}$.

But $I_1 = I_2$ since the wire and the current source remain unchanged. The ratio of the numbers of turns can be found from the formula $N_1/N_2 = D_2/D_1$. This gives

$$\frac{B_2}{B_1} = \frac{L_2 S_1 D_2}{L_1 S_2 D_1} = \frac{L_2 D_1}{L_1 D_2}.$$

Therefore, the magnetic induction in the new coil is

$$B_2 = \frac{B_1 L_2 D_1}{L_1 D_2}.$$

3.56.*Let N_1 be the number of turns of the coil of inductance L_1, and N_2 be the number of turns of the coil of inductance L_2. It should be noted that the required composite coil of inductance L can be treated as a coil with $N = N_1 + N_2$ turns. If the relation between the inductance and the number of turns is known, L can be expressed in terms of L_1 and L_2. For a given geometrical configuration of the coil, such a relation must actually exist because inductance is determined only by geometrical configuration and the number of turns of the coil (we speak of long cylindrical coils with uniform winding). Let us derive this relation.

From the superposition principle for a magnetic field, it follows that the magnetic field produced by a current I in a coil of a given size is proportional to the number of turns in it. Indeed, the doubling of the number of turns in the coil can be treated as a replacement of each turn by two new closely located turns. These two turns will produce twice as strong a field as that produced by a single turn since the fields produced by two turns are added. Therefore, the field in a coil with twice as many turns is twice as strong. Thus, $B \propto N$ (B is the magnetic induction, and the current is fixed). It should be noted that the magnetic flux embraced by the turns of the coil is

$$\Phi = BNS \propto BN \propto N^2.$$

It remains for us to consider that $L = \dfrac{\Phi}{I} \propto N^2$.

Thus, we obtain $L = kN^2$ for a given geometry. Further, we take into account that $N_1 = \sqrt{L_1 / k}$, $N_2 = \sqrt{L_2 / k}$, and hence $L = k\,(N_1 + N_2)^2$. Consequently, $L = L_1 + L_2 + 2\sqrt{L_1 L_2}$.

3.57. For a motor with a separate excitation, we obtain the circuit shown in Fig. 224. In the first case, i.e. when the winch is not loaded, $0 = I_1 = (\xi - \xi_1)/r$, where r is the internal resistance of the motor, and ξ_1 is the induced emf, $\xi_1 = \alpha v_1$. Thus, $\xi_1 = \xi$, whence $\alpha = \xi / v_1$. In the second case, the power consumed by the motor is

$$\xi_2 I_2 = \frac{(\xi - \xi_2)\,\xi_2}{r} = mgv_2.$$

The induced emf is now $\xi_2 = \alpha v_2$. Thus, for the internal resistance of the motor, we obtain $r = \dfrac{(\xi - \alpha v_2)\,\alpha}{mg}$.

For the maximum liberated power, we can write

$$N_{\max} = \frac{(\xi - \xi')\,\xi'}{r} = m' gv',$$

where it can easily be shown that the maximum power $\xi' = \alpha v'$ is liberated under the condition

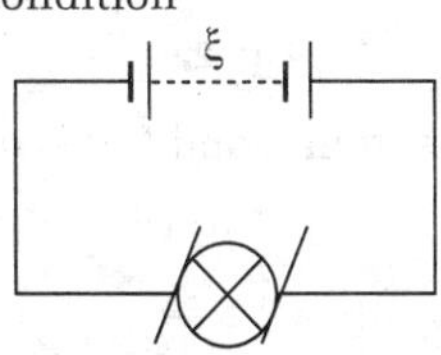

Fig. 224

$\xi' = \xi/2$ (the maximum value of the denominator). Hence

$$v' = \frac{\xi}{2\alpha} = \frac{v_1}{2} = 2\ \text{m/s}.$$

$$m' = \frac{mv_1}{2(v_1 - v_2)} = 10\frac{2}{3} \simeq 6.7\ \text{kg}.$$

3.58. Let us plot the time dependences $U_{ex}(t)$ of the external voltage, $I_c(t)$ of the current in the circuit (which passes only in one direction when the diode is open), the voltage across the capacitor $U_c(t)$, and the voltage across the diode $U_a(t)$ (Fig. 225).

Therefore, the voltage between the anode and the cathode varies between 0 and $-2U_0$.

3.59. Since the current and the voltage vary in phase, and the amplitude of current is $I = \xi_0 / R$

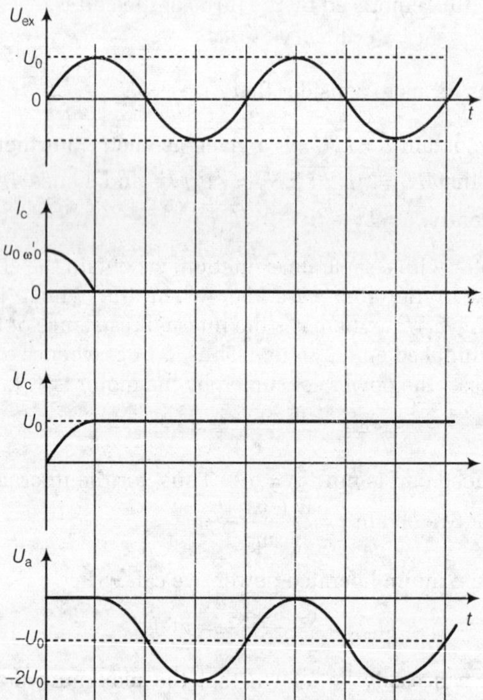

Fig. 225

(i.e. the contributions from C and L are compensated), we have

$$\frac{1}{\omega C} = \omega L.$$

From the relations $U_c = q / C$ and $dq / dt = I$, we obtain

$$U_c = \frac{\xi_0 \sin \omega t}{R\omega C}.$$

Therefore, the amplitude of the voltage across the capacitor plates is

$$U_0 = \frac{\xi_0 \omega L}{R}.$$

3.60. During steady-state oscillations, the work done by the external source of current must be equal to the amount of heat liberated in the resistor. For this the amplitudes of the external voltage and the voltage across the resistor must be equal: $RI_0 = U_0$.

Since the current in the circuit and the charge on the capacitor are connected through the equation $I = dq / dt$, the amplitudes I_0 and q_0 of current and charge can be obtained from the formula

$$I_0 = \omega_0 q_0,$$

where the resonance frequency is $\omega_0 = 1 / \sqrt{LC}$.

By hypothesis, $U_0 = U = \frac{q_1}{C}$,

whence $q_0 = \frac{q_1}{R}\sqrt{\frac{L}{C}} = 10^{-8}$ C.

3.61. For $0 < t < \tau$, charge oscillations will occur in the circuit, and

$$q = \left(\frac{CU}{2}\right)\cos \omega_0 t, \ \omega_0 = \sqrt{\frac{2}{LC}}.$$

At the instant τ, the charge on the capacitor at its breakdown is $(CU/2) \cos \omega_0 \tau$, and the energy of the capacitor is $(CU^2/8) \cos^2 \omega_0 \tau$. After the breakdown, this energy is converted into heat and lost by the system. The remaining energy is

$$W - \frac{CU^2}{4} - \left(\frac{CU^2}{8}\right)\cos^2 \omega_0 \tau.$$

The amplitude of charge oscillations after the breakdown can be determined from the condition $W = q_0^2/(2C)$, whence

$$q_0 = \frac{CU}{2}\sqrt{2 - \cos^2 \omega_0 \tau}.$$

3.62. It is sufficient to shunt the superconducting coil through a resistor with a low resistance which can withstand a high temperature. Then the current in the working state will pass through the coil irrespective of the small value of the resistance of the resistor.

If, however, a part of the winding loses its superconducting properties, i.e. if it has a high resistance, the current will pass through the shunt resistance. In this case, heat will be liberated in the resistor.

4. Optics

4.1. Rays which are singly reflected from the mirror surface of the cone propagate as if they were emitted by an aggregate of virtual point sources arranged on a circle. Each such source is symmetrical to the source S about the corresponding generator of the cone. The image of these sources on a screen is a ring.

It is essential that the beam of rays incident on the lens from a virtual source is plane: it does not pass through the entire surface of the lens but intersects it along its diameter. Therefore, the extent to which such a beam is absorbed by a diaphragm depends on the shape and orientation of the latter.

A symmetrical annular diaphragm (see Fig. 116) absorbs the beams from all virtual sources to the same extent. In this case, the illuminance of the ring on the screen will decrease uniformly. The diaphragm shown in Fig. 117 will completely transmit the beams whose planes form angles $\alpha < \alpha_0$ with the vertical.

Consequently, the illuminance of the upper and lower parts of the ring on the screen will remain unchanged. Other beams will be cut by the diaphragm the more, the closer the plane of a beam to the horizontal plane. For this reason, the illuminance of the lateral regions of the ring will decrease as the angle α varies between α_0 and $\frac{\pi}{2}$.

4.2. Let us first neglect the size of the pupil, assuming that it is point-like. Obviously, only those of the beams passing through the lens will get into the eye which have passed through point B before they fall on the lens (Fig. 226). This point is conjugate to the point at which the pupil is located.

The distance b from the lens to point B can be calculated by using the formula for a thin-lens:

$$\frac{1}{F} = \frac{1}{a} + \frac{1}{b}$$

$$b = \frac{aF}{a - F} = 12\,\text{cm}.$$

It is clear now that the screen must coincide with the real image of the pupil in the plane S. Figure 226 shows that the minimum radius of the screen is

$$R = \frac{b}{a}\, r \simeq 0.5\,\text{mm},$$

and the screen must be placed in the plane S with its centre at point B

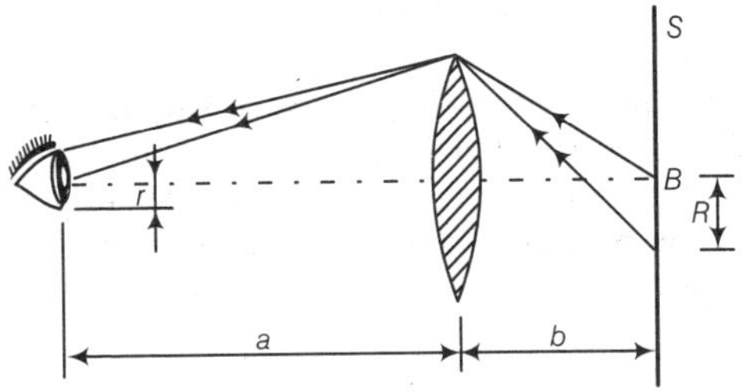

Fig. 226

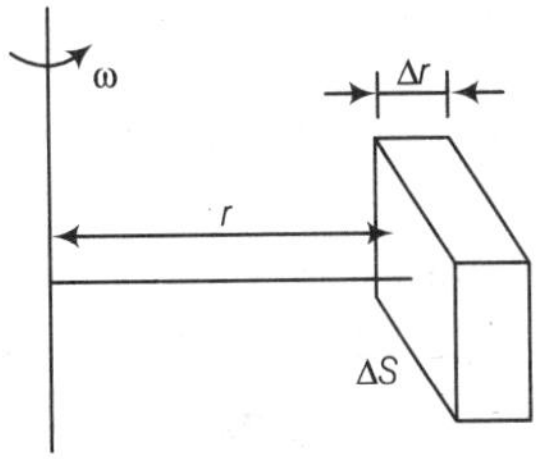

Fig. 227

4.3*. Let us first determine the distribution of the gas pressure near the axis of the vessel. We shall consider the volume element $\Delta r\ \Delta S$ of the gas (Fig. 227). The centripetal acceleration $a = \omega^2 r$ of this element is ensured by the difference in the corresponding pressures:

$[p\,(r + \Delta r) - p\,(r)]\Delta S = \rho \Delta r\ \Delta S\ \omega^2 r.$

Therefore, for the variation of pressure, we obtain the following equation: $\dfrac{dp}{dr} = \rho\omega^2 r.$

Since the relation $\mu p = \rho RT$ is satisfied for an ideal gas (R is the universal gas constant), we obtain

$$\frac{dp}{dr} = p\left(\frac{\mu\omega^2}{RT}\right)r.$$

By hypothesis, for $r \le r_{\text{beam}}$, we have $p(r) - p_0 << p_0$, and hence

$$p(r) \approx p_0\left(1 + \frac{\mu\omega^2}{2RT}r^2\right).$$

Accordingly, for the gas density at $r \le r_{\text{beam}}$, we obtain

$\rho(r) \approx \rho_0\left(1 + \dfrac{\mu\omega^2}{2RT}r^2\right)$, $\rho_0 = p_0\,\dfrac{\mu}{RT}$, and for the refractive index, we get

$$n(r) = n_0 + kr^2,\ n_0 = 1 + \alpha\,\rho_0,\ k = \frac{\alpha p_0}{2}\left(\frac{\mu\omega}{RT}\right)^2.$$

Let us now find the angle of refraction of a ray passing through the vessel at a distance r from the axis. The optical path length in the vessel is $n(r)l$.

The optical path difference δ_{opt} between two close rays emerging from the vessel must be equal to the geometrical path difference δ due to the deflection of the rays from the initial direction of propagation. In this case, the interference of the rays will result in their augmentation (Huygens' principle).

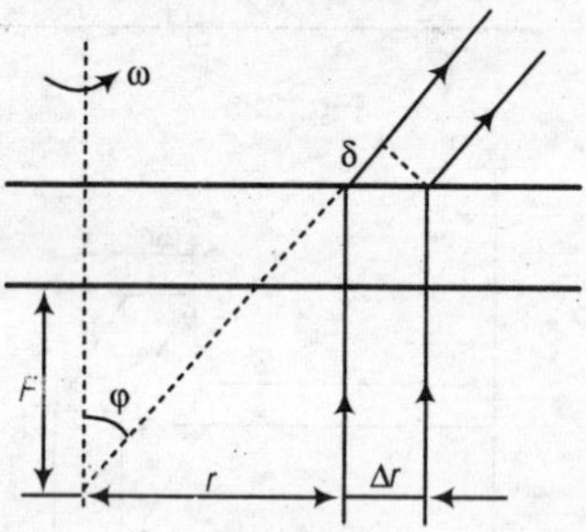

Fig. 228

It follows from Fig. 228 that $\delta_{opt} = [n(r + \Delta r) - n(r)]l$, $\delta = \Delta r \sin\phi$.

Hence

$$\sin\phi = \frac{\delta}{\Delta r} = \frac{[n(r + \Delta r) - n(r)]}{\Delta r} l = 2k\, l\, r.$$

This leads to the following conclusion. If we consider a narrow beam of light such that the deflection angle ϕ is small, then $\phi \propto r$, i.e. the rotating vessel will act as a diverging lens with a focal length $F = (2kl)^{-1}$.

Therefore, for the maximum deflection angle, we obtain $\sin\phi_{max} = 2klr_{beam}$.

Consequently, the required radius of the spot on the screen is

$$R = r_{beam} + L\tan\phi_{max}.$$

In the diverging lens approximation, we obtain

$$R \approx r_{beam} + L\phi_{max} \approx r_{beam} + 2klr_{beam}L$$

$$= r_{beam}\left[1 + \alpha p_0 lL\left(\frac{\mu\omega}{RT}\right)^2\right].$$

4.4. The telescope considered in the problem is of the Kepler type. The angular magnification $k = \frac{F}{f}$, and hence the focal length of the eyepiece is $f = \frac{F}{k} = 2.5$ cm. As the object being observed approaches the observer from infinity to the smallest possible distance a, the image of the object formed by the objective will be displaced from the focal plane towards the eyepiece by a distance x which can be determined from the formula for a thin lens:

$$\frac{1}{a} + \frac{1}{F + x} = \frac{1}{F}, \; \frac{1}{F + x} = \frac{a - F}{aF},$$

$$x = \frac{aF}{a - F} - F \approx \frac{F^2}{a}$$

since $a >> F$. Thus, we must find x. The eyepiece of the telescope is a magnifying glass.

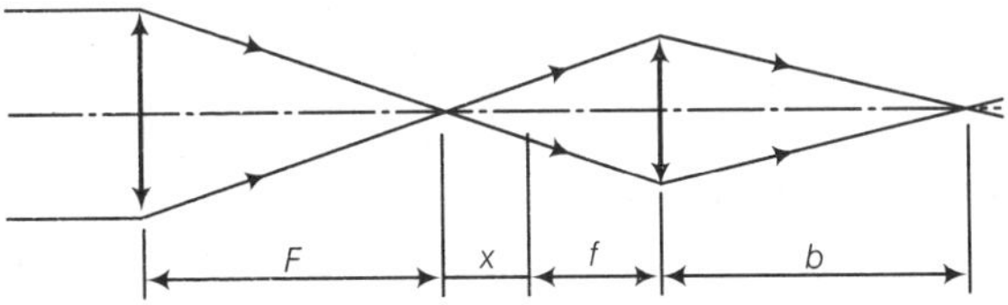

Fig. 229

When an object is viewed through a magnifier by the unstrained eye (accommodated to infinity), the object must be placed in the focal plane of the magnifier. The required distance x is equal to the displacement of the focal plane of the eyepiece during its adjustment. In this case, the eyepiece must obviously be moved away from the objective.

Figure 229 shows that when an infinitely remote object is viewed from the shifted eyepiece, the light beam will converge at the exit.

When a parallel beam of rays is incident on the telescope, such a position of the eyepiece is required for a long-sighted person whose eye has an insufficient focal power for converging the parallel beam on the retina. The maximum shift of the eyepiece corresponds to the focal power $D_+ = +10$ D. The spectacles of such a focal power converge a parallel beam at a distance $b = \frac{1}{D_+}$. This distance b just determines the displacement x :

$$\frac{1}{f + x} + \frac{1}{b} = \frac{1}{f},$$

whence

$$x = \frac{f^2}{b - f} = \frac{5}{6} \text{ cm.}$$

The required distance is

$$a \approx \frac{F^2}{x} = \frac{0.25 \times 6 \text{ m}^2}{5 \times 10^{-2} \text{ m}} = 30 \text{ m}.$$

4.5. Yes, it can. The answer is illustrated by Fig. 230. The sought regions are shown hatched.

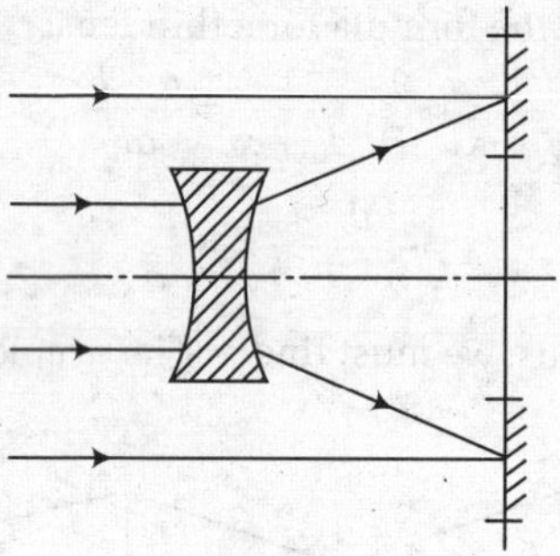

Fig. 230

4.6. When the pencil enters the water, the water surface in its vicinity forms a diverging lens: the rays emerging from the light source are deflected from the axis of the pencil. For this reason, a large dark spot is formed under the pencil (Fig. 231).

When the pencil is drawn out of the water, the water surface near the pencil forms a converging lens:

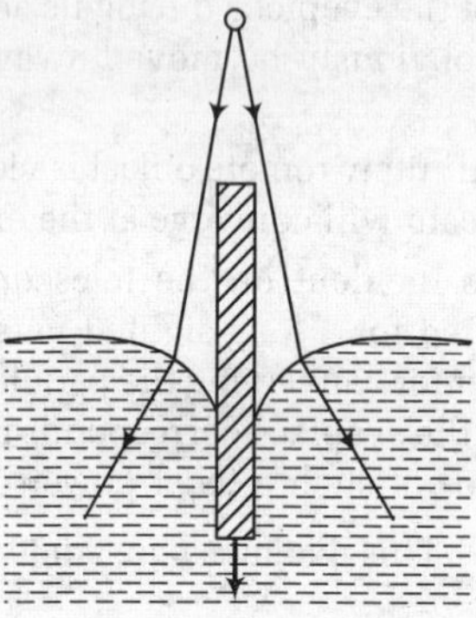

Fig. 231

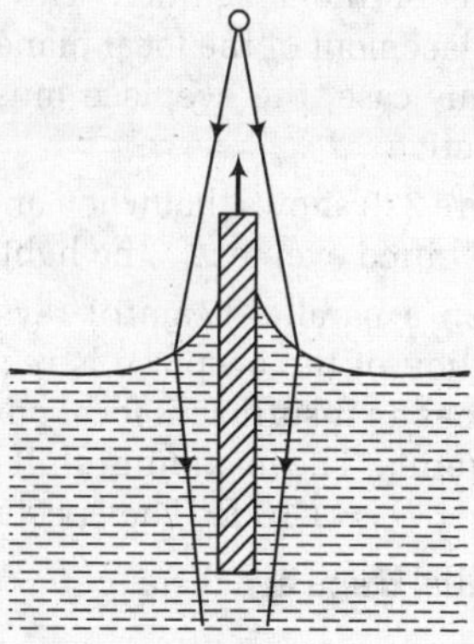

Fig. 232

the rays emerging from the light source are deflected towards the axis of the pencil. For this reason, a bright spot is formed under the pencil (Fig. 232).

4.7. The answer follows from Fig. 233. The first bright ring is formed by the rays which undergo one reflection from the body before they leave it (such a ray is marked by 1). The second bright ring is formed by the rays undergoing two reflections (such a ray is marked by 2), and so on. Clearly, the larger the number of reflections, the more the light absorbed by the body of the ballpoint pen. Therefore, the further a bright ring from the centre, the lower its brightness.

4.8. Let us prove that after refraction all the rays emerging from the point source towards the screen will lie within the cylinder, and after multiple reflections from the lateral surface of the cylinder, will ultimately pass through the hole in the screen.

Indeed, the extreme ray from the point source S, whose angle of incidence on the left base of the cylinder is $\frac{\pi}{2}$, after refraction will form an angle α with the cylinder axis such that $\sin\alpha = \frac{1}{n}$ (according to Snell's law).

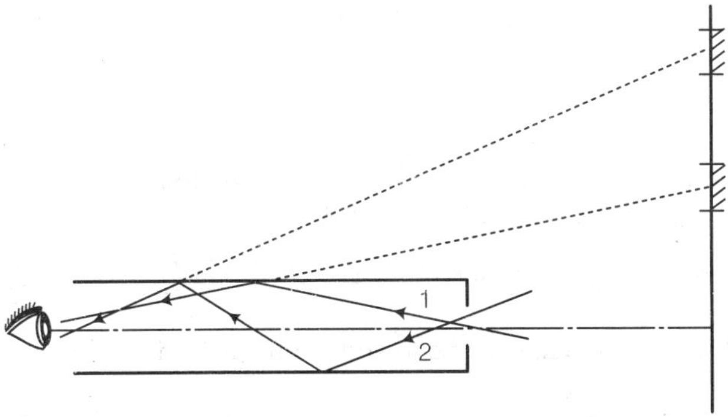

Fig. 233

The angle of incidence ϕ of such a ray on the lateral surface of the cylinder satisfies the condition $\alpha + \phi = \frac{\pi}{2}$ (Fig. 234).

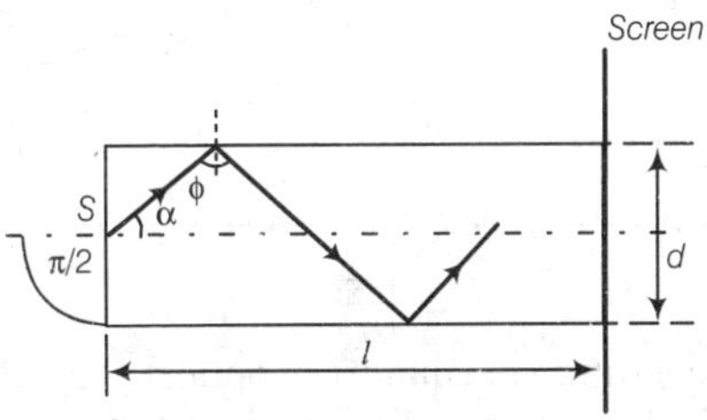

Fig. 234

Since $$\sin\alpha = \frac{1}{n} = \frac{1}{1.5} < \frac{\sqrt{2}}{2},$$

$\alpha < \frac{\pi}{4}$ and $\phi > \frac{\pi}{4}$, i.e. the angle of incidence on the lateral surface of the cylinder will be larger than the critical angle of total internal reflection.

Therefore, this ray cannot emerge from the cylinder at any point other than that lying on the right base. Any other ray emerging from the source towards the screen with a hole and undergoing refraction at the left base of the cylinder will propagate at a smaller angle to the axis, and hence will be incident on the lateral surface at an angle exceeding the critical angle. Thus, the transparent cylinder will "converge" to the hole the rays within a solid angle of 2π sr.

In the absence of the cylinder, the luminous flux confined in a solid angle of $\frac{\pi d^2}{(4l)^2}$ gets into the hole in the screen. Therefore, in the presence of the transparent cylinder, the luminous flux through the hole will increase by a factor of

$$\frac{2\pi}{\pi d^2/(4l)^2} = 8 \times 10^4.$$

4.9. The thickness of the objective lens can be found from geometrical considerations (Fig. 235). Indeed,

$$r_1^2 = (2R_1 - h)h \approx 2R_1 h, \quad h = \frac{r_1^2}{2R_1},$$

where R_1 is the radius of curvature of the objective.

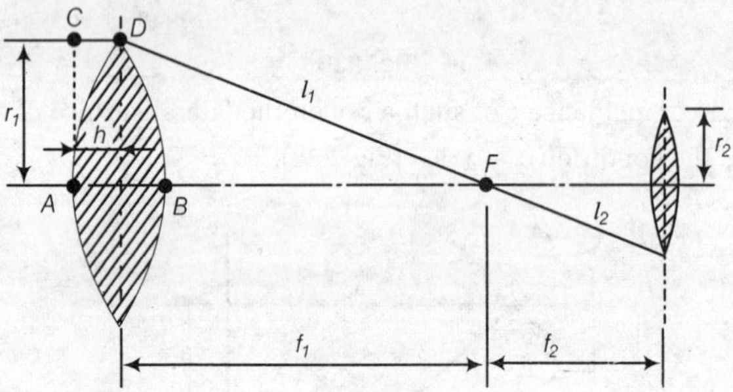

Fig. 235

Let us write the condition of equality of optical paths *ABF* and *CDF* for the case when the telescope is filled with water:

$$(f_1 - h)n_w + 2hn_{gl} = n_w l_1 + h.$$

Here f_1 is the focal length of the objective lens in the presence of water. Substituting the values of h and $l_1 = \sqrt{f_1^2 + r_1^2} \approx f_1 + r_1^2/(2f_1)$, we obtain

$$\frac{r_1^2}{2f_1} n_w = \frac{r_1^2}{2R_1} [(n_{gl} - 1) + (n_{gl} - n_w)].$$

Hence

$$f_1 = \frac{R_1 n_w}{(n_{gl} - 1) + (n_{gl} - n_w)}.$$

When the telescope does not contain water, the focal length of the objective lens is $f_1^{(0)} = \dfrac{R_1}{2(n_{g1} - 1)}$.

Therefore, $f_1 = f_1^{(0)} \dfrac{2(n_{gl} - 1)n_w}{(n_{gl} - 1) + (n_{gl} - n_w)}$.

A similar calculation for the focal lengths f_2 (with water) and $f_2^{(0)}$ (without water) of the eyepiece lens gives the following result:

$$f_2 = f_2^{(0)} \frac{2(n_{gl} - 1)n_w}{(n_{gl} - 1) + (n_{gl} - n_w)}.$$

Therefore, $L = f_1 + f_2 = (f_1^{(0)} + f_2^{(0)}) \dfrac{2(n_{gl} - 1)n_w}{(n_{gl} - 1) + (n_{gl} - n_w)}$.

Since $f_{10}^{(0)} + f_{20}^{(0)} = L_0$, the required distance between the objective and the eyepiece is

$$L = L_0 \frac{2(n_{gl} - 1)n_w}{2n_{gl} - n_w - 1} = 30\,\text{cm}.$$

4.10. Let the spider be at point A (Fig. 236) located above the upper point D of the sphere. The spherical surface corresponding to the arc BDB' of the circle is visible to the spider.

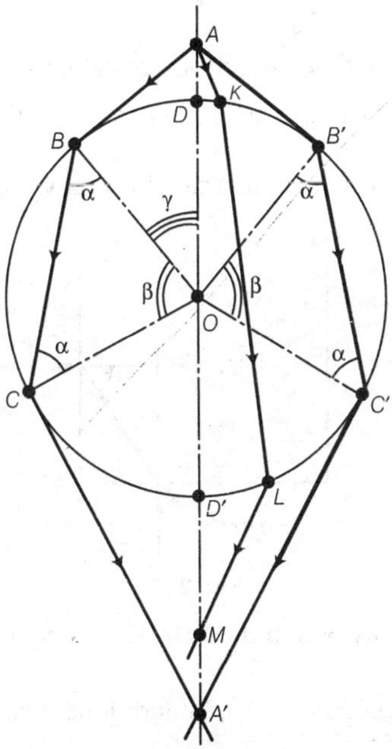

Fig. 236

Points B and B' are the points of intersection of tangents drawn from point A to the surface of the sphere. The ray AB propagates within the sphere along BC. The angle α can be found from the condition

$$\sin\alpha = \frac{1}{n_{gl}},$$

where n_{gl} is the refractive index of glass. This ray will emerge from the sphere along CA'. Therefore, the fraction of the spherical surface corresponding to the arc $CD'C'$ will also be visible (by way of an example, the optical path of the ray $AKLM$ is shown).

The surface of the spherical zone corresponding to the arcs BC and $B'C'$ will be invisible to the spider.

The angle γ is determined from the condition $\cos\gamma = \frac{R}{R+h}$,

where R is the radius of the sphere, and h is the altitude of the spider above the spherical surface. Since $R >> h$ by hypothesis, $\gamma \simeq 0$. We note now that $\beta = \pi - 2\alpha$ and $\sin\alpha = \frac{1}{n_{gl}}$. Therefore,

$$\beta = \pi - 2\arcsin\left(\frac{1}{n_{gl}}\right) \approx \frac{\pi}{2}.$$

Thus, the opposite half of the spherical surface is visible to the spider, and the fly must be there.

4.11. None of the rays will emerge from the lateral surface of the cylinder if for a ray with an angle of incidence $\gamma \approx \frac{\pi}{2}$ (Fig. 237), the angle of incidence α on the inner surface will satisfy the relation $\sin\alpha > \frac{1}{n}$.

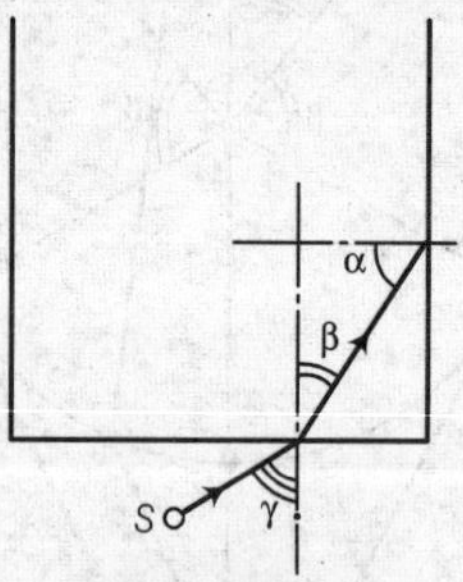

Fig. 237

In this case, the ray will undergo total internal reflection on the lateral surface.

It follows from geometrical considerations that

$$\sin\alpha = \sqrt{1-\sin^2\beta}, \quad \sin\beta = \frac{1}{n}. \quad \text{Thus,} \quad n_{min} = \sqrt{2}.$$

4.12. By hypothesis, the foci of the two lenses are made to coincide, i.e. the separation between the lenses is $3f$, where f is the focal length of a lens with a lower focal power.

In the former case, all the rays entering the tube will emerge from it and form a circular spot of radius $\frac{r}{2}$, where r is the radius of the tube (Fig. 238).

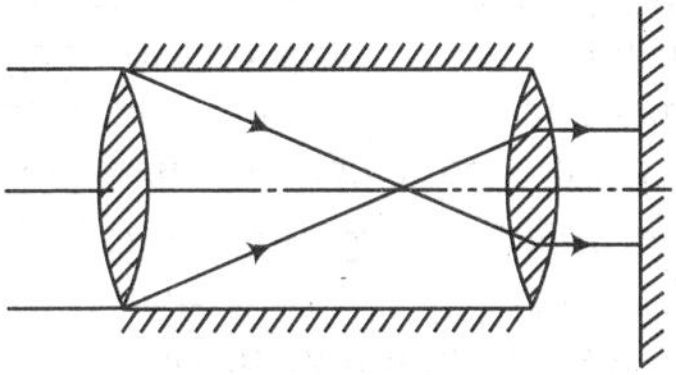

Fig. 238

In the latter case, only the rays which enter the tube at a distance smaller than $\frac{r}{2}$ from the tube axis will emerge from the tube. Such rays will form a circular spot of radius r on the screen (Fig. 239).

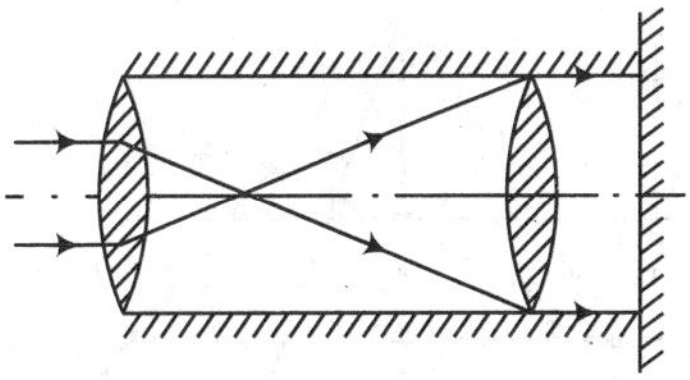

Fig. 239

Thus, if J is the luminous intensity of the light entering the tube, the ratio of the illuminances of the spots before and after the reversal of the tube is

$$E_1 = \frac{J}{\pi(r/2)^2}, \qquad E_2 = \frac{J/4}{\pi r^2}, \qquad \frac{E_2}{E_1} = \frac{1}{16}.$$

4.13. The light entering the camera is reflected from the surface of the facade. It can be assumed that the reflection of light from the plaster is practically independent of the angle of reflection. In this case, the luminous energy incident on the objective of the camera is proportional to the solid angle at which the facade is seen from the objective. As the distance from the object is reduced by half, the solid angle increases by a factor of four, and a luminous energy four times stronger than in the former case is incident on the objective of the same area.

For such large distances from the object, the distance between the objective and the film in the camera does not practically change during the focussing of the object and is equal to the focal length of the objective. The solid angle within which the energy from the objective is incident on the surface of the image depends linearly on the solid angle at which the facade is seen, i.e. on the distance from the object. In this case, the illuminance of the surface of the image (which, by hypothesis, is uniformly distributed over the area of this surface), which determines the exposure, is directly proportional to the corresponding energy incident on the objective from the facade and inversely proportional to the area of the image. Since this ratio is practically independent of the distance from the object under given conditions there is no need to change the exposure.

4.14*. The problem is analogous to the optical problem in which the refraction of a plane wave in a prism is analyzed. According to the laws of geometrical optics, the light ray propagating from point A to point B (Fig. 240) takes the shortest time in comparison with all other paths.

The fisherman must move along the path of a "light ray", i.e. must approach point E of the bay at an angle γ, cross the bay in a boat at right angles to the bisector of the angle α, and then move along the shore in the direction of point B.

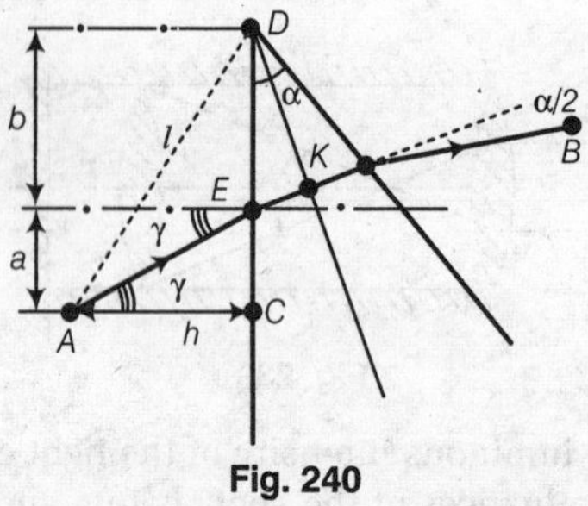

Fig. 240

The angle γ can be determined from Snell's law ($n = 2$):

$$\sin\gamma = n\sin\frac{\alpha}{2}.$$

The distance a is $a = h\tan\gamma = h\dfrac{n\sin(\alpha/2)}{\sqrt{1-n^2\sin^2(\alpha/2)}}$.

The distance b can be determined from the equation $a + b = \sqrt{l^2 - h^2}$. Hence

$$b = \sqrt{l^2 - h^2} - h\frac{n\sin(\alpha/2)}{\sqrt{1-n^2\sin^2(\alpha/2)}}.$$

If $b > 0$, i.e.

$$l^2 - h^2 > h^2\frac{n^2\sin^2(\alpha/2)}{\sqrt{1-n^2\sin^2(\alpha/2)}},$$

the fisherman must use the boat. Separate segment in this case will be

$$EK = p = b\sin\frac{\alpha}{2} = \left(\sqrt{l^2 - h^2} - h\frac{n\sin(\alpha/2)}{\sqrt{1 - n^2\sin^2(\alpha/2)}}\right)\sin\frac{\alpha}{2}$$

$$AE = q = \frac{h}{\cos\gamma} = \frac{h}{\sqrt{1 - n^2\sin^2(\alpha/2)}}.$$

Therefore, if $\frac{l^2 - h^2}{h^2} > \frac{n^2\sin^2(\alpha/2)}{1 - n^2\sin^2(\alpha/2)}$, the required time is

$$t = 2\left(\frac{q}{v} + \frac{p}{v/n}\right) = \frac{2h}{v}\left(\frac{1}{\sqrt{1 - n^2\sin^2(\alpha/2)}} + \frac{n\sqrt{l^2 - h^2}\sin(\alpha/2)}{h} - \frac{n^2\sin^2(\alpha/2)}{\sqrt{1 - n^2\sin^2(\alpha/2)}}\right)$$

$$= \frac{2h}{v}\left(\sqrt{1 - n^2\sin^2\frac{\alpha}{2}} + \frac{\sqrt{l^2 - h^2}}{h}n\sin\frac{\alpha}{2}\right).$$

If $\frac{l^2 - h^2}{h^2} \le \frac{n^2\sin^2(\alpha/2)}{1 - n^2\sin^2(\alpha/2)}$, then $t = \frac{2l}{v}$.

4.15. If follows from symmetry considerations that the image of the point source S will also be at a distance b from the sphere, but on the opposite side (Fig. 241).

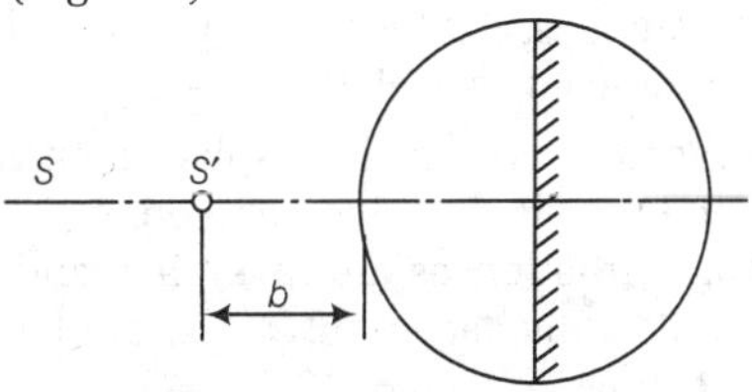

Fig. 241

4.16. An observer on the ship can see only the rays for which $\sin\alpha < \frac{1}{n_{gl}}$ (if $\sin\alpha > \frac{1}{n_{gl}}$, such a ray undergoes total internal reflection and cannot be seen by the observer, Fig. 242). For the angle β, we have the relation $n_w\sin\beta = n_{gl}\sin\alpha$, $\sin\beta = \frac{n_{gl}}{n_w}\sin\alpha$,

where n_{gl} is the refractive index of glass. Since

$|\sin\alpha| < \frac{1}{n_{gl}}$, $|\sin\beta| < \frac{1}{n_w}$.

Therefore, the observer can see only the objects emitting light to the porthole at an angle of incidence $\beta \le \arcsin(1/n_w)$.

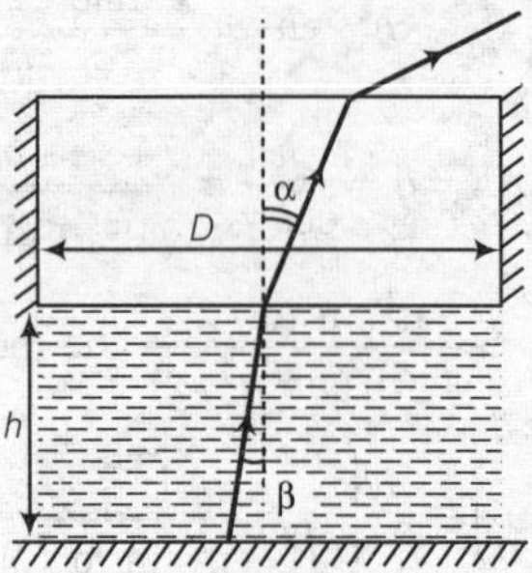

Fig. 242

Figure 242 shows that the radius of a circle at the sea bottom which is accessible to observation is $R \approx h \tan\beta$, and the sought area ($h \tan\beta >> D/2$) is

$$S = \pi R^2 \approx \frac{\pi h^2}{n_w^2 - 1} \simeq 82 \text{ m}^2.$$

4.17*. Short-sighted persons use concave (diverging) glasses which reduce the focal power of their eyes, while long-sighted persons use convex (converging) glasses.

It is clear that behind a diverging lens, the eye will look smaller, and behind a converging lens larger. If, however, you have never seen your companion without glasses, it is very difficult to say whether his eyes are magnified or reduced, especially if the glasses are not very strong.

The easiest way is to determine the displacement of the visible contour of the face behind the glasses relative to other parts of the face: if it is displaced inwards, the lenses are diverging, and your companion is short-sighted, if it is displaced outwards, the lenses are converging, and the person is long-sighted.

4.18. We decompose the velocity vector $\mathbf{v}$ of the person into two components, one parallel to the mirror, $\mathbf{v}_{||}$, and the other perpendicular to the mirror, $\mathbf{v}_{\perp}$, i.e. $\mathbf{v} = \mathbf{v}_{||} + \mathbf{v}_{\perp}$ (Fig. 243).

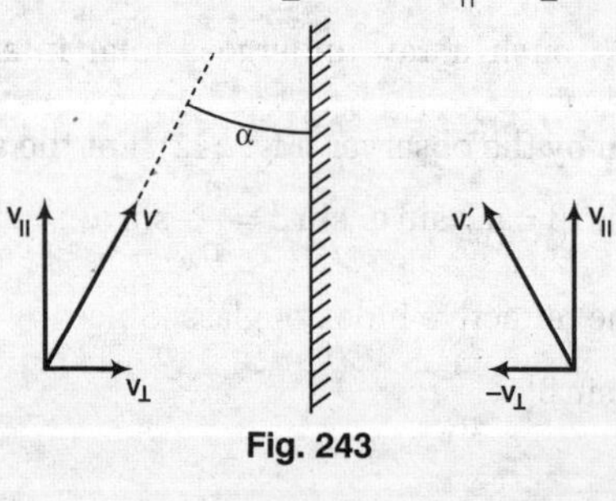

Fig. 243

The velocity of the image will obviously be $\mathbf{v}' = \mathbf{v}_{||} - \mathbf{v}_{\perp}$ Therefore, the velocity at which the person approaches his image is defined as his velocity relative to the image from the formula

$$v_{rel} = 2v_{\perp} = 2v \sin\alpha.$$

4.19. Let O be the centre of the spherical surface of the mirror, ABC the ray incident at a distance BE from the mirror axis, and $OB = R$ (Fig. 244).

From the right triangle OBE, we find that $\sin\alpha = \frac{h}{R}$. The triangle OBC is isosceles since $\angle ABO = \angle OBC$ according to the law of reflection, and $\angle BOC = \angle ABO$ as alternate-interior angles.

Hence $OD = DB = \frac{R}{2}$. From the triangle ODC, we obtain

$$x = \frac{R}{2\cos\alpha} = \frac{R^2}{2\sqrt{R^2 - h^2}}$$

(C is the point of intersection of the ray reflected by the mirror and the optical axis).

For a ray propagating at a distance h_1, the distance $x_1 \approx \frac{R}{2}$, with an error of about 0.5% since $h_1^2 << R^2$. For a ray propagating at a distance h_2, the distance $x_2 = 3.125$ cm. Finally, we obtain

$$\Delta x = x_2 - x_1 \simeq 0.6\,\text{cm} \neq 0\ (!)$$

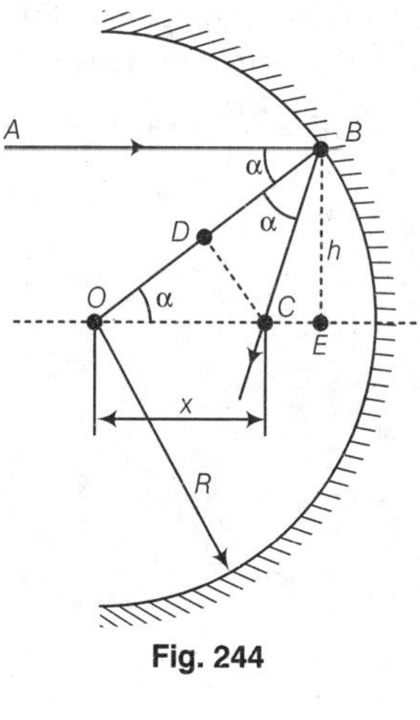

Fig. 244

4.20. Let us consider a certain luminous point A of the filament and an arbitrary ray AB emerging from it.

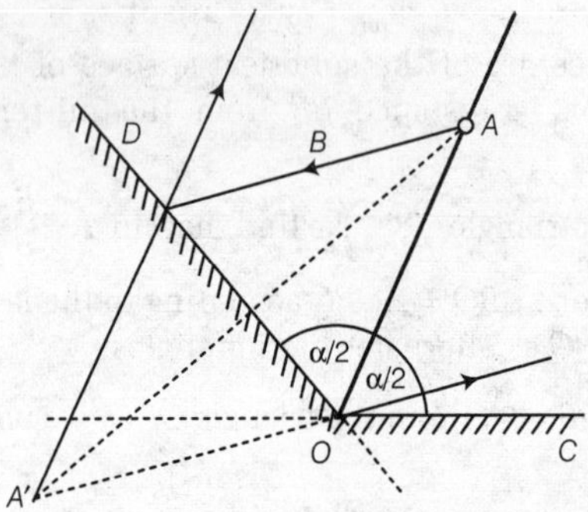

Fig. 245

We draw a plane through the ray and the filament. It follows from geometrical considerations that with all possible reflections, the given ray will remain in the constructed plane (Fig. 245).

After the first reflection at the conical surface, the ray AB will propagate as if it emerged from point A', viz. the virtual image of point A. The necessary condition so that none of the rays emerging from A ever gets on the mirror is that point A' must not be higher than the straight line OC, viz.

the second generator of the cone, lying in the plane of the ray (point O is the vertex of the conical surface). This will be observed if

$$\angle A'OD + \angle AOD + \angle AOC = 3\frac{\alpha}{2} \geq 180°.$$

Consequently, $\alpha_{min} \geq 120°$.